Solutions Manu

for

Essentials of Investments

Ninth Edition

Zvi Bodie
Boston University

Alex Kane
University of California—San Diego

Alan J. Marcus
Boston College

Prepared by
Fiona Chou
University of California—San Diego

The McGraw-Hill Companies

Solutions Manual for
ESSENTIALS OF INVESTMENTS, Ninth Edition
Zvi Bodie, Alex Kane, and Alan J. Marcus

Published by McGraw-Hill/Irwin, an imprint of The McGraw-Hill Companies, Inc., 1221 Avenue of the Americas, New York, NY 10020.

3 4 5 6 7 8 9 0 DOH/DOH 1 0 9 8 7 6 5

ISBN: 978-0-07-750224-9
MHID: 0-07-750224-8

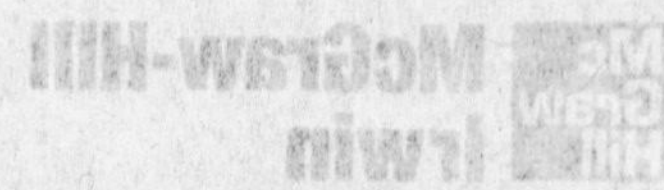

www.mhhe.com

Table of Contents

Table of Contents

CHAPTER 01
INVESTMENTS: BACKGROUND AND ISSUES

1. Equity is a lower-priority claim and represents an ownership share in a corporation, whereas fixed-income (debt) security is a higher-priority claim but does not have an ownership interest. Fixed-income (debt) security pays a specified cash flow at pre-contracted time intervals until the last payment on the maturity date. Equity has an indefinite life.

2. The primary asset has a claim on the real assets of a firm, whereas a derivative asset provides a payoff that depends on the prices of a primary asset but not the claim on real assets.

3. Asset allocation is the allocation of an investment portfolio across broad asset classes. Security selection is the choice of specific securities within each asset class.

4. Agency problems are conflicts of interest between managers and stockholders. They can be addressed through corporate governance mechanisms, such as the design of executive compensation, oversight by the Board, and monitoring from the institutional investors.

5. Real assets are assets used to produce goods and services. Financial assets are claims on real assets or the income generated by them.

6. Investment bankers are firms specializing in the sale of new securities to the public, typically by underwriting the issue. Commercial banks accept deposits and lend the money to other borrowers. After the Glass-Steagall Act was repealed in 1999, some commercial banks started transforming to "universal banks" which provide the services of both commercial banks and investment banks. With the passage of the Dodd–Frank Wall Street Reform and Consumer Protection Act in 2010, Glass-Steagall was partially restored via the Volker Rule.

7.

   a. Toyota creates a real asset—the factory. The loan is a financial asset that is created in the transaction.

   b. When the loan is repaid, the financial asset is destroyed but the real asset continues to exist.

   c. The cash is a financial asset that is traded in exchange for a real asset, inventory.

8.

   a. No. The real estate in existence has not changed, only the perception of its value has.

   b. Yes. The financial asset value of the claims on the real estate has changed, and thus the balance sheet of individual investors has been reduced.

c. The difference between these two answers reflects the difference between real and financial asset values. Real assets still exist, yet the value of the claims on those assets or the cash flows they generate do change. Thus, there is the difference.

9.

a. The bank loan is a financial liability for Lanni. Lanni's IOU is the bank's financial asset. The cash Lanni receives is a financial asset. The new financial asset created is Lanni's promissory note held by the bank.

b. The cash paid by Lanni is the transfer of a financial asset to the software developer. In return, Lanni gets a real asset, the completed software. No financial assets are created or destroyed. Cash is simply transferred from one firm to another.

c. Lanni sells the software, which is a real asset, to Microsoft. In exchange Lanni receives a financial asset, 1,500 shares of Microsoft stock. If Microsoft issues new shares in order to pay Lanni, this would constitute the creation of new financial asset.

d. In selling 1,500 shares of stock for $120,000, Lanni is exchanging one financial asset for another. In paying off the IOU with $50,000, Lanni is exchanging financial assets. The loan is "destroyed" in the transaction, since it is retired when paid.

10.

a.

Assets		*Liabilities & Shareholders' Equity*	
Cash	$ 70,000	Bank loan	$ 50,000
Computers	30,000	Shareholders' equity	50,000
Total	$100,000	Total	$100,000

$$\text{Ratio of real to total assets} = \frac{\$\ 30{,}000}{\$100{,}000} = 0.3$$

b.

Assets		*Liabilities & Shareholders' Equity*	
Software product*	$ 70,000	Bank loan	$ 50,000
Computers	30,000	Shareholders' equity	50,000
Total	$100,000	Total	$100,000

*Value at cost

$$\text{Ratio of real to total assets} = \frac{\$100{,}000}{\$100{,}000} = 1.0$$

c.

Assets		Liabilities & Shareholders' equity	
Microsoft shares	$125,000	Bank loan	$ 50,000
Computers	30,000	Shareholders' equity	105,000
Total	$155,000	Total	$155,000

$$\text{Ratio of real to total assets} = \frac{\$\ 30{,}000}{\$155{,}000} = 0.2$$

Conclusion: When the firm starts up and raises working capital, it will be characterized by a low ratio of real to total assets. When it is in full production, it will have a high ratio of real assets. When the project "shuts down" and the firm sells it, the percentage of real assets to total assets goes down again because the product is again exchanged into financial assets.

11. Passed in 2010, the Dodd-Frank Wall Street Reform and Consumer Protection Act proposes several mechanisms to mitigate systemic risk. The act attempts to limit the risky activities in which the banks can engage and calls for stricter rules for bank capital, liquidity, and risk management practices, especially as banks become larger and their potential failure becomes more threatening to other institutions. The act seeks to unify and clarify the lines of regulatory authority and responsibility in government agencies and to address the incentive issue by forcing employee compensation to reflect longer-term performance. It also mandates increased transparency, especially in derivatives markets.

12. For commercial banks, the ratio is: $\frac{\$\ 157.0}{\$12{,}157.3} = 0.0129$

For non-financial firms, the ratio is: $\frac{\$13{,}661}{\$28{,}196} = 0.4845$

The difference should be expected since the business of financial institutions is to make loans that are financial assets.

13. National wealth is a measurement of the real assets used to produce GDP in the economy. Financial assets are claims on those assets held by individuals.

Financial assets owned by households represent their claims on the real assets of the issuers, and thus show up as wealth to households. Their interests in the issuers, on the other hand, are obligations to the issuers. At the national level, the financial interests and the obligations cancel each other out, so only the real assets are measured as the wealth of the economy. The financial assets are important since they drive the efficient use of real assets and help us allocate resources, specifically in terms of risk return trade-offs.

14.

a. A fixed salary means compensation is (at least in the short run) independent of the firm's success. This salary structure does not tie the manager's immediate compensation to the success of the firm, and thus allows the manager to envision and seek the sustainable operation of the company. However, since the compensation is secured and not tied to the performance of the firm, the manager might not be motivated to take any risk to maximize the value of the company.

b. A salary paid in the form of stock in the firm means the manager earns the most when shareholder wealth is maximized. When the stock must be held for five years, the manager has less of an incentive to manipulate the stock price. This structure is most likely to align the interests of managers with the interests of the shareholders. If stock compensation is used too much, the manager might view it as overly risky since the manager's career is already linked to the firm. This undiversified exposure would be exacerbated with a large stock position in the firm.

c. When executive salaries are linked to firm profits, the firm creates incentives for managers to contribute to the firm's success. However, this may also lead to earnings manipulation or accounting fraud, such as divestment of its subsidiaries or unreasonable revenue recognition. That is what audits and external analysts will look out for.

15. Even if an individual investor has the expertise and capability to monitor and improve the managers' performance, the payoffs would not be worth the effort, since his ownership in a large corporation is so small compared to that of institutional investors. For example, if the individual investor owns $10,000 of IBM stock and can increase the value of the firm by 5%, a very ambitious goal, the benefit would only be: $10,000 × 5% = $500.

In contrast, a bank that has a multimillion-dollar loan outstanding to the firm has a big stake in making sure the firm can repay the loan. It is clearly worthwhile for the bank to spend considerable resources to monitor the firm.

16. Since the traders benefited from profits but did not get penalized by losses, they were encouraged to take extraordinary risks. Since traders sell to other traders, there also existed a moral hazard since other traders might facilitate the misdeed. In the end, this represents an agency problem.

17. Securitization requires access to a large number of potential investors. To attract these investors, the capital market needs:

(1) A safe system of business laws and low probability of confiscatory taxation/regulation;
(2) A well-developed investment banking industry;
(3) A well-developed system of brokerage and financial transactions, and;
(4) Well-developed media, particularly financial reporting.

These characteristics are found in (and make for) a well-developed financial market.

18. Progress in securitization facilitates the shifting of default risk from the intermediates to the investors of such a security. Since the intermediates no longer bear the default risk, their role and motivation in assessing and monitoring the quality of the borrowers is mitigated. For example, when the national market in mortgage-backed securities becomes highly developed, local banks can easily sell their claims on mortgages to the issuers of mortgage-backed securities and then use the money they receive to create more mortgages because the local banks make profits both from making loans and selling loans to the issuers of mortgage-backed securities. This way the local banks are actually incentivized by the volume of the loan that they lend out, instead of by the quality of the loan, and thus they become less cautious in originating subprime mortgages.

19. Mutual funds accept funds from small investors and invest, on behalf of these investors, in the national and international securities markets.

    Pension funds accept funds and then invest, on behalf of current and future retirees, thereby channeling funds from one sector of the economy to another.

    Venture capital firms pool the funds of private investors and invest in start-up firms.

    Banks accept deposits from customers and loan those funds to businesses or use the funds to buy securities of large corporations.

20. Even if the firm does not need to issue stock in any particular year, the stock market is still important to the financial manager. The stock price provides important information about how the market values the firm's investment projects. For example, if the stock price rises considerably, managers might conclude that the market believes the firm's future prospects are bright. This might be a useful signal to the firm to proceed with an investment such as an expansion of the firm's business.

    In addition, the fact that shares can be traded in the secondary market makes the shares more attractive to investors since they know that, when they wish to, they will be able to sell their shares. This in turn makes investors more willing to buy shares in a primary offering, and thus improves the terms on which firms can raise money in the equity market.

21. Treasury bills serve a purpose for investors who prefer a low-risk investment. The lower average rate of return compared to stocks is the price investors pay for predictability of investment performance and portfolio value.

22. You should be skeptical. If the author actually knows how to achieve such returns, one must question why the author would then be so ready to sell the secret to others. Financial markets are very competitive; one of the implications of this fact is that riches do not come easily. High expected returns require bearing some risk, and obvious bargains are few and far between. Odds are that the only one getting rich from this book is its author.

CHAPTER 02
ASSET CLASSES AND FINANCIAL INSTRUMENTS

1. Common stock is an ownership share in a publicly held corporation. Common shareholders have voting rights and may receive dividends. Preferred stock represents nonvoting shares in a corporation, usually paying a fixed stream of dividends. While corporate bonds are long-term debt issued by corporations, the bonds typically pay semi-annual coupons and return the face value of the bond at maturity.

2. While the DJIA has 30 large corporations in the index, it does not represent the overall market nearly as well as the more than 5000 stocks contained in The Wilshire index. The DJIA is simply too small.

3. Money market securities are short-term, relatively low risk, and highly liquid. Also, their unit value almost never changes.

4. The major components of the money market are Treasury bills, certificates of deposit, commercial paper, bankers' acceptances, Eurodollars, repos, reserves, federal funds, and brokers' calls.

5. American Depository Receipts, or ADRs, are certificates traded in U.S. markets that represent ownership in shares of a foreign company. Investors may also purchase shares of foreign companies on foreign exchanges. Lastly, investors may use international mutual funds to own shares indirectly.

6. The coupons paid by municipal bonds are exempt from federal income tax and from state tax in many states. Therefore, the higher the tax bracket that the investor is in, the more valuable the tax-exempt feature to the investor.

7. The London Interbank Offer Rate (LIBOR) is the rate at which large banks in London are willing to lend money among themselves. The Fed funds rate is the rate of interest on very short-term loans among financial institutions in the U.S.

8. General obligation bonds are backed by the taxing power of the local governments, while revenue bonds have proceeds attached to specific projects. A revenue bond has fewer guarantees, it is riskier in terms of default, and, therefore, you expect it to have a higher yield.

9. Corporations may exclude 70% of dividends received from domestic corporations in the computation of their taxable income.

10. Limited liability means that the most shareholders can lose in event of the failure of the corporation is their original investment.

11. (a) A repurchase agreement is the sale of a security with a commitment to repurchase the same security at a specified future date and a designated price.

12. Money market securities are referred to as "cash equivalents" because of their great liquidity. The prices of money market securities are very stable, and they can be converted to cash (i.e., sold) on very short notice and with very low transaction costs.

13. Equivalent taxable yield = $\frac{\text{Rate on municipal bond}}{1-\text{Tax rate}} = \frac{r_m}{1-t} = \frac{.0675}{1-0.35} = .1038$ or 10.38%

14. After-tax yield = Rate on the taxable bond × (1 − Tax rate)

    a. The taxable bond. With a zero tax bracket, the after-tax yield for the taxable bond is the same as the before-tax yield (5%), which is greater than the 4% yield on the municipal bond.

    b. The taxable bond. The after-tax yield for the taxable bond is: 0.05 × (1 − 0.10) = 0.045 or 4.50%.

    c. Neither. The after-tax yield for the taxable bond is: 0.05 × (1 − 0.20) = 0.4 or 4%. The after-tax yield of taxable bond is the same as that of the municipal bond.

    d. The municipal bond. The after-tax yield for the taxable bond is: 0.05 × (1 − 0.30) = 0.035 or 3.5%. The municipal bond offers the higher after-tax yield for investors in tax brackets above 20%.

15. The after-tax yield on the corporate bonds is: 0.09 × (1 − 0.30) = 0.063 or 6.3%. Therefore, the municipals must offer at least 6.3% yields.

16. Using the formula of Equivalent taxable yield (r) = $\frac{r_m}{1-t}$, we get:

    a. $r = \frac{0.04}{1-0} = 0.04$ or 4.00%

    b. $r = \frac{0.04}{1-0.10} = 0.0444$ or 4.44%

    c. $r = \frac{0.04}{1-0.20} = 0.05$ or 5.00%

    d. $r = \frac{0.04}{1-0.30} = 0.0571$ or 5.71%

17.

    a. You would have to pay the asked price of:
    98 = 98% of par = $980.00

b. The coupon rate is 4.25%, implying coupon payments of $42.5 annually or, more precisely, $21.25 (= 42.5/2) semiannually.

c. Given the asked price and coupon rate, we can calculate current yield with the formula:

$$\text{Current yield} = \frac{\text{Annual coupon income}}{\text{Price}} = 4.25/98 = 0.0434 = 4.34\%$$

18.

a. The closing price today is $75.60, which is $0.97 above yesterday's price. Therefore, yesterday's closing price was: $75.60 − $0.97 = $74.63.

b. You would buy 66 shares: $5,000/$75.60 = 66.14.

c. Your annual dividend income on 66 shares would be 66 × $1.88 = $124.08.

d. Earnings per share can be derived from the price-earnings (PE) ratio:
Given price/Earnings = 10.92 and Price = $75.60, we know that Earnings per Share = $75.60/10.92 = $6.92.

19.

a. At $t = 0$, the value of the index is: ($90 + $50 + $100)/3 = 80
At $t = 1$, the value of the index is: ($95 + $45 + $110)/3 = 83.33
The rate of return is: $\frac{V_1}{V_0} - 1 = (83.33/80) - 1 = 0.0417$ or 4.17%

b. In the absence of a split, stock C would sell for $110, and the value of the index would be the average price of the individual stocks included in the index: ($95 + $45 + $110)/3 = $83.33.

After the split, stock C sells at $55; however, the value of the index should not be affected by the split. We need to set the divisor (d) such that:
83.33 = ($95 + $45 + $55)/d
d = 2.34

c. The rate of return is zero. The value of the index remains unchanged since the return on each stock separately equals zero.

20.

a. Total market value at $t = 0$ is:
($90 × 100) + ($50 × 200) + ($200 × 100) = $39,000

Total market value at $t = 1$ is:
($95 × 100) + ($45 × 200) + ($110 × 100) = $40,500

Rate of return = $\frac{V_1}{V_0} - 1 = (\$40{,}500/\$39{,}000) - 1 = 0.0385$ or 3.85%

b. The return on each stock is as follows:

$$R_A = \frac{V_1}{V_0} - 1 = (\$95/\$90) - 1 = 0.0556 \text{ or } 5.56\%$$

$$R_B = \frac{V_1}{V_0} - 1 = (\$45/\$50) - 1 = -0.10 \text{ or } -10.00\%$$

$$R_C = \frac{V_1}{V_0} - 1 = (\$110/\$100) - 1 = 0.10 \text{ or } 10.00\%$$

The equally-weighted average is: [5.56% + (−10.00%) + 10.00%]/3 = 1.85%

21. The fund would require constant readjustment since every change in the price of a stock would bring the fund asset allocation out of balance.

22. In this case, the value of the divisor will increase by an amount necessary to maintain the index value on the day of the change. For example, if the index was comprised of only one stock, it would increase by 2.06 points: ($95 − $31) / $31 = 2.06.

23. Bank discount of 87 days: $0.034 \times \frac{87 \text{ days}}{360 \text{ days}} = 0.008217$

Price: $10,000 × (1 − 0.008217) = $9,917.83

$$\text{Bond equivalent yield} = \frac{\text{Face value} - \text{Purchase price}}{\text{Purchase price} \times T}$$

$$= \frac{\$10{,}000 - \$9{,}917.83}{\$9{,}917.83 \times \frac{87 \text{ days}}{365 \text{ days}}} = 0.0348 \text{ or } 3.48\%$$

24.

a. The higher coupon bond: The 10-year T-bond with a 10% coupon
b. The call with the lower exercise price: The call with the exercise price of $35
c. The put option on the lower priced stock: The put on the stock selling at $50

25.

a. The December maturity futures price is $6.37 per bushel. If the contract closes at $6.43 per bushel in December, your profit / loss on each contract (for delivery of 5,000 bushels of corn) will be: ($6.43 − $6.37) × 5000 = $ 300.00 gain.

b. There are 487,465 contracts outstanding, representing 2,437,325,000 bushels of corn.

26.

a. Yes. As long as the stock price at expiration exceeds the exercise price, it makes sense to exercise the call.
Gross profit is: ($367 − $355) × 100 shares = $1,200
Net profit = ($12 − $13.70) × 100 shares = $170 loss
Rate of return = −$1.70/$13.70 = −0.1241 or 12.41% loss

b. Yes, exercise.
Gross profit is: (\$367 − \$360) × 100 shares = \$700
Net profit = (\$7 − \$11.15) × 100 shares = \$415 loss
Rate of return = −\$4.15/\$11.15 = 0.3722 or 37.22 % loss

c. A put with an exercise price of \$355 would expire worthless for any stock price equal to or greater than \$355. An investor in such a put would have a rate of return over the holding period of −100%.

27.

a. Long call
b. Long put
c. Short put
d. Short call

28. There is always a chance that the option will expire in the money. Investors will pay something for this chance of a positive payoff.

29. Long call for \$4:

	Value of call at expiration	Initial Cost	Profit
a.	0	4	−4
b.	0	4	−4
c.	0	4	−4
d.	5	4	1
e.	10	4	6

Long put for \$6:

	Value of put at expiration	Initial Cost	Profit
a.	10	6	4
b.	5	6	−1
c.	0	6	−6
d.	0	6	−6
e.	0	6	−6

30. The spread will widen. Deterioration of the economy increases credit risk, that is, the likelihood of default. Investors will demand a greater premium on debt securities subject to default risk.

31. Ten stocks have a 52 week high at least 50% above the 52 week low. Individual stocks are much more volatile than a group of stocks.

52-wk high	52-wk low	Price ratio (High-Low)/Low
18.93	11.65	0.62
23.73	16.62	0.43
88.7	44.24	1.00
43.39	22.89	0.90
42.84	25.4	0.69
38.22	22.45	0.70
7.09	4.3	0.65
18.08	6.28	1.88
21.1	11.7	0.80
49.32	21.68	1.27
78.27	55.46	0.41
21.65	13.96	0.55

32. The total before-tax income is $4. The corporations may exclude 70% of dividends received from domestic corporations in the computation of their taxable income; the taxable income is therefore: $4 × 30% = $1.20.
Income tax in the 30% tax bracket: $1.2 × 30% = $0.36
After-tax income = $4 − $0.36 = $3.64
After-tax rate of return = $3.64/$40 = 0.091 or 9.10%

33. A put option conveys the right to sell the underlying asset at the exercise price. A short position in a futures contract carries an obligation to sell the underlying asset at the futures price.

34. A call option conveys the right to buy the underlying asset at the exercise price. A long position in a futures contract carries an obligation to buy the underlying asset at the futures price.

CFA 1

Answer: c. Taxation

CHAPTER 03
SECURITIES MARKETS

1. An IPO is the first time a formerly privately-owned company sells stock to the general public. A seasoned issue is the issuance of stock by a company that has already undergone an IPO.

2. The effective price paid or received for a stock includes items such as bid-ask spread, brokerage fees, commissions, and taxes (when applicable). These reduce the amount received by a seller and increase the cost incurred by a buyer.

3. The primary market is the market where newly-issued securities are sold, while the secondary market is the market for trading existing securities. After firms sell their newly-issued stocks to investors in the primary market, new investors purchase stocks from existing investors in the secondary market.

4. The primary source of income for a securities dealer is the bid-ask spread. This is the difference between the price at which the dealer is willing to purchase a security and the price at which they are willing to sell the same security.

5. When a firm is a willing buyer of securities and wishes to avoid the extensive time and cost associated with preparing a public issue, it may issue shares privately.

6. A stop order is a trade is not to be executed unless stock hits a price limit. The stop-loss is used to limit losses when prices are falling. An order specifying a price at which an investor is willing to buy or sell a security is a limit order, while a market order directs the broker to buy or sell at whatever price is available in the market.

7. Many large investors seek anonymity for fear that their intentions will become known to other investors. Large block trades attract the attention of other traders. By splitting large transactions into smaller trades, investors are better able to retain a degree of anonymity.

8. Underwriters purchase securities from the issuing company and resell them. A prospectus is a description of the firm and the security it is issuing.

9. Margin is a type of leverage that allows investors to post only a portion of the value of the security they purchase. As such, when the price of the security rises or falls, the gain or loss represents a much higher percentage, relative to the actual money invested.

10. a. A market order has price uncertainty but not execution uncertainty.

11. a. An illiquid security in a developing country is most likely to trade in broker markets.

12.

a. In principle, potential losses are unbounded, growing directly with increases in the price of IBM.

b. If the price of IBM shares goes above $200, then the stop-buy order would be executed, limiting the losses from the short sale. If the stop-buy order can be filled at $200, the maximum possible loss per share is $10. The total loss is: $10 × 100 shares = $1000.

13. Answers to this problem will vary.

14.

a. In addition to the explicit fees of $60,000, we should also take into account the implicit cost incurred to DRK from the underpricing in the IPO. The underpricing is $4 per share, or a total of $400,000, implying total costs of $460,000.

b. No. The underwriters do not capture the part of the costs corresponding to the underpricing. However, the underpricing may be a rational marketing strategy to attract and retain long-term relationships with their investors. Without it, the underwriters would need to spend more resources in order to place the issue with the public. The underwriters would then need to charge higher explicit fees to the issuing firm. The issuing firm may be just as well off paying the implicit issuance cost represented by the underpricing.

15.

a. The stock is purchased for $40 × 300 shares = $12,000.

Given that the amount borrowed from the broker is $4,000, Dee's margin is the initial purchase price net borrowing: $12,000 − $4,000 = $8,000.

b. If the share price falls to $30, then the value of the stock falls to $9,000. By the end of the year, the amount of the loan owed to the broker grows to:

Principal × (1 + Interest rate) = $4,000 × (1 + 0.08) = $4,320.

The value of the stock falls to: $30 × 300 shares = $9,000.

The remaining margin in the investor's account is:

$$\text{Margin on long position} = \frac{\text{Equity in account}}{\text{Value of stock}}$$

$$= \frac{\$9{,}000 - \$4{,}320}{\$9{,}000} = 0.52 = 52\%$$

Therefore, the investor will not receive a margin call.

c. $$\text{Rate of return} = \frac{\text{Ending equity in account} - \text{Initial equity in account}}{\text{Initial equity in account}}$$

$$= \frac{\$4{,}680 - \$8{,}000}{\$8{,}000} = -0.4150 = -41.50\%$$

16.

a. The initial margin was: $\$40 \times 1{,}000 \times 0.50 = \$20{,}000$.

As a result of the \$10 increase in the stock price, Old Economy Traders loses: $\$10 \times 1{,}000 \text{ shares} = \$10{,}000$.
Moreover, Old Economy Traders must pay the dividend of \$2 per share to the lender of the shares: $\$2 \times 1{,}000 \text{ shares} = \$2{,}000$.

The remaining margin in the investor's account therefore decreases to: $\$20{,}000 - \$10{,}000 - \$2{,}000 = \$8{,}000$.

b. $$\text{Margin on short position} = \frac{\text{Equity}}{\text{Value of shares owed}}$$

$$= \frac{\$8{,}000}{\$50 \times 1{,}000 \text{ shares}} = 0.16 = 16\%$$

Because the percentage margin falls below the maintenance level of 30%, there will be a margin call.

c. $$\text{The rate of return} = \frac{\text{Ending equity} - \text{Initial equity}}{\text{Initial equity}}$$

$$= \frac{\$8{,}000 - \$20{,}000}{\$20{,}000} = -0.60 = -60\%$$

17.

a. The market-buy order will be filled at \$50.25, the best price of limit-sell orders in the book.

b. The next market-buy order will be filled at \$51.50, the next-best limit-sell order price.

c. As a security dealer, you would want to increase your inventory. There is considerable buying demand at prices just below \$50, indicating that downside risk is limited. In contrast, limit-sell orders are sparse, indicating that a moderate buy order could result in a substantial price increase.

18.

a. Your initial investment is the sum of \$5,000 in equity and \$5,000 from borrowing, which enables you to buy 200 shares of Telecom stock:

$$\frac{\text{Initial investment}}{\text{Stock price}} = \frac{\$10{,}000}{\$50} = 200 \text{ shares}$$

The shares increase in value by 10%: $\$10{,}000 \times 0.10 = \$1{,}000$.
You pay interest of $= \$5{,}000 \times 0.08 = \$400$.

The rate of return will be:

$$\frac{\$1{,}000 - \$400}{\$5{,}000} = 0.12 = 12\%$$

b. The value of the 200 shares is 200*P*. Equity is (200*P* – $5,000), and the required margin is 30%.

Solving $\frac{200P - \$5{,}000}{200P} = 0.30$, we get $P = \$35.71$.

You will receive a margin call when the stock price falls below $35.71.

19.

a. Initial margin is 50% of $5,000, which is $2,500.

b. Total assets are $7,500 ($5,000 from the sale of the stock and $2,500 put up for margin). Liabilities are 100*P*. Therefore, net worth is ($7,500 – 100*P*).

Solving $\frac{\$7{,}500 - 100P}{100P} = 0.30$, we get $P = \$57.69$.

A margin call will be issued when the stock price reaches $57.69 or higher.

20. The broker is instructed to attempt to sell your Marriott stock as soon as the Marriott stock trades at a bid price of $20 or less. Here, the broker will attempt to execute but may not be able to sell at $20, since the bid price is now $19.95. The price at which you sell may be more or less than $20 because the stop-loss becomes a market order to sell at current market prices.

21.

a. The trade will be executed at $55.50.

b. The trade will be executed at $55.25.

c. The trade will not be executed because the bid price is lower than the price specified in the limit-sell order.

d. The trade will not be executed because the asked price is higher than the price specified in the limit-buy order.

22.

a. In an exchange market, there can be price improvement in the two market orders. Brokers for each of the market orders (i.e., the buy and the sell orders) can agree to execute a trade inside the quoted spread. For example, they can trade at $55.37, thus improving the price for both customers by $0.12 or $0.13 relative to the quoted bid and asked prices. The buyer gets the stock for $0.13 less than the quoted asked price, and the seller receives $0.12 more for the stock than the quoted bid price.

b. Whereas the limit order to buy at \$55.37 would not be executed in a dealer market (since the asked price is \$55.50), it could be executed in an exchange market. A broker for another customer with an order to sell at market would view the limit buy order as the best bid price; the two brokers could agree to the trade and bring it to the specialist, who would then execute the trade.

23.

a. You will not receive a margin call. You invest in 1,000 shares of Disney at \$40 per share with \$20,000 in equity and \$20,000 from borrowing. At \$35 per share, the value of the stock becomes \$35,000. Therefore, the equity decreases to \$15,000:

$$\text{Equity} = \text{Value of stock} - \text{Debt} = \$35{,}000 - \$20{,}000 = \$15{,}000$$

$$\text{Percentage margin} = \frac{\text{Equity in account}}{\text{Value of stock}}$$

$$= \frac{\$15{,}000}{\$35{,}000} = 0.4286 \text{ or } 42.86\%$$

The percentage margin still exceeds the required maintenance margin.

b. Solving $\dfrac{1{,}000P - \$20{,}000}{1{,}000P} = 0.35$ or 35%, we get $P = \$30.77$

You will receive a margin call when the stock price falls to \$30.77 or lower.

24. The proceeds from the short sale (net of commission) were: (\$21 × 100) − \$50 = \$2,050.

A dividend payment of \$300 was withdrawn from the account. Covering the short sale at \$15 per share costs (including commission): \$1500 + \$50 = \$1550.

Therefore, the value of your account is equal to the net profit on the transaction: \$2,050 − \$300 − \$1,550 = \$200.

Noted that the profit of \$200 equals (100 shares × profit per share of \$2), your net proceeds per share were:

\$21	Selling price of stock
−\$15	Repurchase price of stock
−\$ 3	Dividend per share
−\$ 1	2 trades × \$0.50 commission per share
\$ 2	

25. The total cost of the purchase is: \$40 × 500 = \$20,000.

Investing \$15,000 from your own funds and borrowing \$5,000 from the broker, you start the margin account with the net worth of \$15,000.

a.

(i) Net worth increases to: ($44 × 500) – $5,000 = $17,000
Percentage gain = ($17,000 – $15,000)/$15,000 = 0.1333 = 13.33%

(ii) With price unchanged, net worth is unchanged.
Percentage gain = zero

(iii) Net worth falls to ($36 × 500) – $5,000 = $13,000
Percentage gain = ($13,000 – $15,000)/$15,000 = –0.1333 = –13.33%

The relationship between the percentage return and the percentage change in the price of the stock is given by:

$$\% \text{ return} = \% \text{ change in price} \times \frac{\text{Total investment}}{\text{Investor's initial equity}}$$

$$= \% \text{ change in price} \times 1.3333$$

For example, when the stock price rises from $40 to $44, the percentage change in price is 10% (0.10), while the percentage gain for the investor is:

$$\% \text{ return} = 0.10 \times \frac{\$20{,}000}{\$15{,}000} = 0.1333 \text{ or } 13.33\%$$

b. The value of the 500 shares is 500*P*. Equity is (500*P* – $5,000). You will receive a margin call when:

$$\frac{500P - \$5{,}000}{500P} = 0.25 \text{ or } 25\%, \text{ when } P = \$13.33 \text{ or lower.}$$

c. The value of the 500 shares is 500*P*. But now you have borrowed $10,000 instead of $5,000. Therefore, equity is (500*P* – $10,000). You will receive a margin call when:

$$\frac{500P - \$10{,}000}{500P} = 0.25 \text{ or } 25\% \text{ when } P = \$26.67.$$

With less equity in the account, you are far more vulnerable to a margin call.

d. By the end of the year, the amount of the loan owed to the broker grows to:

$5,000 × (1 + 0.08) = $5,400

The equity in your account is (500*P* – $5,400). Initial equity was $15,000. Therefore, the rate of return after one year is as follows:

(i) $$\frac{(500 \times \$44) - \$5{,}400 - \$15{,}000}{\$15{,}000} = 0.1067 = 10.67\%$$

(ii) $\frac{(500 \times \$40) - \$5,400 - \$15,000}{\$15,000} = -0.0267 = -2.67\%$

(iii) $\frac{(500 \times \$36) - \$5,400 - \$15,000}{\$15,000} = -0.1600 = -16.00\%$

The relationship between the percentage return and the percentage change in the price of Intel is given by:

$$\%\text{ return} = \left(\%\text{ change in price} \times \frac{\text{Total investment}}{\text{Investor's initial equity}}\right) - \left(8\% \times \frac{\text{Funds borrowed}}{\text{Investor's initial equity}}\right)$$

For example, when the stock price rises from \$40 to \$44, the percentage change in price is 10% (0.10), while the percentage gain for the investor is:

$$\left(.10 \times \frac{\$\ 20,000}{\$15,000}\right) - \left(.08 \times \frac{\$\ 5,000}{\$15,000}\right) = .1067 \text{ or } 10.67\%$$

e. The value of the 500 shares is 500*P*. Equity is (500*P* – \$5,400). I will receive a margin call when:

$$\frac{500P - \$5,400}{500P} = 0.25 \text{ or } 25\% \text{ when } P = \$14.40 \text{ or lower.}$$

26.

a. Given the \$15,000 invested funds and assuming the gain or loss on the short position is (−500 × Δ*P*), we can calculate the rate of return using the following formula:
Rate of return = (−500 × Δ*P*)/15,000

Thus, the rate of return in each of the three scenarios is:
(i) Rate of return = (−500 × \$4)/\$15,000 = −0.1333 = −13.33%
(ii) Rate of return = (−500 × \$0)/\$15,000 = 0%
(iii) Rate of return = [−500 × (−\$4)]/\$15,000 = 0.1333 = 13.33%

Total assets on margin are the sum of the initial margin and the proceeds from the sale of the stock:

\$20,000 + \$15,000 = \$35,000. Liabilities are 500*P*. A margin call will be issued when:

$$\frac{\$35,000 - 500P}{500P} = 0.25 \text{ or } 25\% \text{ when } P = \$56 \text{ or higher.}$$

b. With a $1 dividend, the short position must now pay on the borrowed shares: ($1/share × 500 shares) = $500. Rate of return is now:
$[(-500 \times \Delta P) - 500]/15{,}000$

(i) Rate of return =[(−500 × $4) − $500]/$15,000 = −0.1667 = −16.67%
(ii) Rate of return = [(−500 × $0) − $500]/$15,000 = −0.0333 = −3.33%
(iii) Rate of return = [(−500) × (−$4) − $500]/$15,000 = 0.1000 = 10.00%

Total assets are $35,000, and liabilities are (500*P* + 500). A margin call will be issued when:

$$\frac{\$35{,}000 - 500P - 500}{500P} = 0.25 \text{ or } 25\% \text{ when } P = \$55.20 \text{ or higher.}$$

CFA 1

d. Cannot tell from the information given.
The broker will start to sell when the stock price hits $55 and keep doing so if the price further tumbles.

CFA 2

d. Act as odd-lot dealers.

CHAPTER 04
MUTUAL FUNDS AND OTHER INVESTMENT COMPANIES

1. Mutual funds offer many benefits. Some of those benefits include: the ability to invest with small amounts of money, diversification, professional management, low transaction costs, tax benefits, and the ability to reduce administrative functions. The costs associated with investing in mutual funds are generally operating expenses, marketing, distribution charges, and loads. Loads are fees paid when investors purchase or sell the shares.

2. Close-end funds trade on the open market and are thus subject to market pricing. Open-end funds are sold by the mutual fund and must reflect the NAV of the investments.

3. 12b-1 fees are annual fees charged by a mutual fund to pay for marketing and distribution costs.

4. A unit investment trust is an unmanaged mutual fund. Its portfolio is fixed and does not change due to asset trades, as does a close-end fund. Investors who wish to liquidate their holdings of a unit investment trust may sell the shares back to the trustee for net asset value, while a close-end fund is traded on the open market.

5. Exchange-traded funds can be traded during the day, just as the stocks they represent. They are most tax effective, in that they do not have as many distributions. They have much lower transaction costs. They also do not require load charges, management fees, and minimum investment amounts. The disadvantage is that ETFs must be purchased from brokers for a fee. Moreover, investors may incur a bid-ask spread when purchasing an ETF.

6. Hedge funds have much less regulation since they are part of private partnerships and free from most SEC regulation. They permit investors to take on many risks unavailable to mutual funds. Hedge funds, however, may require higher fees and provide less transparency to investors. This offers significant counter party risk and hedge fund investors need to be more careful about the firm they invest with.

7. An open-end fund will have higher fees since they are actively marketing and managing their investor base. The fund is always looking for new investors. A unit investment trust need not spend too much time on such matters since investors find each other.

8. Asset allocation funds may dramatically vary the proportions allocated to each market in accord with the portfolio manager's forecast of the relative performance of each sector. Hence, these funds are engaged in market timing and are not designed to be low-risk investment vehicles.

9.

a. A unit investment trust offers low costs and stable portfolios. Since they do not change their portfolios, investors know exactly what they own. They are better suited to sophisticated investors.

b. Open-end mutual funds offer higher levels of service to investors. The investors do not have any administrative burdens and their money is actively managed. These are better suited for less knowledgeable investors.

c. Individual securities offer the most sophisticated investors ultimate flexibility. Investors are able to save money since they are only charged the expenses they incur. All decisions are under the control of the investor.

10. Open-end funds must honor redemptions and receive deposits from investors. This flow of money necessitates retaining cash. Close-end funds no longer take and receive money from investors. As such, they are free to be fully invested at all times.

11. The offering price includes a 6% front-end load, or sales commission, meaning that every dollar paid results in only $0.94 going toward the purchase of shares. Therefore:

$$\text{Offering price} = \frac{\text{NAV}}{1-\text{load}} = \frac{\$10.70}{1-0.06} = \$11.38$$

12. NAV = Offering price × (1 − load) = $12.30 × 0.95 = $11.69

13. Given that net asset value equals assets minus liabilities expressed on a per-share basis, we first add up the value of the shares to get the market value of the portfolio:

Stock	Value Held by Fund
A	$ 7,000,000
B	12,000,000
C	8,000,000
D	15,000,000
Total	$42,000,000

Knowing that the accrued management fee, which adjusts the value of the portfolio, totals $30,000, and the number of the shares outstanding is 4,000,000, we can use the NAV equation:

$$\text{Net asset value} = \frac{\text{Market value of assets} - \text{Market value of liabilities}}{\text{Shares outstanding}}$$

$$= \frac{\$42,000,000 - \$30,000}{4,000,000} = \$10.49$$

14. The value of stocks sold and replaced = \$15,000,000.

$$\text{Turnover rate} = \frac{\text{Value of stocks sold or replaced}}{\text{Value of assets}}$$

$$= \frac{\$15{,}000{,}000}{\$42{,}000{,}000} = 0.3571 = 35.71\%$$

15.

a. $$\text{NAV} = \frac{\text{Market value of assets} - \text{Market value of liabilities}}{\text{Shares outstanding}}$$

$$= \frac{\$200{,}000{,}000 - \$3{,}000{,}000}{5{,}000{,}000} = \$39.40$$

b. $$\text{Premium (or discount)} = \frac{\text{Price} - \text{NAV}}{\text{NAV}} = \frac{\$36 - \$39.40}{\$39.40} = -0.0863 = -8.63\%$$

The fund sells at an 8.63% discount from NAV.

16. Given the NAV at the beginning and the end of the period, and the distributions during the period, we can use the equation below to solve for the rate of return of the Corporate Fund:

$$\text{Rate of return} = \frac{\Delta(\text{NAV}) + \text{Distributions}}{\text{Start of year NAV}} = \frac{-\$0.40 + \$1.50}{\$12.50} = 0.0880 = 8.80\%$$

17. As the price of a close-end fund may deviate from its NAV, we instead use the price of the net asset value when we calculate the rate of return:

a. Start of year price = $\$12.00 \times 1.02 = \$12.24$

End of year price $= \$12.10 \times 0.93 = \$11.253$

Although NAV increased, the price of the fund fell by \$0.987.

$$\text{Rate of return} = \frac{\Delta(\text{Price}) + \text{Distributions}}{\text{Start of year price}} = \frac{-\$0.987 + \$1.50}{\$12.24} = 0.0419 = 4.19\%$$

b. An investor holding the same portfolio as the fund manager would have earned a rate of return based on the increase in the NAV of the portfolio:

$$\text{Rate of return} = \frac{\Delta(\text{NAV}) + \text{Distributions}}{\text{Start of year NAV}} = \frac{\$0.10 + \$1.50}{\$12.00} = 0.1333 = 13.33\%$$

18. Assume a hypothetical investment of \$100. The end value of the investment will be equal to $I \times (1 - \text{front-end load}) \times (1 + r - \text{true expense ratio})^T$

Loaded-Up
We add the 12b-1 fee to the operating expenses to obtain the true expense ratio: Expense ratio + (12b-1 fee) = 1% + 0.75% = 1.75%

a. Year 1 = $\$100 \times (1 + 0.06 - 0.0175) = \$104.25$
b. Year 3 = $\$100 \times (1 + 0.06 - 0.0175)^3 = \$113.30$
c. Year 10 = $\$100 \times (1 + 0.06 - 0.0175)^{10} = \$151.62$

Economy fund

a. Year 1 = $\$100 \times 0.98 \times (1 + 0.06 - 0.0025) = \$103.64$
b. Year 3 = $\$100 \times 0.98 \times (1 + 0.06 - 0.0025)^3 = \$115.90$
c. Year 10 = $\$100 \times 0.98 \times (1 + 0.06 - 0.0025)^{10} = \$171.41$

19.

a. $$\text{NAV} = \frac{\text{Market value of assets} - \text{Market value of liabilities}}{\text{Shares outstanding}}$$

$$= \frac{\$450{,}000{,}000 - \$10{,}000{,}000}{44{,}000{,}000} = \$10$$

b. Because 1 million shares are redeemed at NAV = \$10, the value of the portfolio decreases to:
Portfolio value = \$450 million − (\$10 × 1 million) = \$440 million

The number of shares outstanding will be the current shares outstanding minus the number of shares redeemed: 44 million − 1 million = 43 million.

Thus, net asset value after the redemption will be:

$$\text{NAV} = \frac{\text{Market value of assets} - \text{Market value of liabilities}}{\text{Shares outstanding}}$$

$$= \frac{\$440{,}000{,}000 - \$10{,}000{,}000}{43{,}000{,}000} = \$10$$

20.

a. Empirical research indicates that past performance of mutual funds is not highly predictive of future performance, especially for better-performing funds. While there *may* be some tendency for the fund to be an above average performer next year, it is unlikely to once again be a top 10% performer.

b. On the other hand, the evidence is more suggestive of a tendency for poor performance to persist. This tendency is probably related to fund costs and turnover rates. Thus if the fund is among the poorest performers, investors would be concerned that the poor performance will persist.

21. Start of year NAV $= \dfrac{\text{Market value of assets} - \text{Market value of liabilities}}{\text{Shares outstanding}}$

$$= \frac{\$200{,}000{,}000}{10{,}000{,}000} = \$20$$

End of year NAV is based on the 8% price gain, less the 1% 12b-1 fee:

End of year NAV = $\$20 \times 1.08 \times (1 - 0.01) = \$21.384$

Given the dividends per share is \$0.20, we can calculate the rate of return using the following equation:

Rate of return $= \dfrac{\Delta(\text{NAV}) + \text{Distributions}}{\text{Start of year NAV}}$

$$= \frac{(\$21.384 - \$20) + \$0.20}{\$20} = 0.0792 = 7.92\%$$

22. The excess of purchases over sales must be due to new inflows into the fund. Therefore, \$400 million of stock previously held by the fund was replaced by new holdings. So turnover is:

Turnover rate $= \dfrac{\text{Value of stocks sold or replaced}}{\text{Value of assets}}$

$$= \frac{\$400{,}000{,}000}{\$2{,}200{,}000{,}000} = 0.1818 = 18.18\%$$

23. Fees paid to investment managers were: 0.7% × \$2.2 billion = \$15.4 million. Since the total expense ratio was 1.1% and the management fee was 0.7%, we conclude that 0.4% must be for other expenses. Therefore, other administrative expenses were: 0.004 × \$2.2 billion = \$8.8 million.

24. Because the 4% load was paid up front and reduced the actual amount invested, only 96% (1.00 − .04) of the contribution was invested. Given the value of the portfolio increased by 12% and the expense ratio was 1.2%, we can calculate the end value of the investment against the initial contribution:

$1 + r = 0.96 \times (1 + 0.12 - 0.012) = 1.0637$

Thus, the rate of return was: $1.0637 - 1 = 0.0637 = 6.37\%$

Or otherwise, you can calculate the rate of return by the actual amount invested and value changes:

To purchase the shares, you would have had to invest: $\$20{,}000/(1 - 0.04) = \$20{,}833$

The shares increase in value from \$20,000 to $\$20{,}000 \times (1.12 - 0.012) = \$22{,}160$

The rate of return was: $(\$22{,}160 - \$20{,}833)/\$20{,}833 = 0.0637$ or 6.37%

25. Suppose you have \$1000 to invest. The initial investment in Class A shares is \$940 net of the front-end load. After 4 years, your portfolio will be worth:

$\$940 \times (1.10)^4 = \$1{,}376.25$

Class B shares allow you to invest the full \$1,000, but your investment performance net of 12b-1 fees will be only 9.5%, and you will pay a 1% back-end load fee if you sell after 4 years. Your portfolio value after 4 years will be:

$\$1{,}000 \times (1.095)^4 = \$1{,}437.66$

After paying the back-end load fee, your portfolio value will be:

$\$1{,}437.66 \times 0.99 = \$1{,}423.28$

Class B shares are the better choice if your horizon is 4 years.

With a 15-year horizon, the Class A shares will be worth:

$\$940 \times (1.10)^{15} = \$3{,}926.61$

For the Class B shares, there is no back-end load in this case since the horizon is greater than 5 years. Therefore, the value of the Class B shares will be:

$\$1{,}000 \times (1.095)^{15} = \$3{,}901.32$

At this longer horizon, Class B shares are no longer the better choice. The effect of Class B's 0.5% 12b-1 fees cumulates over time and finally overwhelms the 6% load charged to Class A investors.

26.

a. After two years, each dollar invested in a fund with a 4% load and a portfolio return equal to r will grow to: $\$0.96 \times (1 + r - 0.005)^2$

Each dollar invested in the bank CD will grow to: $\$1 \times (1.06)^2$

If the mutual fund is to be the better investment, then the portfolio return, r, must satisfy:

$0.96 \times (1 + r - 0.005)^2 > (1.06)^2$

$0.96 \times (1 + r - 0.005)^2 > 1.1236$

$(1 + r - 0.005)^2 > 1.1704$

$1 + r - 0.005 > 1.0819$

$1 + r > 1.0869$

Therefore, $r > 0.0869 = 8.69\%$

b. If you invest for six years, then the portfolio return must satisfy:

$0.96 \times (1 + r - 0.005)^6 > (1.06)^6 = 1.4185$

$(1 + r - 0.005)^6 > 1.4776$

$1 + r - 0.005 > 1.0672$

$1 + r > 1.0722$

$r > 7.22\%$

The cutoff rate of return is lower for the six year investment because the "fixed cost" (i.e., the one-time front-end load) is spread out over a greater number of years.

c. With a 12b-1 fee instead of a front-end load, the portfolio must earn a rate of return (r) that satisfies:

$1 + r - 0.005 - 0.0075 > 1.06$

In this case, r must exceed 7.25% regardless of the investment horizon.

27. The turnover rate is 50%. This means that, on average, 50% of the portfolio is sold and replaced with other securities each year. Trading costs on the sell orders are 0.4%; the buy orders to replace those securities entail another 0.4% in trading costs. Total trading costs will reduce portfolio returns by: $2 \times 0.004 \times 0.50 = 0.004$ or 0.4%

28. For the bond fund, the fraction of portfolio income given up to fees is:

$$\frac{0.6\%}{4.0\%} = 0.150 = 15.0\%$$

For the equity fund, the fraction of investment earnings given up to fees is:

$$\frac{0.6\%}{12.0\%} = 0.050 = 5.0\%$$

Fees are a much higher fraction of expected earnings for the bond fund, and therefore may be a more important factor in selecting the bond fund.

This may help to explain why unmanaged unit investment trusts are concentrated in the fixed income market. The advantages of unit investment trusts are low turnover and low trading costs and management fees. This is a more important concern to bond-market investors.

29. Equity funds and fixed-income funds contain different types of securities. Therefore, there are numerous differences that make comparison difficult. Equity funds invest primarily in the common stock of publically traded firms. Fixed-income funds invest in corporate bonds, Treasury bonds, mortgage-backed securities, or municipal (tax-free) bonds. The risks associated with stocks are primarily related to economic conditions and the success of the business operations. The risks associated with fixed-income securities are primarily interest rate risk and credit risk.

30. Suppose that finishing in the top half of all portfolio managers is purely luck, and that the probability of doing so in any year is exactly ½. Then the probability that any particular manager would finish in the top half of the sample five years in a row is $(½)^5 = 1/32$. We would then expect to find that [350 × (1/32)] = 11 managers finish in the top half for each of the five consecutive years. This is precisely what we found. Thus, we should not conclude that the consistent performance after five years is proof of skill. We would expect to find eleven managers exhibiting precisely this level of "consistency" even if performance is due solely to luck.

CHAPTER 05
RISK AND RETURN: PAST AND PROLOGUE

1. The 1% VaR will be less than −30%. As percentile or probability of a return declines so does the magnitude of that return. Thus, a 1 percentile probability will produce a smaller VaR than a 5 percentile probability.

2. The geometric return represents a compounding growth number and will artificially inflate the annual performance of the portfolio.

3. No. Since all items are presented in nominal figures, the input should also use nominal data.

4. Decrease. Typically, standard deviation exceeds return. Thus, an underestimation of 4% in each will artificially decrease the return per unit of risk. To return to the proper risk return relationship the portfolio will need to decrease the amount of risk free investments.

5. Using Equation 5.6, we can calculate the mean of the HPR as:

$$E(r) = \sum_{s=1}^{S} p(s)\, r(s) = (0.3 \times 0.44) + (0.4 \times 0.14) + [0.3 \times (-0.16)] = 0.14 \text{ or } 14\%$$

Using Equation 5.7, we can calculate the variance as:

$$Var(r) = \sigma^2 = \sum_{s=1}^{S} p(s)\, [\, r(s) - E(r)]^2$$

$$= [0.3 \times (0.44 - 0.14)^2] + [0.4 \times (0.14 - 0.14)^2] + [0.3 \times (-0.16 - 0.14)^2]$$

$$= 0.054$$

Taking the square root of the variance, we get $SD(r) = \sigma = \sqrt{Var(r)} = \sqrt{0.054} = 0.2324$ or 23.24%

6. We use the below equation to calculate the holding period return of each scenario:

$$HPR = \frac{\text{Ending Price} - \text{Beginning Price} + \text{Cash Dividend}}{\text{Beginning Price}}$$

a. The holding period returns for the three scenarios are:

Boom: $(50 - 40 + 2)/40 = 0.30 = 30\%$

Normal: $(43 - 40 + 1)/40 = 0.10 = 10\%$

Recession: $(34 - 40 + 0.50)/40 = -0.1375 = -13.75\%$

$$E(HPR) = \sum_{s=1}^{S} p(s)\, r(s)$$

$$= [(1/3) \times 0.30] + [(1/3) \times 0.10] + [(1/3) \times (-0.1375)]$$

$$= 0.0875 \text{ or } 8.75\%$$

$$\text{Var(HPR)} = \sum_{s=1}^{S} p(s)\,[\,r(s) - E(r)]^2$$

$$= [(1/3) \times (0.30 - 0.0875)^2] + [(1/3) \times (0.10 - 0.0875)^2]$$

$$+ [(1/3)\,(-0.1375 - 0.0875)^2]$$

$$= 0.031979$$

$$SD(r) = \sigma = \sqrt{Var(r)} = \sqrt{319.79} = 0.1788 \text{ or } 17.88\%$$

b. E(r) = (0.5 × 8.75%) + (0.5 × 4%) = 6.375%

σ = 0.5 × 17.88% = 8.94%

7.

a. Time-weighted average returns are based on year-by-year rates of return.

Year	Return = [(Capital gains + Dividend)/Price]
2010–2011	(110 – 100 + 4)/100 = 0.14 or 14.00%
2011–2012	(90 – 110 + 4)/110 = –0.1455 or –14.55%
2012–2013	(95 – 90 + 4)/90 = 0.10 or 10.00%

Arithmetic mean: [0.14 + (–0.1455) + 0.10]/3 = 0.0315 or 3.15%

Geometric mean: $\sqrt[3]{(1 + 0.14) \times [1 + (-0.1455)] \times (1 + 0.10)} - 1$

= 0.0233 or 2.33%

b.

	Date			
	1/1/2010	1/1/2011	1/1/2012	1/1/2013
Net Cash Flow	–300	–208	110	396

Time	Net Cash flow	Explanation
0	–300	Purchase of three shares at \$100 per share
1	–208	Purchase of two shares at \$110, plus dividend income on three shares held
2	110	Dividends on five shares, plus sale of one share at \$90
3	396	Dividends on four shares, plus sale of four shares at \$95 per share

The dollar-weighted return is the internal rate of return that sets the sum of the present value of each net cash flow to zero:

$$0 = -\$300 + \frac{-\$208}{1+IRR} + \frac{\$110}{(1+IRR)^2} + \frac{\$396}{(1+IRR)^3}$$

Dollar-weighted return = Internal rate of return = –0.1661%

8.

a. Given that A = 4 and the projected standard deviation of the market return = 20%, we can use the below equation to solve for the expected market risk premium:

$$A = 4 = \frac{\text{Average}(r_M) - r_f}{\text{Sample } \sigma_M^2} = \frac{\text{Average}(r_M) - r_f}{(20\%)^2}$$

$$E(r_M) - r_f = A\sigma_M^2 = 4 \times (0.20)^2 = 0.16 \text{ or } 16\%$$

b. Solve $E(r_M) - r_f = 0.09 = A\sigma_M^2 = A \times (0.20)^2$, we can get

$$A = 0.09/0.04 = 2.25$$

c. Increased risk tolerance means decreased risk aversion (A), which results in a decline in risk premiums.

9. From Table 5.4, we find that for the period 1926 – 2010, the mean excess return for S&P 500 over T-bills is 7.98%.

E(r) = Risk-free rate + Risk premium = 5% + 7.98% = 12.98%

10. To answer this question with the data provided in the textbook, we look up the real returns of the large stocks, small stocks, and Treasury Bonds for 1926–2010 from Table 5.2, and the real rate of return of T-Bills in the same period from Table 5.3:

Total Real Return – Geometric Average
Large Stocks: 6.43%
Small Stocks: 8.54%
Long-Term T-Bonds: 2.06%

Total Real Return – Arithmetic Average
Large Stocks: 8.00%
Small Stocks: 13.91%
Long-Term T-Bonds: 1.76%
T-Bills: 0.68% (Table 5.3)

11.

a. The expected cash flow is: (0.5 × \$50,000) + (0.5 × \$150,000) = \$100,000
With a risk premium of 10%, the required rate of return is 15%. Therefore, if the value of the portfolio is X, then, in order to earn a 15% expected return:

Solving X × (1 + 0.15) = \$100,000, we get X = \$86,957

b. If the portfolio is purchased at \$86,957, and the expected payoff is \$100,000, then the expected rate of return, E(r), is:

$$\frac{\$100{,}000 - \$86{,}957}{\$86{,}957} = 0.15 = 15\%$$

The portfolio price is set to equate the expected return with the required rate of return.

c. If the risk premium over T-bills is now 15%, then the required return is:

$$5\% + 15\% = 20\%$$

The value of the portfolio (X) must satisfy:

$$X \times (1 + 0.20) = \$100,000 \Rightarrow X = \$83,333$$

d. For a given expected cash flow, portfolios that command greater risk premiums must sell at lower prices. The extra discount in the purchase price from the expected value is to compensate the investor for bearing additional risk.

12.

a. Allocating 70% of the capital in the risky portfolio *P*, and 30% in risk-free asset, the client has an expected return on the complete portfolio calculated by adding up the expected return of the risky proportion (y) and the expected return of the proportion $(1 - y)$ of the risk-free investment:

$$E(r_C) = y \times E(r_P) + (1 - y) \times r_f$$

$$= (0.7 \times 0.17) + (0.3 \times 0.07) = 0.14 \text{ or } 14\% \text{ per year}$$

The standard deviation of the portfolio equals the standard deviation of the risky fund times the fraction of the complete portfolio invested in the risky fund:

$$\sigma_C = y \times \sigma_P = 0.7 \times 0.27 = 0.189 \text{ or } 18.9\% \text{ per year}$$

b. The investment proportions of the client's overall portfolio can be calculated by the proportion of risky portfolio in the complete portfolio times the proportion allocated in each stock.

Security		Investment Proportions
T-Bills		30.0%
Stock A	0.7 × 27% =	18.9%
Stock B	0.7 × 33% =	23.1%
Stock C	0.7 × 40% =	28.0%

c. We calculate the reward-to-variability ratio (Sharpe ratio) using Equation 5.14.

For the risky portfolio:

$$S = \frac{\text{Portfolio Risk Premium}}{\text{Standard Deviation of Portfolio Excess Return}}$$

$$= \frac{E(r_P) - r_f}{\sigma_P} = \frac{0.17 - 0.07}{0.27} = 0.3704$$

For the client's overall portfolio:

$$S = \frac{E(r_C) - r_f}{\sigma_C} = \frac{0.14 - 0.07}{0.189} = 0.3704$$

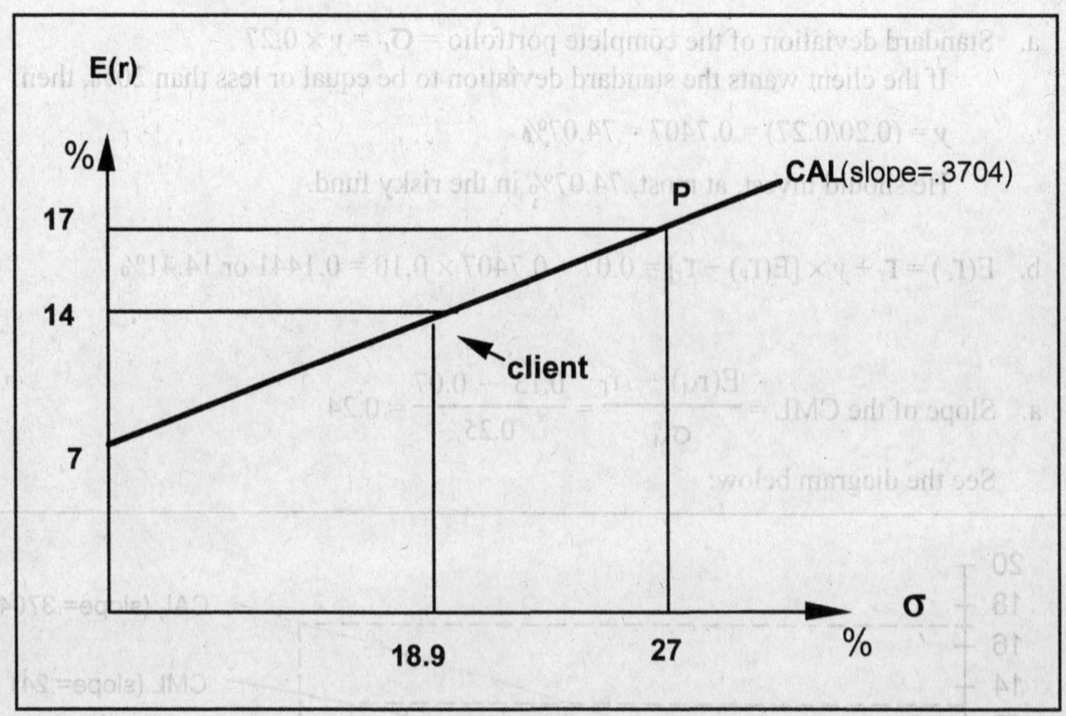

13.

a. $E(r_C) = y \times E(r_P) + (1 - y) \times r_f$

$= y \times 0.17 + (1 - y) \times 0.07 = 0.15$ or 15% per year

Solving for y, we get $y = \frac{0.15 - 0.07}{0.10} = 0.8$

Therefore, in order to achieve an expected rate of return of 15%, the client must invest 80% of total funds in the risky portfolio and 20% in T-bills.

b. The investment proportions of the client's overall portfolio can be calculated by the proportion of risky asset in the whole portfolio times the proportion allocated in each stock.

Security		Investment Proportions
T-Bills		20.0%
Stock A	$0.8 \times 27\% =$	21.6%
Stock B	$0.8 \times 33\% =$	26.4%
Stock C	$0.8 \times 40\% =$	32.0%

c. The standard deviation of the complete portfolio is the standard deviation of the risky portfolio times the fraction of the portfolio invested in the risky asset:

$$\sigma_C = y \times \sigma_P = 0.8 \times 0.27 = 0.216 \text{ or } 21.6\% \text{ per year}$$

14.

a. Standard deviation of the complete portfolio = $\sigma_C = y \times 0.27$

If the client wants the standard deviation to be equal or less than 20%, then:

$y = (0.20/0.27) = 0.7407 = 74.07\%$

He should invest, at most, 74.07% in the risky fund.

b. $E(r_C) = r_f + y \times [E(r_P) - r_f] = 0.07 + 0.7407 \times 0.10 = 0.1441$ or 14.41%

15.

a. Slope of the CML $= \dfrac{E(r_M) - r_f}{\sigma_M} = \dfrac{0.13 - 0.07}{0.25} = 0.24$

See the diagram below:

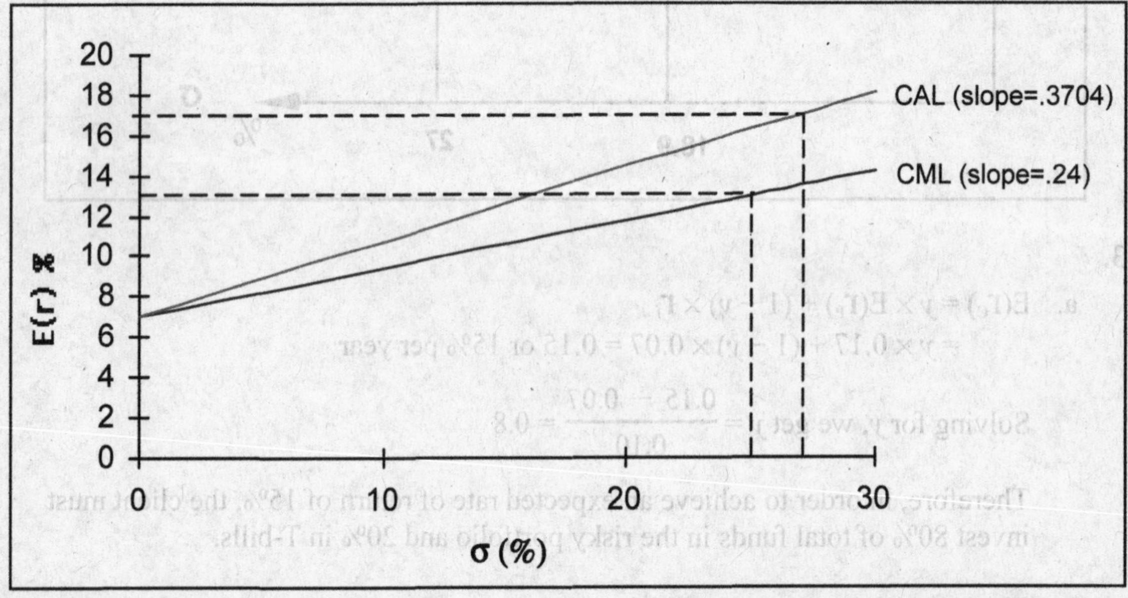

b. Your fund allows an investor to achieve a higher expected rate of return for any given standard deviation than would a passive strategy, i.e., a higher expected return for any given level of risk.

16.

a. With 70% of his money in your fund's portfolio, the client has an expected rate of return of 14% per year and a standard deviation of 18.9% per year. If he shifts that money to the passive portfolio (which has an expected rate of return of 13% and standard deviation of 25%), his overall expected return and standard deviation would become:

$$E(r_C) = r_f + 0.7 \times [E(r_M) - r_f]$$

In this case, $r_f = 7\%$ and $E(r_M) = 13\%$. Therefore:

$$E(r_C) = 0.07 + (0.7 \times 0.06) = 0.112 \text{ or } 11.2\%$$

The standard deviation of the complete portfolio using the passive portfolio would be:

$$\sigma_C = 0.7 \times \sigma_M = 0.7 \times 0.25 = 0.175 \text{ or } 17.5\%$$

Therefore, the shift entails a decline in the mean from 14% to 11.2% and a decline in the standard deviation from 18.9% to 17.5%. Since both mean return *and* standard deviation fall, it is not yet clear whether the move is beneficial. The disadvantage of the shift is apparent from the fact that, if your client is willing to accept an expected return on his total portfolio of 11.2%, he can achieve that return with a lower standard deviation using your fund portfolio rather than the passive portfolio. To achieve a target mean of 11.2%, we first write the mean of the complete portfolio as a function of the proportions invested in your fund portfolio, y:

$$E(r_C) = 7\% + y \times (17\% - 7\%) = 7\% + 10\% \times y$$

Because our target is $E(r_C) = 11.2\%$, the proportion that must be invested in your fund is determined as follows:

$$11.2\% = 7\% + 10\% \times y \Rightarrow y = \frac{11.2\% - 7\%}{10\%} = 0.42$$

The standard deviation of the portfolio would be:

$$\sigma_C = y \times 27\% = 0.42 \times 27\% = 11.34\%$$

Thus, by using your portfolio, the same 11.2% expected rate of return can be achieved with a standard deviation of only 11.34% as opposed to the standard deviation of 17.5% using the passive portfolio.

b. The fee would reduce the reward-to-variability ratio, i.e., the slope of the CAL. Clients will be indifferent between your fund and the passive portfolio if the slope of the after-fee CAL and the CML are equal. Let f denote the fee:

$$\text{Slope of CAL with fee} = \frac{17\% - 7\% - f}{27\%} = \frac{10\% - f}{27\%}$$

$$\text{Slope of CML (which requires no fee)} = \frac{13\% - 7\%}{25\%} = 0.24$$

Setting these slopes equal and solving for f:

$$\frac{10\% - f}{27\%} = 0.24$$

$$10\% - f = 27\% \times 0.24 = 6.48\%$$

$$f = 10\% - 6.48\% = 3.52\% \text{ per year}$$

17. Assuming no change in tastes, that is, an unchanged risk aversion, investors perceiving higher risk will demand a higher risk premium to hold the same portfolio they held before. If we assume that the risk-free rate is unaffected, the increase in the risk premium would require a higher expected rate of return in the equity market.

18. Expected return for your fund = T-bill rate + risk premium = 6% + 10% = 16%
Expected return of client's overall portfolio = (0.6 × 16%) + (0.4 × 6%) = 12%
Standard deviation of client's overall portfolio = 0.6 × 14% = 8.4%

19. Reward to volatility ratio $= \dfrac{\text{Portfolio Risk Premium}}{\text{Standard Deviation of Portfolio Excess Return}}$

$$= \frac{10\%}{14\%} = 0.7143$$

20.

Excess Return (%)

	Average	**Std Dev**	**Sharpe Ratio**	**5% VaR**
1926–2010	13.91	37.56	0.37	−65.13
1926–1955	20.02	49.25	0.41	−78.60
1956–1985	12.18	32.31	0.38	−49.53
1986–2010	8.66	25.82	0.34	−49.16

a. In three out of four time frames presented, small stocks provide worse ratios than large stocks.

b. Small stocks show a declining trend in risk, but the decline is not stable.

21. For geometric real returns, we take the geometric average return and the real geometric return data from Table 5.2 and then calculate the inflation in each time frame using the equation: Inflation rate = (1 + Nominal rate)/(1 + Real rate) − 1.

Geometric Real Returns (%) - Large Stocks

	Average	Inflation	Real Return
1926–2010	9.62	3.00	6.43
1926–1955	9.66	1.36	8.18
1956–1985	9.52	4.80	4.51
1986–2010	9.71	2.83	6.68

Risk Return Ratio - Large Stocks

	Arithmetic Real Return	Std Dev	Real Return to Risk
1926–2010	8.47	20.38	0.42
1926–1955	11.20	25.18	0.44
1956–1985	5.93	17.15	0.35
1986–2010	8.24	17.75	0.46

The VaR is not calculated, since the values used to determine the VaR in Table 5.4 are not provided.

Comparing with the excess return statistics in Table 5.4, in three out of four time frames the arithmetic real return is larger than the excess return, and the standard deviation of the real return in each time frame is lower than that of the excess return.

22.

Nominal Returns (%) - Small Stocks

	Nominal Return	Standard Deviation	Return to Risk
1926–2010	17.57	36.98	0.48
1926–1955	21.11	48.89	0.43
1956–1985	18.01	31.84	0.57
1986–2010	12.81	25.20	0.51

Real Returns (%) - Small Stocks

	Real Return (Arithmetic)	Standard Deviation	Return to Risk
1926–2010	14.19	36.32	0.39
1926–1955	19.32	48.12	0.40
1956–1985	12.76	30.82	0.41
1986–2010	9.75	24.83	0.39

The VaR is not calculated, since the values used to determine the VaR in Table 5.4 are not provided.

Comparing the nominal rate with the real rate of return, the real rates in all time frames and their standard deviation are lower than those of the nominal returns.

23.

Results	T Bill	S&P 500	Market
Average	3.56	5.57	5.63
SD	2.96	20.33	20.41
Skew	0.90	-0.87	-0.88
Kurtosis	0.70	1.06	0.92
Percentile (5%)	0.05	-31.51	-35.04
Normal (5%)	-1.31	-27.86	-27.93
Min	-0.04	-61.89	-59.69
Max	13.73	43.24	45.13
Serial corr	0.91	0.05	0.06
Corr(SP500,Mkt)		0.99	
Corr(pf, risk-free)		-0.12	-0.15

Comparison

The combined market index represents the Fama-French market factor (Mkt). It is better diversified than the S&P 500 index since it contains approximately ten times as many stocks. The total market capitalization of the additional stocks, however, is relatively small compared to the S&P 500. As a result, the performance of the value-weighted portfolios is expected to be quite similar, and the correlation of the excess returns very high. Even though the sample contains 84 observations, the standard deviation of the annual returns is relatively high, but the difference between the two indices is very small. When comparing the continuously compounded excess returns, we see that the difference between the two portfolios is indeed quite small, and the correlation coefficient between their returns is 0.99. Both deviate from the normal distribution as seen from the negative skew and positive kurtosis. Accordingly, the VaR (5% percentile) of the two is smaller than what is expected from a normal distribution with the same mean and standard deviation. This is also indicated by the lower minimum excess return for the period. The serial correlation is also small and indistinguishable across the portfolios.

As a result of all this, we expect the risk premium of the two portfolios to be similar, as we find from the sample. It is worth noting that the excess return of both portfolios has a small negative correlation with the risk-free rate. Since we expect the risk-free rate to be highly correlated with the rate of inflation, this suggests that equities are not a perfect hedge against inflation. More rigorous analysis of this point is important, but beyond the scope of this question.

CFA 1

Answer: $V(12/31/2011) = V(1/1/2005) \times (1 + g)^7 = \$100{,}000 \times (1.05)^7 = \$140{,}710.04$

CFA 2

Answer: *a.* and *b.* are true. The standard deviation is non-negative.

CFA 3

Answer: c. Determines most of the portfolio's return and volatility over time.

CFA 4

Answer: Investment 3.

For each portfolio: Utility = $E(r) - (0.5 \times 4 \times \sigma^2)$

Investment	E(r)	σ	Utility
1	0.12	0.30	−0.0600
2	0.15	0.50	−0.3500
3	0.21	0.16	0.1588
4	0.24	0.21	0.1518

We choose the portfolio with the highest utility value.

CFA 5

Answer: Investment 4.
When an investor is risk neutral, A = 0 so that the portfolio with the highest utility is the portfolio with the highest expected return.

CFA 6

Answer: b. Investor's aversion to risk.

CFA 7

Answer:

$E(r_X) = [0.2 \times (-0.20)] + (0.5 \times 0.18) + (0.3 \times 0.50) = 0.20$ or 20%

$E(r_Y) = [0.2 \times (-0.15)] + (0.5 \times 0.20) + (0.3 \times 0.10) = 0.10$ or 10%

CFA 8

Answer:

$\sigma_X^2 = [0.2 \times (-0.20 - 0.20)^2] + [0.5 \times (0.18 - 0.20)^2] + [0.3 \times (0.50 - 0.20)^2] = 0.0592$

$\sigma_X = 0.2433 = 24.33\%$

$\sigma_Y^2 = [0.2 \times (-0.15 - 0.10)^2] + [0.5 \times (0.20 - 0.10)^2] + [0.3 \times (0.10 - 0.10)^2] = 0.0175$

$\sigma_Y = 0.1323 = 13.23\%$

CFA 9

Answer:

$E(r) = (0.9 \times 0.20) + (0.1 \times 0.10) = 0.19$ or 19%

CFA 10

Answer:

The probability is 0.5 that the state of the economy is neutral. Given a neutral economy, the probability that the performance of the stock will be poor is 0.3, and the probability of both a neutral economy and poor stock performance is:

$0.3 \times 0.5 = 0.15$

CFA 11

Answer:

$E(r) = (0.1 \times 0.15) + (0.6 \times 0.13) + (0.3 \times 0.07) = 0.114$ or 11.4%

CHAPTER 06
EFFICIENT DIVERSIFICATION

1. So long as the correlation coefficient is below 1.0, the portfolio will benefit from diversification because returns on component securities will not move in perfect lockstep. The portfolio standard deviation will be *less* than a weighted average of the standard deviations of the component securities.

2. The covariance with the other assets is more important. Diversification is accomplished via correlation with other assets. Covariance helps determine that number.

3. *a* and *b* will have the same impact of increasing the Sharpe ratio from .40 to .45.

4. The expected return of the portfolio will be impacted if the asset allocation is changed. Since the expected return of the portfolio is the first item in the numerator of the Sharpe ratio, the ratio will be changed.

5. Total variance = Systematic variance + Residual variance = β^2 Var(r_M) + Var(e)
When $\beta = 1.5$ and $\sigma(e) = .3$, variance $= 1.5^2 \times .2^2 + .3^2 = .18$. In the other scenarios:

s_M	s(e)	b	TOTAL Variance	Corr Coeff
0.2	0.3	1.65	0.1989	0.7399
0.2	0.33	1.5	0.1989	0.6727

a. Both will have the same impact. Total variance will increase from .18 to .1989.

b. Even though the increase in the total variability of the stock is the same in either scenario, the increase in residual risk will have less impact on *portfolio* volatility. This is because residual risk is diversifiable. In contrast, the increase in beta increases systematic risk, which is perfectly correlated with the market-index portfolio and therefore has a greater impact on portfolio risk.

6.

a. Without doing any math, the severe recession is worse and the boom is better. Thus, there appears to be a higher variance, yet the mean is probably the same since the spread is equally large on both the high and low side. The mean return, however, should be higher since there is higher probability given to the higher returns.

b. Calculation of mean return and variance for the stock fund:

(A) Scenario	(B) Probability	(C) Rate of Return	(D) Col. B × Col. C	(E) Deviation from Expected Return	(F) Squared Deviation	(G) Col. B × Col. F
Severe recession	0.05	-40	-2.0	-51.2	2621.44	131.07
Mild recession	0.25	-14	-3.5	-25.2	635.04	158.76
Normal growth	0.40	17	6.8	5.8	33.64	13.46
Boom	0.30	33	9.9	21.8	475.24	142.57
	Expected Return =		11.2		Variance =	445.86
					Standard Deviation =	21.12

c. Calculation of covariance:

(A) Scenario	(B) Probability	(C) Deviation from Mean Return: Stock Fund	(D) Deviation from Mean Return: Bond Fund	(E) Col. C × Col. D	(F) Col. B × Col. E
Severe recession	0.05	-51.2	-14	716.8	35.84
Mild recession	0.25	-25.2	10	-252	-63.00
Normal growth	0.40	5.8	3	17.4	6.96
Boom	0.30	21.8	-10	-218	-65.40
				Covariance =	-85.6

Covariance has increased because the stock returns are more extreme in the recession and boom periods. This makes the tendency for stock returns to be poor when bond returns are good (and vice versa) even more dramatic.

7.

a. One would expect variance to increase because the probabilities of the extreme outcomes are now higher.

b. Calculation of mean return and variance for the stock fund:

Scenario	Probability	Stock Rate of Return	Col. B × Col. C	Deviation from Expected Return	Squared Deviation	Col. B × Col. F
Severe recession	0.10	-0.37	-0.037	-0.465	0.2162	0.0216
Mild recession	0.20	-0.11	-0.022	-0.205	0.0420	0.0084
Normal growth	0.35	0.14	0.049	0.045	0.0020	0.0007
Boom	0.35	0.30	0.105	0.205	0.0420	0.0147
	Expected Return =		0.095		Variance =	0.0454
					Standard Deviation =	0.2132

c. Calculation of covariance

		Deviation from Mean Return			
Scenario	Probability	Stock Fund	Bond Fund	Col. C × Col. D	Col. B × Col. E
Severe recession	0.1	-0.465	-0.122	0.05673	0.00567
Mild recession	0.2	-0.205	0.119	-0.024395	-0.0049
Normal growth	0.35	0.045	0.049	0.002205	0.00077
Boom	0.35	0.205	-0.082	-0.01681	-0.0059
		Expected return =	-0.036	Covariance =	-0.0043

Covariance has decreased because the probabilities of the more extreme returns in the recession and boom periods are now higher. This gives more weight to the extremes in the mean calculation, thus making their deviation from the mean less pronounced.

8. The parameters of the opportunity set are:

$E(r_S) = 15\%$, $E(r_B) = 9\%$, $\sigma_S = 32\%$, $\sigma_B = 23\%$, $\rho = 0.15$, $r_f = 5.5\%$

From the standard deviations and the correlation coefficient we generate the covariance matrix [note that $Cov(r_S, r_B) = \rho\sigma_S\sigma_B$]:

	Bonds	Stocks
Bonds	529.0	110.4
Stocks	110.4	1024.0

The minimum-variance portfolio proportions are:

$$w_{Min}(S) = \frac{\sigma_B^2 - Cov(r_S, r_B)}{\sigma_S^2 + \sigma_B^2 - 2Cov(r_S, r_B)} = \frac{529 - 110.4}{1{,}024 + 529 - (2 \times 110.4)} = .3142$$

$$w_{Min}(B) = 1 - .3142 = .6858$$

The mean and standard deviation of the minimum variance portfolio are:

$$E(r_{Min}) = (.3142 \times 15\%) + (.6858 \times 9\%) = 10.89\%$$

$$\sigma_{Min} = [w_S^2\sigma_S^2 + w_B^2\sigma_B^2 + 2\, w_S\, w_B\, Cov(r_S, r_B)]^{1/2}$$

$$= [(.3142^2 \times 1024) + (.6858^2 \times 529) + (2 \times .3142 \times .6858 \times 110.4)]^{1/2}$$

$$= 19.94\%$$

% in stocks	% in bonds	Exp. Return	Std dev.	Sharpe Ratio	
0.00	1.00	0.09	0.23	0.15	
0.20	0.80	0.10	0.20	0.23	
0.3142	0.6858	0.1089	0.1994	0.2701	Minimum Variance Portfolio
0.40	0.60	0.11	0.20	0.29	
0.60	0.40	0.13	0.23	0.32	
0.6466	0.3534	0.1288	0.233382	0.3162	Tangency Portfolio
0.80	0.20	0.14	0.27	0.31	
1.00	0.00	0.15	0.32	0.30	

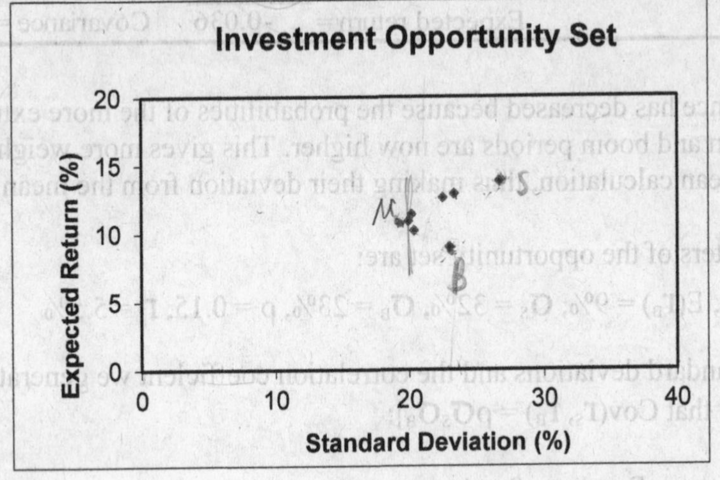

9.

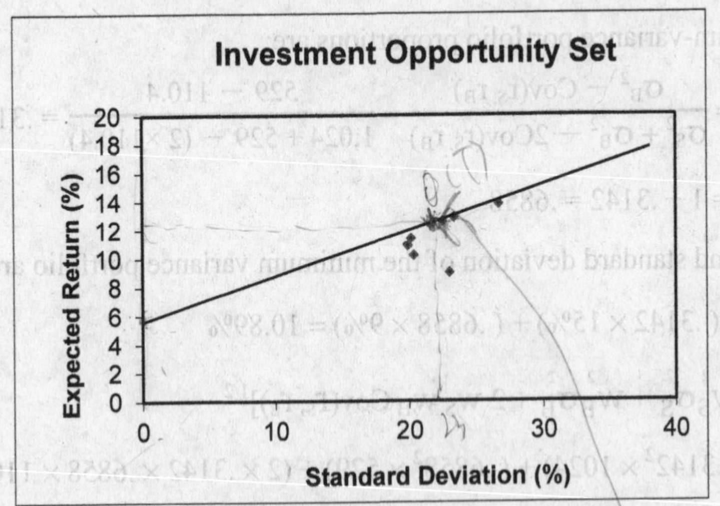

The graph approximates the points:

	E(r)	σ
Minimum variance portfolio	10.89%	19.94%
Tangency portfolio	12.88%	23.3382%

10. The reward-to-variability ratio (Sharpe ratio) of the optimal CAL is:

$$\frac{E(r_P) - r_f}{\sigma_P} = \frac{12.88 - 5.5}{23.34} = .3162$$

11.

a. The equation for the CAL is:

$$E(r_C) = r_f + \frac{E(r_P) - r_f}{\sigma_P}\sigma_C = 5.5 + .3162\sigma_C$$

Setting $E(r_C)$ equal to 12% yields a standard deviation of 20.5566%.

b. The mean of the complete portfolio as a function of the proportion invested in the risky portfolio (y) is:

$$E(r_C) = (1 - y)r_f + yE(r_P) = r_f + y[E(r_P) - r_f] = 5.5 + y(12.88 - 5.5)$$

Setting $E(r_C) = 12\% \Rightarrow y = .8808$ (88.08% in the risky portfolio)

$1 - y = .1192$ (11.92% in T-bills)

To prevent rounding error, we use the spreadsheet with the calculation of the previous parts of the problem to compute the proportion in each asset in the complete portfolio:

σ(c)	0.205559955 = (12% - 5.5%)/Sharpe ratio(risky portfolio)
W(risky portfolio)	0.880786822 = σ(c)/σ(risky portfolio)

Proportion of stocks in complete portfolio
W(s) = W(risky portfolio)*% in stock of the risky portfolio
= 0.569541021

Proportion of bonds in complete portfolio
W(b) = W(risky portfolio)*% in bonds of the risky portfolio
= 0.311245801

12. Using only the stock and bond funds to achieve a mean of 12%, we solve:

$$12 = 15w_S + 9(1 - w_S) = 9 + 6w_S \Rightarrow w_S = .5$$

Investing 50% in stocks and 50% in bonds yields a mean of 12% and standard deviation of: $\sigma_P = [(.50^2 \times 1{,}024) + (.50^2 \times 529) + (2 \times .50 \times .50 \times 110.4)]^{1/2} = 21.06\%$

The efficient portfolio with a mean of 12% has a standard deviation of only 20.61%. Using the CAL reduces the standard deviation by 45 basis points.

13.

a. Although it appears that gold is dominated by stocks, gold can still be an attractive diversification asset. If the correlation between gold and stocks is sufficiently low, gold will be held as a component in the optimal portfolio.

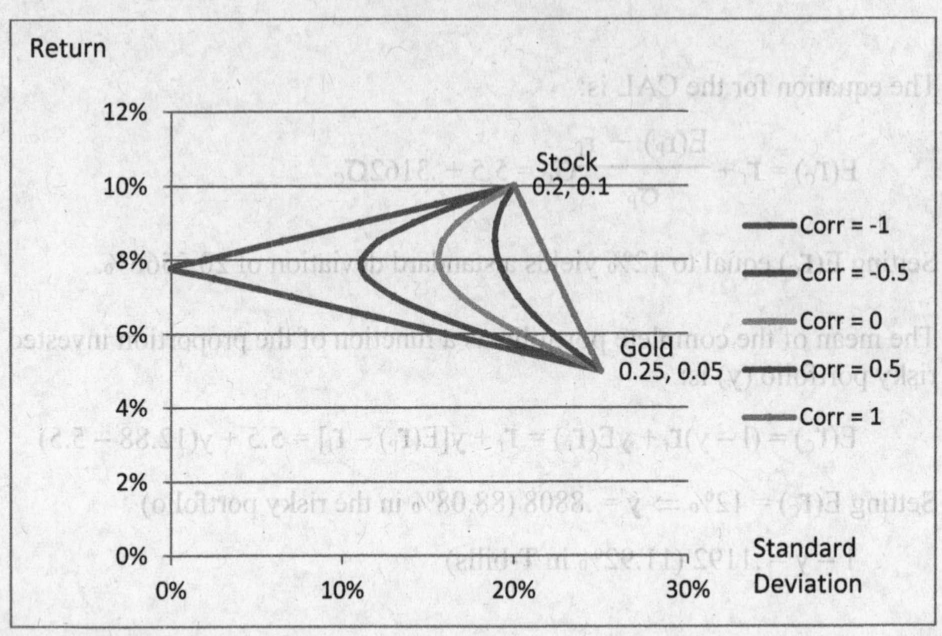

b. If gold had a perfectly positive correlation with stocks, gold would not be a part of efficient portfolios. The set of risk/return combinations of stocks and gold would plot as a straight line with a negative slope. (Refer to the above graph when correlation is 1.) The graph shows that when the correlation coefficient is 1, holding gold provides no benefit of diversification. The stock-only portfolio dominates any portfolio containing gold. This cannot be an equilibrium; the price of gold must fall and its expected return must rise.

14. Since Stock A and Stock B are perfectly negatively correlated, a risk-free portfolio can be created and the rate of return for this portfolio in equilibrium will always be the risk-free rate. To find the proportions of this portfolio [with w_A invested in Stock A and $w_B = (1 - w_A)$ invested in Stock B], set the standard deviation equal to zero. With perfect negative correlation, the portfolio standard deviation reduces to:

$$\sigma_P = ABS[w_A\sigma_A - w_B\sigma_B]$$

$$0 = 40\ w_A - 60(1 - w_A) \Rightarrow w_A = .60$$

The expected rate of return on this risk-free portfolio is:

$$E(r) = (.60 \times .08) + (.40 \times .13) = 10.0\%$$

Therefore, the risk-free rate must also be 10.0%.

15. Since these are annual rates and the risk-free rate was quite variable during the sample period of the recent 20 years, the analysis has to be conducted with continuously compounded rates in excess of T-bill rates. Notice that to obtain cc rates we must convert percentage return to decimal. The decimal cc rate, ln(1 + percentage rate/100), can then be multiplied by 100 to return to percentage rates. Recall also that with cc rates, excess returns are just the difference between total returns and the risk-free (T-bill) rates.

	Annual returns from Table 2			Continuously compounded rates			Excess returns	
Year	Large Stock	Long-Term T-Bonds	T-Bills	Large Stock	Long-Term T-Bonds	T-Bills	Large Stock	Long-Term T-Bonds
1989	31.34	19.49	8.38	27.26	17.81	8.05	19.21	9.76
1990	-3.20	7.13	7.84	-3.25	6.89	7.55	-10.80	-0.66
1991	30.66	18.39	5.60	26.74	16.88	5.45	21.29	11.43
1992	7.71	7.79	3.50	7.43	7.50	3.44	3.99	4.06
1993	9.87	15.48	2.90	9.41	14.39	2.86	6.55	11.53
1994	1.29	-7.18	3.91	1.28	-7.45	3.84	-2.55	-11.29
1995	37.71	31.67	5.60	32.00	27.51	5.45	26.55	22.06
1996	23.07	-0.81	5.20	20.76	-0.81	5.07	15.69	-5.88
1997	33.17	15.08	5.25	28.65	14.05	5.12	23.53	8.93
1998	28.58	13.52	4.85	25.14	12.68	4.74	20.40	7.94
1999	21.04	-8.74	4.69	19.10	-9.15	4.58	14.51	-13.73
2000	-9.10	20.27	5.88	-9.54	18.46	5.71	-15.25	12.74
2001	-11.89	4.21	3.86	-12.66	4.12	3.79	-16.45	0.34
2002	-22.10	16.79	1.63	-24.97	15.52	1.62	-26.59	13.90
2003	28.69	2.38	1.02	25.22	2.35	1.01	24.21	1.34
2004	10.88	7.71	1.19	10.33	7.43	1.18	9.14	6.24
2005	4.91	6.50	2.98	4.79	6.30	2.94	1.86	3.36
2006	11.78	-1.21	4.81	11.14	-1.22	4.70	6.44	-5.92
2007	3.53	10.25	4.67	3.47	9.76	4.56	-1.10	5.20
2008	-38.49	1.34	1.55	-48.60	1.33	1.54	-50.14	-0.21
						Average	3.53	4.06
						SD	19.64	8.88
						Corr(stocks,bonds)	0.13	

	Weights in		Portfolio	
	Stocks	Bonds	Mean	SD
	0.0	1	4.06	8.88
	0.1	0.9	4.01	8.47
	0.2	0.8	3.95	8.55
	0.3	0.7	3.90	9.10
	0.4	0.6	3.85	10.05
	0.5	0.5	3.79	11.29
	0.6	0.4	3.74	12.74
	0.7	0.3	3.69	14.34
	0.8	0.2	3.63	16.04
	0.9	0.1	3.58	17.81
	1.0	0	3.53	19.64
Min-Var	0.1338	0.8662	3.99	8.44

The bond portfolio is less risky as represented by its lower standard deviation. Yet, as the portfolio table shows, mixing .87% of bonds with 13% stocks would have produced a portfolio less risky than bonds. In this sample of these 20 years, the average return on the less risky portfolio of bonds was higher than that of the riskier portfolio of stocks. This is exactly what is meant by "risk." Expectation will not always be realized.

16. If the lending and borrowing rates are equal and there are no other constraints on portfolio choice, then the optimal risky portfolios of all investors will be identical. However, if the borrowing and lending rates are not equal, then borrowers (who are relatively risk averse) and lenders (who are relatively risk tolerant) will have different optimal risky portfolios.

17. No, it is not possible to get such a diagram. Even if the correlation between A and B were 1.0, the frontier would be a straight line connecting A and B.

18. In the special case that all assets are perfectly positively correlated, the portfolio standard deviation is equal to the weighted average of the component-asset standard deviations. Otherwise, as the formula for portfolio variance (Equation 6.6) shows, the portfolio standard deviation is *less* than the weighted average of the component-asset standard deviations. The portfolio *variance* is a weighted *sum* of the elements in the covariance matrix, with the products of the portfolio proportions as weights.

19. The probability distribution is:

Probability	Rate of Return
.7	100%
.3	−50%

Expected return = $(.7 \times 1) + .3 \times (-.5) = 0.55$ or 55%

Variance = $[.7 \times (1 - 0.55)^2] + [.3 \times (-0.50 - 0.55)^2] = 0.4725$

Standard Deviation = $\sqrt{0.4725} = 0.6874$ or 68.74%

20. The expected rate of return on the stock will change by beta times the unanticipated change in the market return: $1.2 \times (.08 - .10) = -2.4\%$

Therefore, the expected rate of return on the stock should be revised to:

$.12 - .024 = 9.6\%$

21.

a. The risk of the diversified portfolio consists primarily of systematic risk. Beta measures systematic risk, which is the slope of the security characteristic line (SCL). The two figures depict the stocks' SCLs. Stock B's SCL is steeper, and hence Stock B's systematic risk is greater. The slope of the SCL, and hence the systematic risk, of Stock A is lower. Thus, for this investor, stock B is the riskiest.

b. The undiversified investor is exposed primarily to firm-specific risk. Stock A has higher firm-specific risk because the deviations of the observations from the SCL are larger for Stock A than for Stock B. Deviations are measured by the vertical distance of each observation from the SCL. Stock A is therefore riskiest to this investor.

22. Using "Regression" command from Excel's Data Analysis menu, we can run a regression of GM's excess returns against those of S&P 500, and obtain the following data. The Beta of GM is .87.

SUMMARY OUTPUT

Regression Statistics	
Multiple R	0.37
R Square	0.14
Adjusted R Square	0.12
Standard Error	8.32
Observations	60.00

	Coefficients	*Standard Error*	*t Stat*	*P-value*
Intercept	(1.65)	1.08	(1.52)	0.13
S&P 500	0.87	0.28	3.05	0.00

23. A scatter plot results in the following diagram. The slope of the regression line is 2.0 and intercept is 1.0.

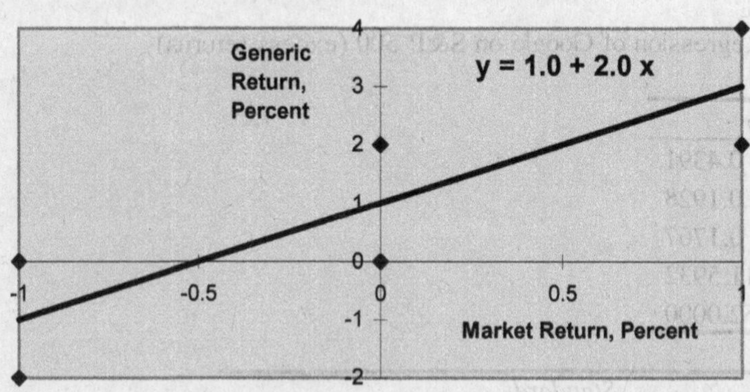

24.

a. Regression output produces the following:
alpha = 3.1792, beta = 1.3916, Residual St Dev = 11.5932

b. Sharpe Ratio of S&P $= \dfrac{E(r_{S\&P}) - r_f}{\sigma_{S\&P}} = -.6123/4.0316 = -.1519$

	Alpha	Beta	E(r) - rf	VAR	SD
S&P			-0.6123	16.2541	4.0316
Google	3.1792	1.3916	2.3271	163.2443	12.7767

c. Information Ratio $= \alpha_G/\sigma(e_G) = 3.1792/11.5932 = .2742$

d. We use Equation 6.16 to compute w_G^O

$$w_G^O = \frac{\alpha_G/\sigma^2(e_G)}{R_{S\&P}/\sigma^2_{S\&P}} = \frac{3.1792/(11.5932^2)}{-.6123/(4.0316^2)} = -62.79\%$$

Then, plug w_G^O into Equation 6.17 to compute the optimal position of Google in the optimal risky portfolio and the weight in the market index:

$$w_G^* = -.6279 / [1 + (-.6279 \times (1 - 1.3916)] = -50.40\%$$

$$w_M^* = 1 - w_G^* = 49.60\%$$

e. $S_O = \sqrt{\left(\dfrac{\alpha_G}{\sigma(e_G)}\right)^2 + (S_M)^2} = \sqrt{\left(\dfrac{3.1792}{11.5932}\right)^2 + (-.1519)^2} = .3135$

Sharpe ratio increases from $-.1519$ to $.3135$.

SUMMARY OUTPUT: Regression of Google on S&P 500 (excess returns)

Regression Statistics	
Multiple R	0.4391
R Square	0.1928
Adjusted R Square	0.1767
Standard Error	11.5932
Observations	52.0000

	Coefficients	*Standard Error*	*t Stat*	*P-value*
Intercept	3.1792	1.6265	1.9546	0.0562
S&P 500	1.3916	0.4027	3.4560	0.0011

	Google	*Spy*
Google	1.00	
S&P 500	0.44	1.00

CFA 1

Answer:

$E(r_P) = (.5 \times 15) + (.4 \times 10) + (.10 \times 6) = 12.1\%$

CFA 2

Answer:

Fund D represents the single best addition to complement Stephenson's current portfolio, given his selection criteria. First, Fund D's expected return (14.0 percent) has the potential to increase the portfolio's return somewhat. Second, Fund D's relatively low correlation with his current portfolio (+ .65) indicates that Fund D will provide greater diversification benefits than any of the other alternatives except Fund B. The result of adding Fund D should be a portfolio with approximately the same expected return and somewhat lower volatility compared to the original portfolio.

The other three funds have shortcomings in terms of either expected return enhancement or volatility reduction through diversification benefits. Fund A offers the potential for increasing the portfolio's return, but is too highly correlated to provide substantial volatility reduction benefits through diversification. Fund B provides substantial volatility reduction through diversification benefits, but is expected to generate a return well below the current portfolio's return. Fund C has the greatest potential to increase the portfolio's return, but is too highly correlated to provide substantial volatility reduction benefits through diversification.

CFA 3

Answer:

a. Subscript OP refers to the original portfolio, ABC to the new stock, and NP to the new portfolio.

i. $E(r_{NP}) = w_{OP}\, E(r_{OP}) + w_{ABC}\, E(r_{ABC}) = (.9 \times .67) + (.1 \times 1.25) = .7280\%$

ii. $Cov_{OP,\, ABC} = Corr_{OP,\, ABC} \times \sigma_{OP} \times \sigma_{ABC} = .40 \times 2.37 \times 2.95 = 2.7966$

iii. $\sigma_{NP} = [w_{OP}^2\, \sigma_{OP}^2 + w_{ABC}^2\, \sigma_{ABC}^2 + 2\, w_{OP}\, w_{ABC}\, (Cov_{OP,\, ABC})]^{1/2}$

$= [(.9^2 \times 2.37^2) + (.1^2 \times 2.95^2) + (2 \times .9 \times .1 \times 2.7966)]^{1/2}$

$= 2.2672\%$

b. Subscript OP refers to the original portfolio, GS to government securities, and NP to the new portfolio.

i. $E(r_{NP}) = w_{OP}\, E(r_{OP}) + w_{GS}\, E(r_{GS}) = (.9 \times .67) + (.1 \times .42) = .6450\%$

ii. $Cov_{OP,\, GS} = Corr_{OP,\, GS} \times \sigma_{OP} \times \sigma_{GS} = 0 \times 2.37 \times 0 = 0$

iii. $\sigma_{NP} = [w_{OP}^2\, \sigma_{OP}^2 + w_{GS}^2\, \sigma_{GS}^2 + 2\, w_{OP}\, w_{GS}\, (Cov_{OP,\, GS})]^{1/2}$

$= [(.9^2 \times 2.37^2) + (.1^2 \times 0) + (2 \times .9 \times .1 \times 0)]^{1/2}$

$= 2.1330\%$

c. Adding the risk-free government securities would result in a lower beta for the new portfolio. The new portfolio beta will be a weighted average of the individual security betas in the portfolio; the presence of the risk-free securities would lower that weighted average.

d. The comment is not correct. Although the respective standard deviations and expected returns for the two securities under consideration are identical, the correlation coefficients between each security and the original portfolio are unknown, making it impossible to draw the conclusion stated. For instance, if the correlation between the original portfolio and XYZ stock is smaller than that between the original portfolio and ABC stock, replacing ABC stocks with XYZ stocks would result in a lower standard deviation for the portfolio as a whole. In such a case, XYZ socks would be the preferred investment, assuming all other factors are equal.

e. Grace clearly expressed the sentiment that the risk of loss was more important to her than the opportunity for return. Using variance (or standard deviation) as a measure of risk in her case has a serious limitation because standard deviation does not distinguish between positive and negative price movements.

CFA 4

Answer:

a. Restricting the portfolio to 20 stocks, rather than 40 to 50, will very likely increase the risk of the portfolio, due to the reduction in diversification. Such an increase might be acceptable if the expected return is increased sufficiently.

b. Hennessy could contain the increase in risk by making sure that he maintains reasonable diversification among the 20 stocks that remain in his portfolio. This entails maintaining a low correlation among the remaining stocks. As a practical matter, this means that Hennessy would need to spread his portfolio among many industries, rather than concentrating in just a few.

CFA 5

Answer:

Risk reduction benefits from diversification are not a linear function of the number of issues in the portfolio. (See Figures 6.1 and 6.2 in the text.) Rather, the incremental benefits from additional diversification are most important when the portfolio is least diversified. Restricting Hennessy to 10 issues, instead of 20 issues, would increase the risk of his portfolio by a greater amount than reducing the size of the portfolio from 30 to 20 stocks.

CFA 6

Answer:

The point is well taken because the committee should be concerned with the volatility of the entire fund. Since Hennessy's portfolio is only one of six well-diversified portfolios, and is smaller than the average, the concentration in fewer issues might have a minimal effect on the diversification of the total fund. Hence, unleashing Hennessy to do stock picking may be advantageous.

CFA 7

Answer:

a. Systematic risk refers to fluctuations in asset prices caused by macroeconomic factors that are common to all risky assets; hence systematic risk is often referred to as market risk. Examples of systematic risk factors include the business cycle, inflation, monetary policy, and technological changes.

   Firm-specific risk refers to fluctuations in asset prices caused by factors that are independent of the market, such as industry characteristics or firm characteristics. Examples of firm-specific risk factors include litigation, patents, management, and financial leverage.

b. Trudy should explain to the client that picking only the five best ideas would most likely result in the client holding a much more risky portfolio. The total risk of a portfolio, or portfolio variance, is the combination of systematic risk and firm-specific risk.

   The systematic component depends on the sensitivity of the individual assets to market movements, as measured by beta. Assuming the portfolio is well-diversified, the number of assets will not affect the systematic risk component of portfolio variance. The portfolio beta depends on the individual security betas and the portfolio weights of those securities.

   On the other hand, the components of firm-specific risk (sometimes called nonsystematic risk) are not perfectly positively correlated with each other and, as more assets are added to the portfolio, those additional assets tend to reduce portfolio risk. Hence, increasing the number of securities in a portfolio reduces firm-specific risk. For example, a patent expiration for one company would not affect the other securities in the portfolio. An increase in oil prices might hurt an airline stock but aid an energy stock. As the number of randomly selected securities increases, the total risk (variance) of the portfolio approaches its systematic variance.

CHAPTER 07
CAPITAL ASSET PRICING AND ARBITRAGE PRICING THEORY

1. The required rate of return on a stock is related to the required rate of return on the stock market via beta. Assuming the beta of Google remains constant, the increase in the risk of the market will increase the required rate of return on the market, and thus increase the required rate of return on Google.

2. An example of this scenario would be an investment in the SMB and HML. As of yet, there are no vehicles (index funds or ETFs) to directly invest in SMB and HML. While they may prove superior to the single index model, they are not yet practical, even for professional investors.

3. a. False. According to CAPM, when beta is zero, the "excess" return should be zero.

   b. False. CAPM implies that the investor will only require risk premium for systematic risk. Investors are not rewarded for bearing higher risk if the volatility results from the firm-specific risk, and thus, can be diversified.

   c. False. We can construct a portfolio with the beta of .75 by investing .75 of the investment budget in the market portfolio and the remainder in T-bills.

4. $E(r) = r_f + \beta\,[E(r_M) - r_f]$, $r_f = 4\%$, $r_M = 6\%$

   \$1 Discount Store: $E(r) = 4\% + 1.5 \times 6\% = 13\%$

   Everything \$5: $E(r) = 4\% + 1.0 \times 6\% = 10\%$

5. \$1 Discount Store is overpriced; Everything \$5 is underpriced.

6. a. 15%. Its expected return is exactly the same as the market return when beta is 1.0.

7. Statement *a* is most accurate.

   The flaw in statement *b* is that beta represents only the systematic risk. If the firm-specific risk is low enough, the stock of Kaskin, Inc. could still have less total risk than that of Quinn, Inc.

   Statement *c* is incorrect. Lower beta means the stock carries less systematic risk.

8. The APT may exist without the CAPM, but not the other way. Thus, statement *a* is possible, but not *b*. The reason is that the APT accepts the principle of risk and return,

which is central to CAPM, without making any assumptions regarding individual investors and their portfolios. However, these assumptions are necessary to CAPM.

9. $E(r_p) = r_f + \beta\,[E(r_M) - r_f]$ Given $r_f = 5\%$ and $E(r_M) = 15\%$, we can calculate β:

$$20\% = 5\% + \beta(15\% - 5\%) \Rightarrow \beta = 1.5$$

10. If the beta of the security doubles, then so will its risk premium. The current risk premium for the stock is: (13% − 7%) = 6%, so the new risk premium would be 12%, and the new discount rate for the security would be: 12% + 7% = 19%

If the stock pays a constant dividend in perpetuity, then we know from the original data that the dividend (D) must satisfy the equation for a perpetuity:

Price = Dividend/Discount rate

$$40 = D/0.13 \Rightarrow D = 40 \times 0.13 = \$5.20$$

At the new discount rate of 19%, the stock would be worth: $5.20/0.19 = $27.37
The increase in stock risk has lowered the value of the stock by 31.58%.

11. The cash flows for the project comprise a 10-year annuity of $10 million per year plus an additional payment in the tenth year of $10 million (so that the total payment in the tenth year is $20 million). The appropriate discount rate for the project is:

$$r_f + \beta\,[E(r_M) - r_f] = 9\% + 1.7 \times (19\% - 9\%) = 26\%$$

Using this discount rate:

$$NPV = -20 + \sum_{t=1}^{10} \frac{10}{1.26^t} + \frac{10}{1.26^{10}}$$

$$= -20 + [10 \times \text{Annuity factor }(26\%, 10\text{ years})] + [10 \times \text{PV factor }(26\%, 10\text{ years})]$$

$$= 15.64$$

The internal rate of return on the project is 49.55%. The highest value that beta can take before the hurdle rate exceeds the IRR is determined by:

$$49.55\% = 9\% + \beta(19\% - 9\%) \Rightarrow \beta = 40.55/10 = 4.055$$

12.

a. The beta is the sensitivity of the stock's return to the market return, or, the change in the stock return per unit change in the market return. We denote the aggressive stock *A* and the defensive stock *D*, and then compute each stock's beta by calculating the difference in its return across the two scenarios divided by the difference in market return.

$$\beta_A = \frac{2 - 32}{5 - 20} = 2.00$$

$$\beta_D = \frac{3.5 - 14}{5 - 20} = 0.70$$

b. With the two scenarios equally likely, the expected rate of return is an average of the two possible outcomes:

$$E(r_A) = 0.5 \times (2\% + 32\%) = 17\%$$

$$E(r_D) = 0.5 \times (3.5\% + 14\%) = 8.75\%$$

c. The SML is determined by the following: Expected return is the T-bill rate = 8% when beta equals zero; beta for the market is 1.0; and the expected rate of return for the market is:

$$0.5 \times (20\% + 5\%) = 12.5\%$$

Thus, we graph the SML as following:

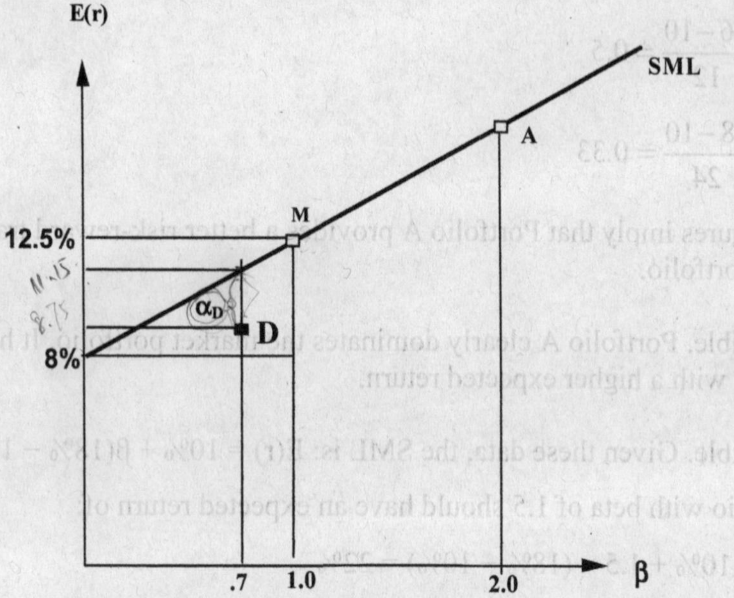

The equation for the security market line is: $E(r) = 8\% + \beta(12.5\% - 8\%)$

d. The aggressive stock has a fair expected rate of return of:

$$E(r_A) = 8\% + 2.0 \times (12.5\% - 8\%) = 17\%$$

The security analyst's estimate of the expected rate of return is also 17%. Thus the alpha for the aggressive stock is zero. Similarly, the required return for the defensive stock is:

$$E(r_D) = 8\% + 0.7 \times (12.5\% - 8\%) = 11.15\%$$

The security analyst's estimate of the expected return for D is only 8.75%, and hence:

$$\alpha_D = \text{actual expected return} - \text{required return predicted by CAPM}$$

$$= 8.75\% - 11.15\% = -2.4\%$$

The points for each stock are plotted on the graph above.

e. The hurdle rate is determined by the project beta (i.e., 0.7), not by the firm's beta. The correct discount rate is therefore 11.15%, the fair rate of return on stock D.

13. Not possible. Portfolio A has a higher beta than Portfolio B, but the expected return for Portfolio A is lower.

14. Possible. If the CAPM is valid, the expected rate of return compensates only for systematic (market) risk as measured by beta, rather than the standard deviation, which includes nonsystematic risk. Thus, Portfolio A's lower expected rate of return can be paired with a higher standard deviation, as long as Portfolio A's beta is lower than that of Portfolio B.

15. Not possible. The reward-to-variability ratio for Portfolio A is better than that of the market, which is not possible according to the CAPM, since the CAPM predicts that the market portfolio is the most efficient portfolio. Using the numbers supplied:

$$S_A = \frac{16-10}{12} = 0.5$$

$$S_M = \frac{18-10}{24} = 0.33$$

These figures imply that Portfolio A provides a better risk-reward tradeoff than the market portfolio.

16. Not possible. Portfolio A clearly dominates the market portfolio. It has a lower standard deviation with a higher expected return.

17. Not possible. Given these data, the SML is: $E(r) = 10\% + \beta(18\% - 10\%)$

A portfolio with beta of 1.5 should have an expected return of:

$$E(r) = 10\% + 1.5 \times (18\% - 10\%) = 22\%$$

The expected return for Portfolio A is 16% so that Portfolio A plots below the SML (i.e., has an alpha of −6%), and hence is an overpriced portfolio. This is inconsistent with the CAPM.

18. Not possible. The SML is the same as in Problem 18. Here, the required expected return for Portfolio A is: $10\% + (0.9 \times 8\%) = 17.2\%$

This is still higher than 16%. Portfolio A is overpriced, with alpha equal to: −1.2%

19. Possible. Portfolio A's ratio of risk premium to standard deviation is less attractive than the market's. This situation is consistent with the CAPM. The market portfolio should provide the highest reward-to-variability ratio.

20.

a.

	Ford	GM	Toyota	S&P	
Beta 5 years	1.81	0.86	0.71	1.00	
Beta first two years	2.01	1.05	0.47	3.78	SD
Beta last two years	1.97	0.69	0.49		
SE of residual	12.01	8.34	5.14		
SE beta 5 years	0.42	0.29	0.18		
Intercept 5 years	-0.93	-1.44	0.45		
Intercept first two years	-2.37	-1.82	1.80		
Intercept last two years	0.81	-3.41	-1.91		

b.

As a first pass, we note that large standard deviation of the beta estimates. None of the subperiod estimates deviate from the overall period estimate by more than two standard deviations. That is, the t-statistic of the deviation from the overall period is not significant for any of the subperiod beta estimates. Looking beyond the aforementioned observation, the differences can be attributed to different alpha values during the subperiods. The case of Toyota is most revealing: The alpha estimate for the first two years is positive and for the last two years negative (both large). Following a good performance in the "normal" years prior to the crisis, Toyota surprised investors with a negative performance, beyond what could be expected from the index. This suggests that a beta of around 0.5 is more reliable. The shift of the intercepts from positive to negative when the index moved to largely negative returns, explains why the line is steeper when estimated for the overall period. Draw a line in the positive quadrant for the index with a slope of 0.5 and positive intercept. Then draw a line with similar slope in the negative quadrant of the index with a negative intercept. You can see that a line that reconciles the observations for both quadrants will be steeper. The same logic explains part of the behavior of subperiod betas for Ford and GM.

21. Since the stock's beta is equal to 1.0, its expected rate of return should be equal to that of the market, that is, 18%.

$$E(r) = \frac{D + P_1 - P_0}{P_0}$$

$$0.18 = \frac{9 + P_1 - 100}{100} \Rightarrow P_1 = \$109$$

22. If beta is zero, the cash flow should be discounted at the risk-free rate, 8%:
PV = $1,000/0.08 = $12,500

If, however, beta is actually equal to 1, the investment should yield 18%, and the price paid for the firm should be:

PV = \$1,000/0.18 = \$5,555.56

The difference (\$6944.44) is the amount you will overpay if you erroneously assume that beta is zero rather than 1.

23. Using the SML: $6\% = 8\% + \beta(18\% - 8\%) \Rightarrow \beta = -2/10 = -0.2$

24. We denote the first investment advisor *1*, who has $r_1 = 19\%$ and $\beta_1 = 1.5$, and the second investment advisor *2*, as $r_2 = 16\%$ and $\beta_2 = 1.0$. In order to determine which investor was a better selector of individual stocks, we look at the abnormal return, which is the ex-post alpha; that is, the abnormal return is the difference between the actual return and that predicted by the SML.

a. Without information about the parameters of this equation (i.e., the risk-free rate and the market rate of return), we cannot determine which investment adviser is the better selector of individual stocks.

b. If $r_f = 6\%$ and $r_M = 14\%$, then (using alpha for the abnormal return):

$$\alpha_1 = 19\% - [6\% + 1.5 \times (14\% - 6\%)] = 19\% - 18\% = 1\%$$

$$\alpha_2 = 16\% - [6\% + 1.0 \times (14\% - 6\%)] = 16\% - 14\% = 2\%$$

Here, the second investment adviser has the larger abnormal return and thus appears to be the better selector of individual stocks. By making better predictions, the second adviser appears to have tilted his portfolio toward under-priced stocks.

c. If $r_f = 3\%$ and $r_M = 15\%$, then:

$$\alpha_1 = 19\% - [3\% + 1.5 \times (15\% - 3\%)] = 19\% - 21\% = -2\%$$

$$\alpha_2 = 16\% - [3\% + 1.0 \times (15\% - 3\%)] = 16\% - 15\% = 1\%$$

Here, not only does the second investment adviser appear to be a better stock selector, but the first adviser's selections appear valueless (or worse).

25.

a. Since the market portfolio, by definition, has a beta of 1.0, its expected rate of return is 12%.

b. $\beta = 0$ means the stock has no systematic risk. Hence, the portfolio's expected rate of return is the risk-free rate, 4%.

c. Using the SML, the *fair* rate of return for a stock with $\beta = -0.5$ is:

$$E(r) = 4\% + (-0.5) \times (12\% - 4\%) = 0.0\%$$

The *expected* rate of return, using the expected price and dividend for next year:

$$E(r) = (\$41 + \$3)/\$40 - 1 = 0.10 = 10\%$$

Because the expected return exceeds the fair return, the stock must be under-priced.

26. The data can be summarized as follows:

	Expected Return	Beta	Deviation
Portfolio A	11%	0.8	10%
Portfolio B	14%	1.5	31%
S & P 500	12%	1	20%
T-bills	6%	0	0%

a. Using the SML, the expected rate of return for any portfolio P is:

$$E(r_P) = r_f + \beta[E(r_M) - r_f]$$

Substituting for portfolios A and B:

$$E(r_A) = 6\% + 0.8 \times (12\% - 6\%) = 10.8\% < 11\%$$

$$E(r_B) = 6\% + 1.5 \times (12\% - 6\%) = 15.0\% > 14\%$$

Hence, Portfolio A is desirable and Portfolio B is not.

b. The slope of the CAL supported by a portfolio P is given by:

$$S = \frac{E(r_P) - r_f}{\sigma_P}$$

Computing this slope for each of the three alternative portfolios, we have:

S (S&P 500) = (12% – 6%)/20% = 6/20

S (A) = (11% – 6%)/10% = 5/10 > S(S&P 500)

S (B) = (14% – 6%)/31% = 8/31 < S(S&P 500)

Hence, portfolio A would be a good substitute for the S&P 500.

27. Since the beta for Portfolio F is zero, the expected return for Portfolio F equals the risk-free rate.

For Portfolio A, the ratio of risk premium to beta is: (10 – 4)/1 = 6

The ratio for Portfolio E is higher: (9 – 4)/(2/3) = 7.5

This implies that an arbitrage opportunity exists. For instance, by taking a long position in Portfolio E and a short position in Portfolio F (that is, borrowing at the risk-free rate and investing the proceeds in Portfolio E), we can create another portfolio which has the same beta (1.0) but higher expected return than Portfolio A. For the beta of the new portfolio to equal 1.0, the proportion (w) of funds invested in E must be: 3/2 = 1.5.

Portfolio Weight	In Asset	Contribution to β	Contribution to Excess Return
−1	Portfolio A	$-1 \times \beta_A = -1.0$	$-1.0 \times (10\% - 4\%) = -6\%$
1.5	Portfolio E	$1.5 \times \beta_E = 1.0$	$1.5 \times (9\% - 4\%) = 7.5\%$
−0.5	Portfolio F	$-0.5 \times 0 = 0$	0
Investment = 0		$\beta_{Arbitrage} = 0$	$\alpha = 1.5\%$

As summarized above, taking a short position in portfolio A and a long position in the new portfolio, we produce an arbitrage portfolio with zero investment (all proceeds from the short sale of Portfolio A are invested in the new portfolio), zero risk (because β = 0 and the portfolios are well diversified), and a positive return of 1.5%.

28. Substituting the portfolio returns and betas in the mean-beta relationship, we obtain two equations in the unknowns, the risk-free rate (r_f) and the factor return (F):

$$14.0\% = r_f + 1 \times (F - r_f)$$

$$14.8\% = r_f + 1.1 \times (F - r_f)$$

From the first equation we find that F = 14%. Substituting this value for F into the second equation, we get:

$$14.8\% = r_f + 1.1 \times (14\% - r_f) \Rightarrow r_f = 6\%$$

29.

a. Shorting equal amounts of the 10 negative-alpha stocks and investing the proceeds equally in the 10 positive-alpha stocks eliminates the market exposure and creates a zero-investment portfolio. Using equation 7.5 and denoting the market factor as R_M, the expected dollar return is [noting that the expectation of residual risk (*e*) in equation 7.8 is zero]:

$$\$1{,}000{,}000 \times [0.03 + (1.0 \times R_M)] - \$1{,}000{,}000 \times [(-0.03) + (1.0 \times R_M)]$$

$$= \$1{,}000{,}000 \times 0.06 = \$60{,}000$$

The sensitivity of the payoff of this portfolio to the market factor is zero because the exposures of the positive alpha and negative alpha stocks cancel out. (Notice that the terms involving R_M sum to zero.) Thus, the systematic component of total risk also is zero. The variance of the analyst's profit is not zero, however, since this portfolio is not well diversified.

For *n* = 20 stocks (i.e., long 10 stocks and short 10 stocks) the investor will have a $100,000 position (either long or short) in each stock. Net market exposure is zero, but firm-specific risk has not been fully diversified. The variance of dollar returns from the positions in the 20 firms is:

$$20 \times [(100{,}000 \times 0.30)^2] = 18{,}000{,}000{,}000$$

The standard deviation of dollar returns is $134,164.

b. If $n = 50$ stocks (i.e., 25 long and 25 short), $40,000 is placed in each position, and the variance of dollar returns is:

$$50 \times [(40{,}000 \times 0.30)^2] = 7{,}200{,}000{,}000$$

The standard deviation of dollar returns is $84,853.

Similarly, if $n = 100$ stocks (i.e., 50 long and 50 short), $20,000 is placed in each position, and the variance of dollar returns is:

$$100 \times [(20{,}000 \times 0.30)^2] = 3{,}600{,}000{,}000$$

The standard deviation of dollar returns is $60,000.

Notice that when the number of stocks increases by a factor of 5 (from 20 to 100), standard deviation falls by a factor of $\sqrt{5} = 2.236$, from $134,164 to $60,000.

30. Any pattern of returns can be "explained" if we are free to choose an indefinitely large number of explanatory factors. If a theory of asset pricing is to have value, it must explain returns using a reasonably limited number of explanatory variables (i.e., systematic factors).

31. The APT factors must correlate with major sources of uncertainty, i.e., sources of uncertainty that are of concern to many investors. Researchers should investigate factors that correlate with uncertainty in consumption and investment opportunities. GDP, the inflation rate, and interest rates are among the factors that can be expected to determine risk premiums. In particular, industrial production (IP) is a good indicator of changes in the business cycle. Thus, IP is a candidate for a factor that is highly correlated with uncertainties related to investment and consumption opportunities in the economy.

32. The revised estimate of the expected rate of return of the stock would be the old estimate plus the sum of the unexpected changes in the factors times the sensitivity coefficients, as follows:

$$\text{Revised estimate} = 14\% + [(1 \times 1\%) + (0.4 \times 1\%)] = 15.4\%$$

33. Equation 7.11 applies here:

$$E(r_P) = r_f + \beta_{P1}\,[E(r_1) - r_f] + \beta_{P2}\,[E(r_2) - r_f]$$

We need to find the risk premium for these two factors:

$\gamma_1 = [E(r_1) - r_f]$ and

$\gamma_2 = [E(r_2) - r_f]$

To find these values, we solve the following two equations with two unknowns:

$40\% = 7\% + 1.8\gamma_1 + 2.1\gamma_2$

$10\% = 7\% + 2.0\gamma_1 + (-0.5)\gamma_2$

The solutions are: $\gamma_1 = 4.47\%$ and $\gamma_2 = 11.86\%$

Thus, the expected return-beta relationship is:

$E(r_P) = 7\% + 4.47\beta_{P1} + 11.86\beta_{P2}$

34. The first two factors (the return on a broad-based index and the level of interest rates) are most promising with respect to the likely impact on Jennifer's firm's cost of capital. These are both macro factors (as opposed to firm-specific factors) that cannot be diversified away; consequently, we would expect that there is a risk premium associated with these factors. On the other hand, the risk of changes in the price of hogs, while important to some firms and industries, is likely to be diversifiable, and therefore is not a promising factor in terms of its impact on the firm's cost of capital.

35. Since the risk free rate is not given, we assume a risk free rate of 0%. The APT required (i.e., equilibrium) rate of return on the stock based on r_f and the factor betas is:

Required $E(r) = 0 + (1 \times 6) + (0.5 \times 2) + (0.75 \times 4) = 10\%$

According to the equation for the return on the stock, the actually expected return on the stock is 6% (because the expected surprises on all factors are zero by definition). Because the actually expected return based on risk is less than the equilibrium return, we conclude that the stock is overpriced.

CFA 1

Answer:

a, c, and *d* are true; *b* is incorrect because the SML doesn't require all investors to invest in the market portfolio but provides a benchmark to evaluate investment performance for both portfolios and individual assets.

CFA 2

Answer:

a. $E(r_X) = 5\% + 0.8 \times (14\% - 5\%) = 12.2\%$

$\alpha_X = 14\% - 12.2\% = 1.8\%$

$E(r_Y) = 5\% + 1.5 \times (14\% - 5\%) = 18.5\%$

$\alpha_Y = 17\% - 18.5\% = -1.5\%$

b.

i. For an investor who wants to add this stock to a well-diversified equity portfolio, Kay should recommend Stock X because of its positive alpha, while Stock Y has a negative alpha. In graphical terms, Stock X's expected return/risk profile plots above the SML, while Stock Y's profile plots below the SML. Also, depending on the individual risk preferences of Kay's clients, Stock X's lower beta may have a beneficial impact on overall portfolio risk.

ii. For an investor who wants to hold this stock as a single-stock portfolio, Kay should recommend Stock Y, because it has higher forecasted return and lower standard deviation than Stock X. Stock Y's Sharpe ratio is:

$$(0.17 - 0.05)/0.25 = 0.48$$

Stock X's Sharpe ratio is only:

$$(0.14 - 0.05)/0.36 = 0.25$$

The market index has an even more attractive Sharpe ratio:

$$(0.14 - 0.05)/0.15 = 0.60$$

However, given the choice between Stock X and Y, Y is superior. When a stock is held in isolation, standard deviation is the relevant risk measure. For assets held in isolation, beta as a measure of risk is irrelevant. Although holding a single asset in isolation is not typically a recommended investment strategy, some investors may hold what is essentially a single-asset portfolio (e.g., the stock of their employer company). For such investors, the relevance of standard deviation versus beta is an important issue.

CFA 3

Answer:

a. McKay should borrow funds and invest those funds proportionally in Murray's existing portfolio (i.e., buy more risky assets on margin). In addition to increased expected return, the alternative portfolio on the capital market line (CML) will also have increased variability (risk), which is caused by the higher proportion of risky assets in the total portfolio.

b. McKay should substitute low beta stocks for high beta stocks in order to reduce the overall beta of York's portfolio. By reducing the overall portfolio beta, McKay will reduce the systematic risk of the portfolio and therefore the portfolio's volatility relative to the market. The security market line (SML) suggests such action (moving down the SML), even though reducing beta may result in a slight loss of portfolio efficiency unless full diversification is maintained. York's primary objective, however, is not to maintain efficiency but to reduce risk exposure; reducing portfolio beta meets that objective. Because York does not permit borrowing or lending, McKay cannot reduce risk by selling equities and using the proceeds to buy risk free assets (i.e., by lending part of the portfolio).

CFA 4

Answer:

a. "Both the CAPM and APT require a mean-variance efficient market portfolio." This statement is incorrect. The CAPM requires the mean-variance efficient portfolio, but APT does not.

b. "The CAPM assumes that one specific factor explains security returns but APT does not." This statement is correct.

CFA 5

Answer:

a. A security's expected return as a function of its systematic risk (β).

CFA 6

Answer:

d. The expect return on the market, r_M:

$$E(r) = r_f + \beta[E(r_M) - r_f] = r_f + 1.0 \times [E(r_M) - r_f] = E(r_M)$$

CFA 7

Answer:

d. Insufficient data given. We need to know the risk-free rate.

CFA 8

Answer:

d. Insufficient data given. We need to know the risk-free rate.

CFA 9

Answer:

Under the CAPM, the only risk that investors are compensated for bearing is the risk that cannot be diversified away (i.e., systematic risk). Because systematic risk (measured by beta) is equal to 1.0 for each of the two portfolios, an investor would expect the same rate of return from each portfolio. Moreover, since both portfolios are well diversified, it does not matter whether the specific risk of the individual securities is high or low. The firm-specific risk has been diversified away from both portfolios.

CFA 10

Answer:

b. Offer an arbitrage opportunity:

$r_f = 8\%$ and $E(r_M) = 16\%$

$$E(r_X) = r_f + \beta_X[E(r_M) - r_f] = 8\% + 1.0 \times (16\% - 8\%) = 16\%$$

$$E(r_Y) = r_f + \beta_Y[E(r_M) - r_f] = 8\% + 0.25 \times (16\% - 8\%) = 10\%$$

Therefore, there is an arbitrage opportunity.

CFA 11

Answer:

c. Positive alpha investment opportunities will quickly disappear, because once such opportunity is observed, the arbitrageurs will take the large position in it, and therefore push the price back to equillibirum.

CFA 12

Answer:

d. A risk-free arbitrage opportunity exists.

CFA 13

Answer:

c. Investors will take on as large a position as possible only if the mispricing opportunity is an arbitrage. Otherwise, considerations of risk and diversification will limit the position they attempt to take in the mispriced security.

CFA 14

Answer:

d. APT does not require the restrictive assumptions concerning the market portfolio. It takes merely the actions of few arbitrageurs to enforce the fair market price.

CHAPTER 08
THE EFFICIENT MARKET HYPOTHESIS

1. The correlation coefficient should be zero. If it were not zero, then one could use returns from one period to predict returns in later periods and therefore earn abnormal profits.

2. The phrase would be correct if it were modified to say "expected risk adjusted returns." Securities all have the same risk adjusted expected return if priced fairly; however, actual results can and do vary. Unknown events cause certain securities to outperform others. This is not known in advance, so expectations are set by known information.

3. Over the long haul, there is an expected upward drift in stock prices based on their fair expected rates of return. The fair expected return over any single day is very small (e.g., 12% per year is only about 0.03% per day), so that on any day the price is virtually equally likely to rise or fall. However, over longer periods, the small expected daily returns cumulate, and upward moves are indeed more likely than downward ones.

4. No, this is not a violation of the EMH. Microsoft's continuing large profits do not imply that stock market investors who purchased Microsoft shares after its success already was evident would have earned a high return on their investments.

5. No. The notion of random walk naturally expects there to be some people who beat the market and some people who do not. The information provided, however, fails to consider the risk of the investment. Higher risk investments should have higher returns. As presented, it is possible to believe him without violating the EMH.

6. b. This is the definition of an efficient market.

7. d. It is not possible to offer a higher risk-return trade off if markets are efficient.

8. Strong-form efficiency includes all information: historical, public, and private.

9. Incorrect. In the short term, markets reflect a random pattern. Information is constantly flowing in the economy and investors each have different expectations that vary constantly. A fluctuating market accurately reflects this logic. Furthermore, while increased variability may be the result of an increase in unknown variables, this merely increases risk and the price is adjusted downward as a result.

10. c. If the stocks are overvalued, without regulative restrictions or other constraints on the trading, some investors observing this trend would be able to form a trading strategy to profit from the mispricing, thereby exploiting the inefficiency and forcing the price to the correct level.

11. c. This is a predictable pattern of returns, which should not occur if the stock market is weakly efficient.

12. c. This is a filter rule, a classic technical trading rule, which would appear to contradict the weak form of the efficient market hypothesis.

13. c. The P/E ratio is public information so this observation would provide evidence against the semi-strong form of the efficient market theory.

14. No, it is not more attractive as a possible purchase. Any value associated with dividend predictability is already reflected in the stock price.

15. No, this is not a violation of the EMH. This empirical tendency does not provide investors with a tool that will enable them to earn abnormal returns; in other words, it does not suggest that investors are failing to use all available information. An investor could not use this phenomenon to choose undervalued stocks today. The phenomenon instead reflects the fact that dividends occur as a response to good performance. After the fact, the stocks that happen to have performed the best will pay higher dividends, but this does not imply that you can identify the best performers early enough to earn abnormal returns.

16. While positive beta stocks respond well to favorable new information about the economy's progress through the business cycle, the stock's returns should be predictable and should not show abnormal returns around already anticipated events. If a recovery, for example, is already anticipated, the actual recovery is not news. The stock price should already reflect the coming recovery. The level of the stock price will be unpredictable only when responding to new information.

17.
   a. Consistent. Half of all managers should outperform the market based on pure luck in any year.

   b. Violation. This would be the basis for an "easy money" rule: Simply invest with last year's best managers.

   c. Consistent. Predictable volatility does not convey a means to earn abnormal returns.

   d. Violation. The abnormal performance ought to occur in January, when the increased earnings are announced.

   e. Violation. Reversals offer a means to earn easy money: Simply buy last week's losers.

18. An anomaly is considered an EMH exception because there are historical data to substantiate a claim that says anomalies have produced excess risk-adjusted abnormal returns in the past. Several anomalies regarding fundamental analysis have been uncovered. These include the P/E effect, the momentum effect, the small-firm-in-January

effect, the neglected- firm effect, post–earnings-announcement price drift, and the book-to-market effect. Whether these anomalies represent market inefficiency or poorly understood risk premiums is still a matter of debate. There are rational explanations for each, but not everyone agrees on the explanation. One dominant explanation is that many of these firms are also neglected firms, due to low trading volume, thus they are not part of an efficient market or offer more risk as a result of their reduced liquidity.

19. Implicit in the dollar-cost averaging strategy is the notion that stock prices fluctuate around a "normal" level. Otherwise, there is no meaning to statements such as "when the price is high." How do we know, for example, whether a price of $25 today will be viewed as high or low compared to the stock price in six months from now?

20. The market responds positively to new news. If the eventual recovery is anticipated, then the recovery is already reflected in stock prices. Only a better-than-expected recovery (or a worse-than-expected recovery) should affect stock prices.

21. You should buy the stock. The firm's management is not as bad as everyone else believes it to be, therefore, the firm is undervalued by the market. You are less pessimistic about the firm's prospects than the beliefs built into the stock price.

22. The market may have anticipated even greater earnings. Compared to prior expectations, the announcement was a disappointment.

23. This is not a violation of EMH. A possible explanation might be that the market index, which is comprised of large firms, is not a proper benchmark for evaluating shares of small firms. Some other risks, such as liquidity, might not be fully captured by the beta and the benchmark.

24. The negative abnormal returns (downward drift in CAR) just prior to stock purchases suggest that insiders deferred their purchases until after bad news was released to the public. This is evidence of valuable inside information. The positive abnormal returns after purchase suggest insider purchases in anticipation of good news. The analysis is symmetric for insider sales.

25.

a. If a shift were actually predictable, it would be a violation of EMH. Such shifts would be expected to occur as a result of a recession, but the recession is not predictable; thus it is not actually a violation of EMH. That being said, such a shift is consistent with EMH since the shift occurs after a recession or recovery occurs. As the news hits the market, the risk premiums are adjusted.

b. The reason this is perceived as an overreaction is because there are two events occurring. First, recessions lead to reduced profits, impacting the numerator in a fundamental analysis. This reduced cash flow represses stock prices. Simultaneously, the recession causes risk premiums to rise, thus increasing the denominator in the fundamental analysis calculation. An increase in the denominator further reduces the price. The result is the appearance of an overreaction.

CFA 1

Answer: b.

Public information constitutes semi-string efficiency, while the addition of private information leads to strong form efficiency.

CFA 2

Answer: a.

The information should be absorbed instantly.

CFA 3

Answer: b.

Since information is immediately included in stock prices, there is no benefit to buying stock after an announcement.

CFA 4

Answer: c.

Stocks producing abnormal excess returns will increase in price to eliminate the positive alpha.

CFA 5

Answer: c.

A random walk reflects no other information and is thus random.

CFA 6

Answer: d.

Unexpected results are by definition an anomaly.

CFA 7

Answer:

Assumptions supporting passive management are:

a. informational efficiency
b. primacy of diversification motives

Active management is supported by the opposite assumptions, in particular, that pockets of market inefficiency exist.

CFA 8

Answer:

a. The grandson is recommending taking advantage of (i) the small firm anomaly and (ii) the January anomaly. In fact, this seems to be one anomaly: the small-firm-in-January anomaly.

b.

(i) Concentration of one's portfolio in stocks having very similar attributes may expose the portfolio to more risk than is desirable. The strategy limits the potential for diversification.

(ii) Even if the study results are correct as described, each such study covers a specific time period. There is no assurance that future time periods would yield similar results.

(iii) After the results of the studies became publicly known, investment decisions might nullify these relationships. If these firms in fact offered investment bargains, their prices may be bid up to reflect the now-known opportunity.

CFA 9

a. The efficient market hypothesis (EMH) states that a market is efficient if security prices immediately and fully reflect all available relevant information. If the market fully reflects information, the knowledge of that information would not allow an investor to profit from the information because stock prices already incorporate the information.

The *weak form* of the EMH asserts that stock prices reflect all the information that can be derived by examining market trading data such as the history of past prices and trading volume.

A strong body of evidence supports weak-form efficiency in the major U.S. securities markets. For example, test results suggest that technical trading rules do not produce superior returns after adjusting for transaction costs and taxes.

The *semistrong form* states that a firm's stock price reflects all publicly available information about a firm's prospects. Examples of publicly available information are company annual reports and investment advisory data.

Evidence strongly supports the notion of semistrong efficiency, but occasional studies (e.g., those identifying market anomalies such as the small-firm-in-January or book-to-market effects) and events (such as the stock market crash of October 19, 1987) are inconsistent with this form of market efficiency. However, there is a question concerning the extent to which these "anomalies" result from data mining.

The *strong form* of the EMH holds that current market prices reflect *all* information (whether publicly available or privately held) that can be relevant to the valuation of the firm.

Empirical evidence suggests that strong-form efficiency does not hold. If this form were correct, prices would fully reflect all information. Therefore even insiders could not earn excess returns. But the evidence is that corporate officers do have access to pertinent information long enough before public release to enable them to profit from trading on this information.

b.

(i) *Technical analysis* involves the search for recurrent and predictable patterns in stock prices in order to enhance returns. The EMH implies that technical analysis is without value. If past prices contain no useful information for predicting future prices, there is no point in following any technical trading rule.

(ii) *Fundamental analysis* uses earnings and dividend prospects of the firm, expectations of future interest rates, and risk evaluation of the firm to determine proper stock prices. The EMH predicts that most fundamental analysis is doomed to failure. According to semistrong-form efficiency, no investor can earn excess returns from trading rules based on publicly available information. Only analysts with unique insight achieve superior returns.

In summary, the EMH holds that the market appears to adjust so quickly to information about both individual stocks and the economy as a whole that no technique of selecting a portfolio using either technical or fundamental analysis can consistently outperform a strategy of simply buying and holding a diversified portfolio of securities, such as those comprising the popular market indexes.

c. Portfolio managers have several roles and responsibilities even in perfectly efficient markets. The most important responsibility is to identify the risk/return objectives for a portfolio given the investor's constraints. In an efficient market, portfolio managers are responsible for tailoring the portfolio to meet the investor's needs, rather than to beat the market, which requires identifying the client's return requirements and risk tolerance. Rational portfolio management also requires examining the investor's constraints, including liquidity, time horizon, laws and regulations, taxes, and unique preferences and circumstances such as age and employment.

CFA 10

a. The earnings (and dividend) growth rates of growth stocks may be consistently overestimated by investors. Investors may extrapolate recent earnings (and dividend) growth too far into the future and thereby downplay the inevitable slowdown. At any given time, growth stocks are likely to revert to (lower) mean returns and value stocks are likely to revert to (higher) mean returns, often over an extended future time horizon.

b. In efficient markets, the current prices of stocks already reflect all known, relevant information. In this situation, growth stocks and value stocks provide the same risk-adjusted expected return.

CFA 11

a. Some empirical evidence that supports the EMH is:

(i) professional money managers do not typically earn higher returns than comparable risk, passive index strategies;

(ii) event studies typically show that stocks respond immediately to the public release of relevant news;

(iii) most tests of technical analysis find that it is difficult to identify price trends that can be exploited to earn superior risk-adjusted investment returns.

b. Some evidence that is difficult to reconcile with the EMH concerns simple portfolio strategies that apparently would have provided high risk-adjusted returns in the past. Some examples of portfolios with attractive historical returns:

(i) low P/E stocks;
(ii) high book-to-market ratio stocks;
(iii) small firms in January;
(iv) firms with very poor stock price performance in the last few months.

Other evidence concerns post-earnings-announcement stock price drift and intermediate-term price momentum.

c. An investor might choose not to index even if markets are efficient because he or she may want to tailor a portfolio to specific tax considerations or to specific risk management issues, for example, the need to hedge (or at least not add to) exposure to a particular source of risk (e.g., industry exposure).

CHAPTER 09
BEHAVIORAL FINANCE AND TECHNICAL ANALYSIS

1. Note the following matches:
   a. Investors are slow to update their beliefs when given new evidence – Conservatism bias

   b. Investors are reluctant to bear losses due to their unconventional decisions – Regret avoidance

   c. Investors exhibit less risk tolerance in their retirement accounts versus their other stock accounts – Mental accounting

   d. Investors are reluctant to sell stocks with "paper" losses – Disposition effect

   e. Investors disregard sample size when forming views about the future from the past – Representation bias

2. Representativeness bias. The sample size is not considered when making future decisions.

3. Fundamental risk means that even if a security is mispriced, it still can be risky to attempt to exploit the mispricing because the correction to price could happen after the trader's investing horizon. This limits the actions of arbitrageurs who take positions in mispriced securities. Thus, the bias may persist since no one takes advantage of it.

4. The premise of behavioral finance is that conventional financial theory ignores how real people make decisions and that people make a difference. Behavioral finance may cite examples of market inefficiencies, but they give no insight into how to exploit such phenomenon. The strength of their argument relies upon observed market inefficiencies and unexplained market behavior. There are many anomalies, yet many can be reverse engineered or explained. Also, while anomalies exist, they rarely meet the test of statistical significance.

5. An unfortunate consequence of behavioral finance (BF) is a tendency for investors to assume more than actually is claimed by the field. While BF is highly critical of EMH and claims to offer alternative theories, it does not propose to be a predictor of future returns. Investors should be wary of people purporting to offer excess returns under the façade of BH. Such claims are likely to be false.

6. c. Loss aversion.

7. a. Fear of regret.

8. a. Selling losers quickly.

9. Statement *b,* that a price has moved above its 52 week moving average, is considered a bullish sign.

10. After the fact, you can always find patterns and trading rules that would have generated enormous profits. This is called data mining. For technical analysts, this is a problem since they rarely can be reproduced to predict future profits.

11. Grinblatt and Han (2005) show that the disposition effect can lead to momentum in stock prices even if fundamental values follow a random walk. This momentum may not lead to abnormal profits but may cause capital to flow to investments that appear to benefit from the momentum, in contrast to where it would otherwise flow.

12. Arbitrage assumes the ability to initiate trades based on arbitrage information. A severe limit of the theory is that similar assets should be priced similarly (law of one price). An example of a limit in which such a trade is not possible is the case of Royal Dutch Petroleum and Shell. This is a case of "Siamese twin" companies, where the value was not proportional to the profit distribution. Attempts to profit from the incorrect pricing would result in substantial loss. An equity carve out is another example. In this, the sale of a portion of the company does not necessarily generate the exact percentage one would expect based on the percentage taken from the original company. The last example involved closed end funds that typically sell for less than NAV.

13. Some people may say it is consistent with both. This is consistent with efficient markets since the price does approach intrinsic value. Behavioral would say it is consistent since the price slowly approaches intrinsic value after the market has a track record of time showing no other shocks are imminent. Lacking information about another shock, EMH says the price should go directly to the new value. Behavioral finance says that may take time.

14. $\text{Trin} = \dfrac{\text{Volume Declining/Number Declining}}{\text{Value Advancing/Number Advancing}} = \dfrac{231{,}468{,}687/270}{4{,}681{,}742{,}414/2{,}787} = 0.5103$

This trin ratio, which is below 1.0, would be taken as a bullish signal.

15. Breadth:

Advances	Declines	Net Advancing
2,787	270	2,517

Breadth is positive. This is a bullish signal (although no one would actually use a one-day measure as in this example).

16. This exercise is left to the student.

17. The confidence index increases from 5%/7% = 0.7143 to 6%/8% = 0.7500. This indicates slightly higher confidence. But the real reason for the increase in the index is the expectation of higher inflation, not higher confidence about the economy.

18. At the beginning of the period the relative strength of Computers, Inc., the price of the stock divided by the industry index, was 19.63/50.0 = 0.3926; by the end of the period, the ratio had increased to 28/56.1 = 0.4991. As the ratio increased over the period, it appears that Computers, Inc. outperformed other firms in its industry. The overall trend, therefore, indicates relative strength, although some fluctuation existed during the period, with the ratio falling to a low point of 17.50/52.9 = 0.33 on day 19.

19. Five day moving averages:

Trading Day	5-Day Moving Average		
Days 1–5	(19.63 + 20 + 20.50 + 22 + 21.13)/5 =	20.652	
Days 2–6	(20 + 20.50 + 22 + 21.13 + 22)/5 =	21.126	
Days 3–7	(20.50 + 22 + 21.13 + 22 + 21.88)/5 =	21.502	
Days 4–8	(22 + 21.13 + 22 + 21.88 + 22.50)/5 =	21.902	
Days 5–9	(21.13 + 22 + 21.88 + 22.50 + 23.13)/5 =	22.128	
Days 6–10	(22 + 21.88 + 22.50 + 23.13 + 23.88)/5 =	22.678	
Days 7–11	(21.88 + 22.50 + 23.13 + 23.88 + 24.50)/5 =	23.178	
Days 8–12	(22.50 + 23.13 + 23.88 + 24.50 + 23.25)/5 =	23.452	
Days 9–13	(23.13 + 23.88 + 24.50 + 23.25 + 22.13)/5 =	23.378	
Days 10–14	(23.88 + 24.50 +23.25 + 22.13 + 22)/5 =	23.152	
Days 11–15	(24.50 + 23.25 + 22.13 + 22 + 20.63)/5 =	22.502	
Days 12–16	(23.25 + 22.13 + 22 + 20.63 + 20.25)/5 =	21.652	Sell signal (day 12 price < moving average)
Days 13–17	(22.13 + 22 + 20.63 + 20.25 + 19.75)/5 =	20.952	
Days 14–18	(22 + 20.63 + 20.25 + 19.75 + 18.75)/5 =	20.276	
Days 15–19	(20.63 + 20.25 + 19.75 + 18.75 + 17.50)/5 =	19.376	
Days 16–20	(20.25 + 19.75 + 18.75 + 17.50 + 19)/5 =	19.050	
Days 17–21	(19.75 + 18.75 + 17.50 + 19 + 19.63)/5 =	18.926	
Days 18–22	(18.75 + 17.50 + 19 + 19.63 + 21.50)/5 =	19.276	
Days 19–23	(17.50 + 19 + 19.63 + 21.50 + 22)/5 =	19.926	
Days 20–24	(19 + 19.63 + 21.50 +22 + 23.13)/5 =	21.052	
Days 21–25	(19.63 + 21.50 + 22 + 23.13 + 24)/5 =	22.052	Buy signal (day 21 price > moving average)
Days 22–26	(21.50 + 22 + 23.13 + 24 + 25.25)/5 =	23.176	
Days 23–27	(22 + 23.13 + 24 + 25.25 +26.25)/5 =	24.126	
Days 24–28	(23.13 + 24 + 25.25 + 26.25 + 27)/5 =	25.126	
Days 25–29	(24 + 25.25 + 26.25 + 27 + 27.50)/5 =	26.000	
Days 26–30	(25.25 + 26.25 + 27 + 27.50 + 28)/5 =	26.800	
Days 27–31	(26.25 + 27 + 27.50 + 28 + 28.50)/5 =	27.450	
Days 28–32	(27 + 27.50 + 28 + 28.50 + 28)/5 =	27.800	
Days 29–33	(27.50 + 28 + 28.50 + 28 + 27.50)/5 =	27.900	
Days 30–34	(28 + 28.50 + 28 + 27.50 + 29)/5 =	28.200	
Days 31–35	(28.50 + 28 + 27.50 + 29 + 29.25)/5 =	28.450	
Days 32–36	(28 + 27.50 + 29 + 29.25 + 29.50)/5 =	28.650	
Days 33–37	(27.50 + 29 + 29.25 + 29.50 + 30)/5 =	29.050	Sell signal (day 33 price < moving average)
Days 34–38	(29 + 29.25 + 29.50 + 30 + 28.50)/5 =	29.250	
Days 35–39	(29.25 + 29.50 + 30 + 28.50 + 27.75)/5 =	29.000	
Days 36–40	(29.50 + 30 + 28.50 + 27.75 + 28)/5 =	28.750	

20.

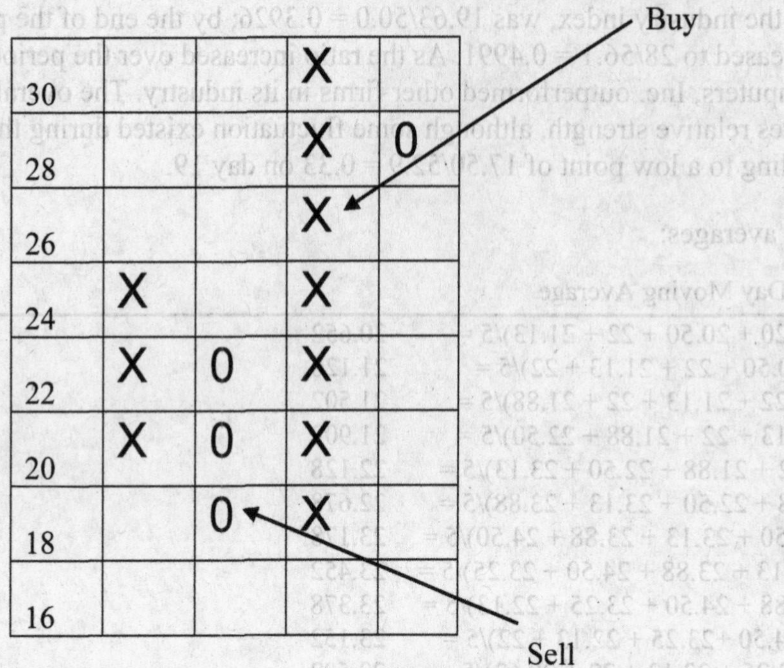

A sell signal occurs at a price of approximately $19, which is similar to a sell signal derived from the moving average rule. However, the buy signals are not the same.

21. This pattern shows a lack of breadth. Even though the index is up, more stocks declined than advanced, which indicates a "lack of broad-based support" for the rise in the index.

22.

Day	Advances	Declines	Net Advances	Cumulative Breadth
1	906	704	202	202
2	653	986	−333	−131
3	721	789	−68	−199
4	503	968	−465	−664
5	497	1,095	−598	−1,262
6	970	702	268	−994
7	1,002	609	393	−601
8	903	722	181	−420
9	850	748	102	−318
10	766	766	0	−318

The signal is bearish as cumulative breadth is negative; however, the negative number is declining in magnitude, indicative of improvement. Perhaps the worst of the bear market has passed.

23. $\text{Trin} = \dfrac{\text{Volume Declining/Number Declining}}{\text{Value Advancing/Number Advancing}} = \dfrac{900{,}000{,}000/704}{1{,}100{,}000{,}000/906} = 1.0529$

This is a slightly bearish indicator, with average volume in advancing issues a bit greater than average volume in declining issues.

24. $\text{Confidence Index} = \dfrac{\text{Yield on Top–Rated Corporate Bonds}}{\text{Yield on Intermediate–Grade Corporate Bonds}}$

This year: Confidence Index = 8%/10.5% = 0.7619

Last year: Confidence Index = 8.5%/10% = 0.8500

Thus, the confidence index is decreasing.

25. [Note: In order to create the 26-week moving average for the S&P 500, we first converted the weekly returns to weekly index values, using a base of 100 for the week prior to the first week of the data set.]

a. The graph below summarizes the data for the 26-week moving average. The graph also shows the values of the S&P 500 index.

b. The S&P 500 crosses through its moving average from below fifteen times, as indicated in the table below. The index increases eight times in weeks following a cross-through and decreases seven times.

c. The S&P 500 crosses through its moving average from above sixteen times, as indicated in the table below. The index increases ten times in weeks following a cross-through and decreases six times.

d. It is obvious from the data presented that the rule did not work in recent years.

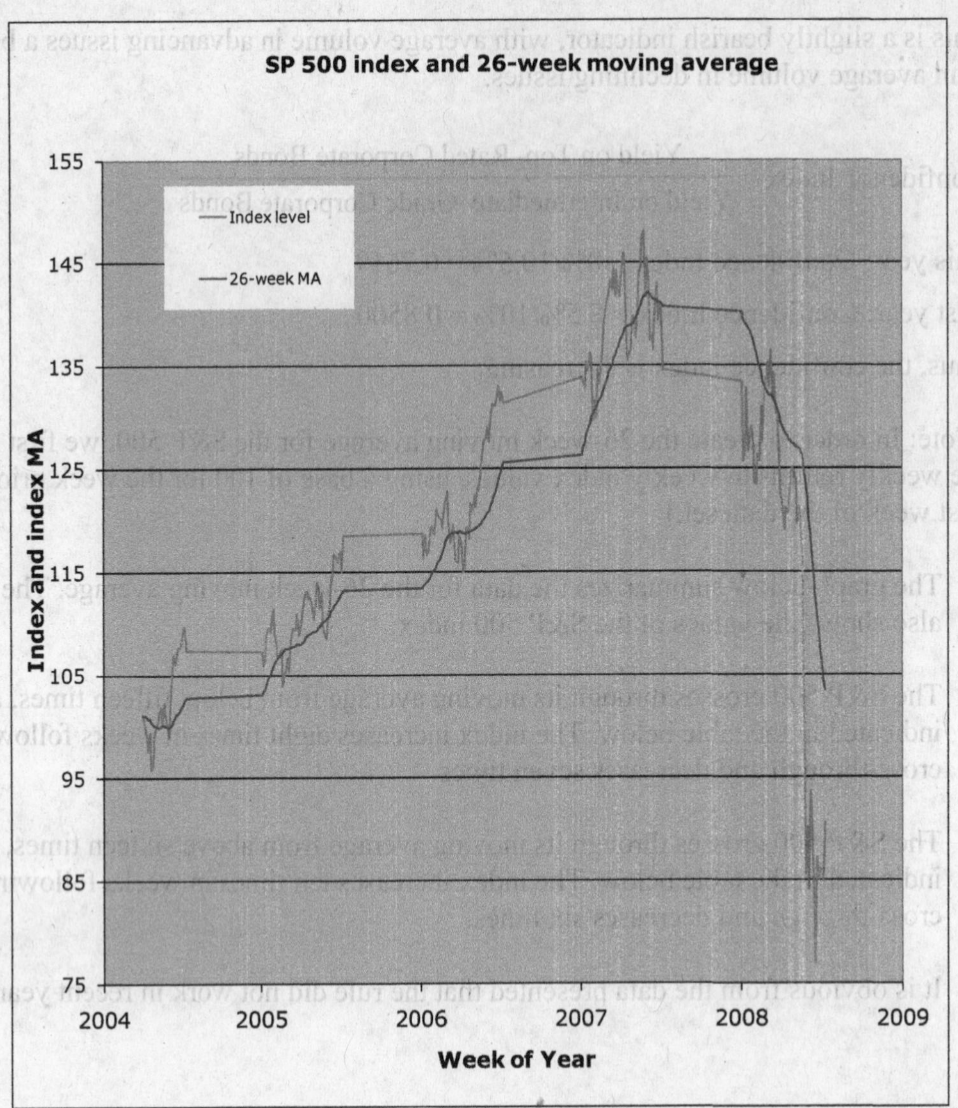

26. [Note: In order to create the relative strength measure, we convert the weekly returns for the Fidelity Banking Fund and for the S&P 500 to base 100 weekly index values.]

    a. The graphs summarize the relative strength of data for the Fidelity Banking Fund.

    b. Over five-week intervals, relative strength increased by more than 5% sixteen times, out of 255 instances. The Fidelity Banking Fund underperformed the S&P 500 index ten times and outperformed the S&P 500 index six times in weeks following an increase of more than 5%.

    c. Over five-week intervals, relative strength decreases by more than 5% thirty one times, out of 255 instances. The Fidelity Banking Fund underperformed the S&P 500 index seventeen times and outperformed the S&P 500 index fourteen times in weeks following a decrease of more than 5%.

d. An increase in relative strength, as in part (b) above, is regarded as a bullish signal. However, in our sample, the Fidelity Banking Fund is more likely to underperform the S&P 500 index than it is to outperform the index following such a signal. A decrease in relative strength, as in part (c), is regarded as a bearish signal. In our sample, the Fidelity Banking Fund underperformed the index as expected. However, there is no statistical difference in the performance following a substantial change in the relative strength. The subsequent performance appears to be random.

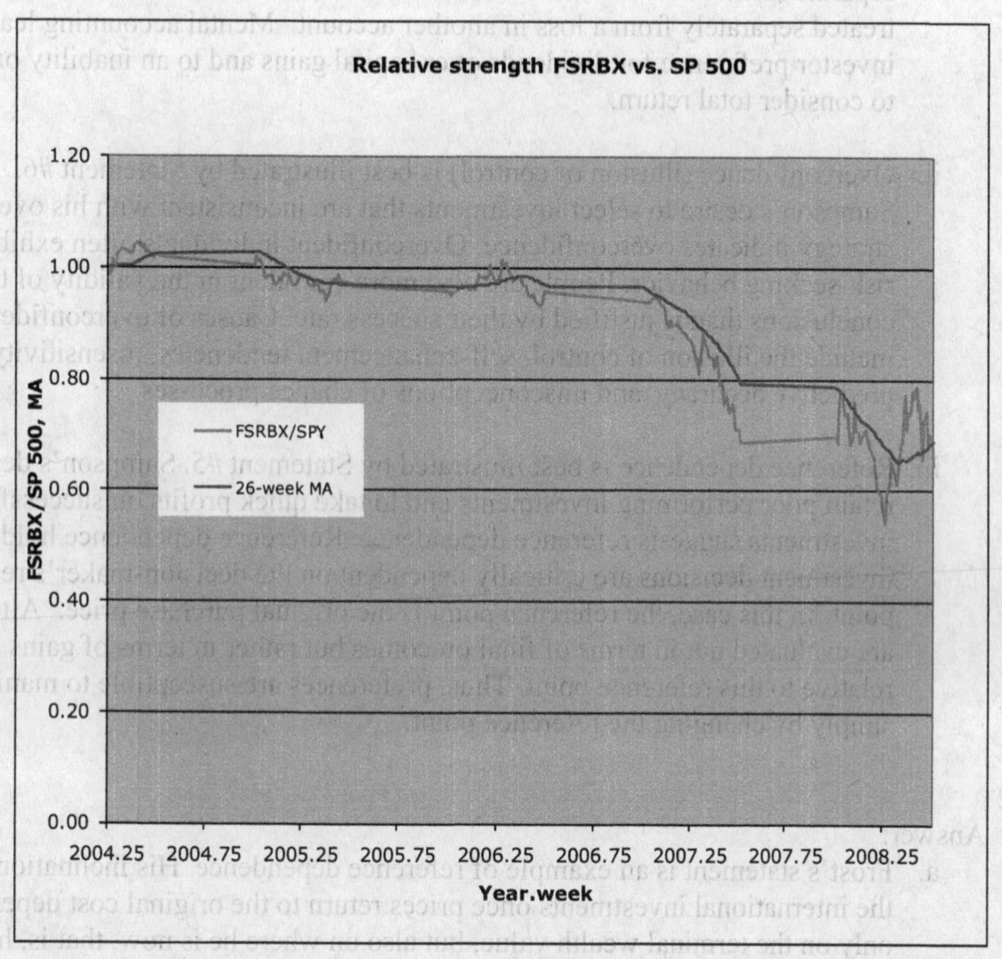

27. Pontiff (1996) demonstrates that deviations of price from net asset value in closed-end funds tend to be higher in funds that are more difficult to arbitrage, for example, those with more idiosyncratic volatility. Since well diversified funds represent less of an opportunity for arbitrage by removing the impact of individual stock anomalies, they would likely have smaller deviations from NAV.

CFA 1

Answer:

i. Mental accounting is best illustrated by Statement #3. Sampson's requirement that his income needs be met via interest income and stock dividends is an example of mental accounting. Mental accounting holds that investors segregate funds into mental accounts (e.g., dividends and capital gains), maintain a set of separate mental accounts, and do not combine outcomes; a loss in one account is treated separately from a loss in another account. Mental accounting leads to an investor preference for dividends over capital gains and to an inability or failure to consider total return.

ii. Overconfidence (illusion of control) is best illustrated by Statement #6. Sampson's desire to select investments that are inconsistent with his overall strategy indicates overconfidence. Overconfident individuals often exhibit risk-seeking behavior. People are also more confident in the validity of their conclusions than is justified by their success rate. Causes of overconfidence include the illusion of control, self-enhancement tendencies, insensitivity to predictive accuracy, and misconceptions of chance processes.

iii. Reference dependence is best illustrated by Statement #5. Sampson's desire to retain poor performing investments and to take quick profits on successful investments suggests reference dependence. Reference dependence holds that investment decisions are critically dependent on the decision-maker's reference point. In this case, the reference point is the original purchase price. Alternatives are evaluated not in terms of final outcomes but rather in terms of gains and losses relative to this reference point. Thus, preferences are susceptible to manipulation simply by changing the reference point.

CFA 2

Answer:

a. Frost's statement is an example of reference dependence. His inclination to sell the international investments once prices return to the original cost depends not only on the terminal wealth value, but also on where he is now, that is, his reference point. This reference point, which is below the original cost, has become a critical factor in Frost's decision.

In standard finance, alternatives are evaluated in terms of terminal wealth values or final outcomes, not in terms of gains and losses relative to some reference point such as original cost.

b. Frost's statement is an example of susceptibility to cognitive error, in at least two ways. First, he is displaying the behavioral flaw of overconfidence. He likely is more confident about the validity of his conclusion than is justified by his rate of success. He is very confident that the past performance of Country XYZ indicates future performance. Behavioral investors could, and often do, conclude that a five-year record is ample evidence to suggest future performance. Second, by choosing to invest in the securities of only Country XYZ, Frost is also exemplifying the behavioral finance phenomenon of asset segregation. That is, he is evaluating Country XYZ investment in terms of its anticipated gains or losses viewed in isolation.

Individuals are typically more confident about the validity of their conclusions than is justified by their success rate or by the principles of standard finance, especially with regard to relevant time horizons. In standard finance, investors know that five years of returns on Country XYZ securities relative to all other markets provide little information about future performance. A standard finance investor would not be fooled by this "law of small numbers." In standard finance, investors evaluate performance in portfolio terms, in this case defined by combining the Country XYZ holding with all other securities held. Investments in Country XYZ, like all other potential investments, should be evaluated in terms of the anticipated contribution to the risk- reward profile of the entire portfolio.

c. Frost's statement is an example of mental accounting. Mental accounting holds that investors segregate money into mental accounts (e.g., safe versus speculative), maintain a set of separate mental accounts, and do not combine outcomes; a loss in one account is treated separately from a loss in another account. One manifestation of mental accounting, in which Frost is engaging, is building a portfolio as a pyramid of assets, layer by layer, with the retirement account representing a layer separate from the "speculative" fund. Each layer is associated with different goals and attitudes toward risk. He is more risk averse with respect to the retirement account than he is with respect to the "speculative" fund account. The money in the retirement account is a down side protection layer, designed to avoid future poverty. The money in the "speculative" fund account is the upside potential layer, designed for a chance at being rich.

In standard finance, decisions consider the risk and return profile of the entire portfolio rather than anticipated gains or losses on any particular account, investment, or class of investments. Alternatives should be considered in terms of final outcomes in a total portfolio context rather than in terms of contributions to a "safe" or a "speculative" account. Standard finance investors seek to maximize the mean-variance structure of the portfolio as a whole and consider covariances between assets as they construct their portfolios. Standard finance investors have consistent attitudes toward risk across their entire portfolio.

CFA 3

Answer:

a. *Illusion of knowledge*: Maclin believes he is an expert on, and can make accurate forecasts about, the real estate market solely because he has studied housing market data on the Internet. He may have access to a large amount of real estate-related information, but he may not understand how to analyze the information nor have the ability to apply it to a proposed investment.

Overconfidence: Overconfidence causes us to misinterpret the accuracy of our information and our skill in analyzing it. Maclin has assumed that the information he collected on the internet is accurate without attempting to verify it or consult other sources. He also assumes he has skill in evaluating and analyzing the real estate-related information he has collected, although there is no information in the question that suggests he possesses such ability.

b. *Reference point*: Maclin's reference point for his bond position is the purchase price, as evidenced by the fact that he will not sell a position for less than he paid for it. This fixation on a reference point, and the subsequent waiting for the price of the security to move above that reference point before selling the security, prevents Maclin from undertaking a risk/return-based analysis of his portfolio position.

c. *Familiarity*: Maclin is evaluating his holding of company stock based on his familiarity with the company rather than on sound investment and portfolio principles. Company employees, because of this familiarity, may have a distorted perception of their own company, assuming a "good company" will also be a good investment. Irrational investors believe an investment in a company with which they are familiar will produce higher returns and have less risk than non-familiar investments.

Representativeness: Maclin is confusing his company (which may well be a good company) with the company's stock (which may or may not be an appropriate holding for his portfolio and/or a good investment) and its future performance. This can result in employees' overweighting their company stock, resulting in an under-diversified portfolio

CFA 4

Answer:

a. The behavioral finance principle of biased expectations/overconfidence is most consistent with the investor's first statement. Petrie stock provides a level of confidence and comfort for the investor because of the circumstances in which she acquired the stock and her recent history with the returns and income from the stock. However, the investor exhibits overconfidence in the stock given the needs of the Trust and the brevity of the recent performance history. Maintaining a 15 percent position in a single stock is inconsistent with the overall strategy of the Trust, and the investor's level of confidence should reflect the stock's overall record, not just the past two years.

b. The behavioral finance principle of mental accounting is most consistent with the investor's second statement. The investor has segregated the monies distributed from the Trust into two "accounts": the returns that the Trust receives from the Petrie stock and the remaining funds that the Trust receives for her benefit. She is maintaining a separate set of mental accounts with regard to the total funds distributed. The investor's "specific uses" should be viewed in the overall context of the spending needs of the Trust and should consider the risk and return profile of the entire Trust.

CFA 5

Answer:

i. *Overconfidence (Biased Expectations and Illusion of Control)*: Pierce is basing her investment strategy for supporting her parents on her confidence in the economic forecasts. This is a cognitive error reflecting overconfidence in the form of both biased expectations and an illusion of control. Pierce is likely more confident in the validity of those forecasts than is justified by the accuracy of prior forecasts. Analysts' consensus forecasts have proven routinely and widely inaccurate. Pierce also appears to be overly confident that the recent performance of the Pogo Island economy is a good indicator of future performance. Behavioral investors often conclude that a short track record is ample evidence to suggest future performance.

Standard finance investors understand that individuals typically have greater confidence in the validity of their conclusions than is justified by their success rate. The calibration paradigm, which compares confidence to predictive ability, suggests that there is significantly lower probability of success than the confidence levels reported by individuals. In addition, standard finance investors know that recent performance provides little information about future performance and are not deceived by this "law of small numbers."

ii. *Loss Aversion (Risk Seeking)*: Pierce is exhibiting *risk aversion* in deciding to sell the Core Bond Fund despite its gains and favorable prospects. She prefers a certain gain over a possibly larger gain coupled with a smaller chance of a loss. Pierce is exhibiting *loss aversion* (risk seeking) by holding the High Yield Bond Fund despite its uncertain prospects. She prefers the modest possibility of recovery coupled with the chance of a larger loss over a certain loss. People tend to exhibit risk seeking, rather than risk aversion, behavior when the probability of loss is large. There is considerable evidence indicating that risk aversion holds for gains and risk seeking behavior holds for losses, and that attitudes toward risk vary depending on particular goals and circumstances.

Standard finance investors are consistently risk averse, and systematically prefer a certain outcome over a gamble with the same expected value. Such investors also take a symmetrical view of gains and losses of the same magnitude, and their sensitivity (aversion) to changes in value is not a function of a specified value reference point.

iii. *Reference Dependence:* Pierce's inclination to sell her Small Company Fund once it returns to her original cost is an example of *reference dependence.* Her sell decision is predicated on the current value as related to original cost, her reference point. Her decision does not consider any analysis of expected terminal value or the impact of this sale on her total portfolio. This reference point of original cost has become a critical but inappropriate factor in Pierce's decision.

In standard finance, alternatives are evaluated in terms of terminal wealth values or final outcomes, not in terms of gains and losses relative to a reference point such as original cost. Standard finance investors also consider the risk and return profile of the entire portfolio rather than anticipated gains or losses on any particular investment or asset class.

CHAPTER 10
BOND PRICES AND YIELDS

1.
   a. Catastrophe bond: Typically issued by an insurance company. They are similar to an insurance policy in that the investor receives coupons and par value, but takes a loss in part or all of the principal if a major insurance claim is filed against the issuer. This is provided in exchange for higher than normal coupons.

   b. Eurobond: They are bonds issued in the currency of one country but sold in other national markets.

   c. Zero-coupon bond: Zero-coupon bonds are bonds that pay no coupons but do pay a par value at maturity.

   d. Samurai bond: Yen-denominated bonds sold in Japan by non-Japanese issuers are called Samurai bonds.

   e. Junk bond: Those rated BBB or above (S&P, Fitch) or Baa and above (Moody's) are considered investment grade bonds, while lower-rated bonds are classified as speculative grade or junk bonds.

   f. Convertible bond: Convertible bonds may be exchanged, at the bondholder's discretion, for a specified number of shares of stock. Convertible bondholders "pay" for this option by accepting a lower coupon rate on the security.

   g. Serial bond: A serial bond is an issue in which the firm sells bonds with staggered maturity dates. As bonds mature sequentially, the principal repayment burden for the firm is spread over time just as it is with a sinking fund. Serial bonds do not include call provisions.

   h. Equipment obligation bond: A bond that is issued with specific equipment pledged as collateral against the bond.

   i. Original issue discount bonds: Original issue discount bonds are less common than coupon bonds issued at par. These are bonds that are issued intentionally with low coupon rates that cause the bond to sell at a discount from par value.

   j. Indexed bond: Indexed bonds make payments that are tied to a general price index or the price of a particular commodity.

2. Callable bonds give the issuer the option to extend or retire the bond at the call date, while the extendable or puttable bond gives this option to the bondholder.

3.

a. YTM will drop since the company has more money to pay the interest on its bonds.

b. YTM will increase since the company has more debt and the risk to the existing bondholders is now increased.

c. YTM will decrease since the firm has either fewer current liabilities or an increase in various current assets.

4. Semi-annual coupon = $1,000 × 6% × 0.5 = $30.

$$\text{Accrued Interest} = \frac{\text{Annual Coupon Payment}}{2} \times \frac{\text{Days since Last Coupon Payment}}{\text{Days Separating Coupon Payment}}$$

$$= \$30 \times (30/182) = \$4.945$$

At a price of 117, the invoice price is: $1,170 + $4.945 = $1,174.95

5. Using a financial calculator, PV = −746.22, FV = 1,000, n = 5, PMT = 0. The YTM is 6.0295%.

Using a financial calculator, PV = −730.00, FV = 1,000, n = 5, PMT = 0. The YTM is 6.4965%.

6. A bond's coupon interest payments and principal repayment are not affected by changes in market rates. Consequently, if market rates increase, bond investors in the secondary markets are not willing to pay as much for a claim on a given bond's fixed interest and principal payments as they would if market rates were lower. This relationship is apparent from the inverse relationship between interest rates and present value. An increase in the discount rate (i.e., the market rate) decreases the present value of the future cash flows.

7. The bond callable at 105 should sell at a lower price because the call provision is more valuable to the firm. Therefore, its yield to maturity should be higher.

8. The bond price will be lower. As time passes, the bond price, which is now above par value, will approach par.

9. $$\text{Current yield} = \frac{\text{Annual Coupon}}{\text{Bond Price}} = \frac{\$1{,}000 \times 4.8\%}{\$970} = 4.95\%$$

10. a. The purchase of a credit default swap. The investor believes the bond may increase in credit risk, which raises the prices of the credit default swaps because of the widened swap spread.

11. c. When credit risk increases, the swap premium increases because of higher chances of default on the firm. When the interest rate risk increases, the price of the CDS decreases because the cash flows are discounted at a higher rate for bearing more risk.

12. The current yield and the annual coupon rate of 6% imply that the bond price was at par a year ago.

Using a financial calculator, FV = 1,000, n =7, PMT = 60, and i =7 gives us a selling price of $946.11 this year.

$$\text{Holding period return} = \frac{-\$1{,}000 + \$946.11 + \$60}{\$1{,}000}$$

$$= 0.0061 = 0.61\%$$

13. Zero coupon bonds provide no coupons to be reinvested. Therefore, the final value of the investor's proceeds comes entirely from the principal of the bond and is independent of the rate at which coupons could be reinvested (if they were paid). There is no reinvestment rate uncertainty with zeros.

14.

a. Effective annual rate on a three-month T-bill:

$$\left(\frac{\$100{,}000}{\$97{,}645}\right)^4 - 1 = (1.02412)^4 - 1 = 0.1000 = 10\%$$

b. Effective annual interest rate on coupon bond paying 5% semiannually:

$(1 + 0.05)^2 - 1 = 0.1025 = 10.25\%$

Therefore, the coupon bond has the higher effective annual interest rate.

15. The effective annual yield on the semiannual coupon bonds is $(1.04)^2 = 8.16\%$. If the annual coupon bonds are to sell at par they must offer the same yield, which requires an annual coupon of 8.16%.

16.

a. The bond pays $50 every six months.
Current price:
[$50 × Annuity factor(4%, 6)] + [$1000 × PV factor(4%, 6)] = $1,052.42

Assuming the market interest rate remains 4% per half year, price six months from now:
[$50 × Annuity factor(4%, 5)] + [$1000 × PV factor(4%, 5)] = $1,044.52

b. $$\text{Rate of Return} = \frac{\$50 + (\$1{,}044.52 - \$1{,}052.42)}{\$1{,}052.42} = \frac{\$50 - \$7.90}{\$1{,}052.42}$$

$$= 0.0400 = 4.00\% \text{ per six months.}$$

17.

a. Use the following inputs: $n = 40$, FV = 1,000, PV = −950, PMT = 40. We will find that the yield to maturity on a semi-annual basis is 4.26%. This implies a bond equivalent yield to maturity of: 4.26% × 2 = 8.52%

Effective annual yield to maturity = $(1.0426)^2 - 1 = 0.0870 = 8.70\%$

b. Since the bond is selling at par, the yield to maturity on a semi-annual basis is the same as the semi-annual coupon, 4%. The bond equivalent yield to maturity is 8%.

Effective annual yield to maturity = $(1.04)^2 - 1 = 0.0816 = 8.16\%$

c. Keeping other inputs unchanged but setting PV = −1,050, we find a bond equivalent yield to maturity of 7.52%, or 3.76% on a semi-annual basis.

Effective annual yield to maturity = $(1.0376)^2 - 1 = 0.0766 = 7.66\%$

18. Since the bond payments are now made annually instead of semi-annually, the bond equivalent yield to maturity is the same as the effective annual yield to maturity. The inputs are: $n = 20$, FV = 1000, PV = −price, PMT = 80. The resulting yields for the three bonds are:

Bond Price	Bond equivalent yield Effective annual yield
$ 950	8.53%
$1,000	8.00%
$1,050	7.51%

The yields computed in this case are lower than the yields calculated with semi-annual coupon payments. All else equal, bonds with annual payments are less attractive to investors because more time elapses before payments are received. If the bond price is the same with annual payments, then the bond's yield to maturity is lower.

19.

$$\text{Nominal Return} = \frac{\text{Interest} + \text{Price Appreciation}}{\text{Initial Price}}$$

$$\text{Real Return} = \frac{1 + \text{Nominal Return}}{1 + \text{Inflation Rate}} - 1$$

<u>The second year</u>

$$\text{Nominal Return} = \frac{\$42.02 + \$30.60}{\$1{,}020.00} = 0.071196 = 7.12\%$$

$$\text{Real Return} = \frac{1 + 0.071196}{1 + 0.03} - 1 = \frac{1.071196}{1.03} - 1 = 1.0400 - 1 = 4.00\%$$

<u>The third year</u>

$$\text{Nominal Return} = \frac{\$42.44 + \$10.51}{\$1{,}050.60} = 0.050400\%$$

$$\text{Real Return} = \frac{1 + 0.050400}{1 + 0.01} - 1 = \frac{1.050400}{1.01} - 1 = 1.0400 - 1 = 4.00\%$$

The real rate of return in each year is precisely the 4% real yield on the bond.

20. Remember that the convention is to use semi-annual periods:

$$\text{Price of a Zero-Coupon Bond} = \frac{\text{Face Value}}{(1+\text{Semiannual YTM})^{T}}$$

$$\text{Bond Equivalent YTM} = \text{Semi-annual YTM} \times 2$$

Price	Maturity (years)	Maturity (half-years)	Semi-annual YTM	Bond equivalent YTM
$400.00	20	40	2.32%	**4.63%**
$500.00	20	40	1.75%	**3.50%**
$500.00	10	20	3.53%	**7.05%**
$376.89	10	20	5.00%	10.00%
$456.39	10	20	4.00%	8.00%
$400.00	**11.68**	23.36	4.00%	8.00%

21. Using a financial calculator, input PV = −800, FV = 1,000, n = 10, PMT = 80. The YTM is 11.46%.

Using a financial calculator, FV = 1,000, n = 9, PMT = 80, i = 11.4. The new price will be 811.70. Thus, the capital gain is $11.70.

22. The reported bond price is: 100 2/32 percent of par = $1,000.6250

15 days have passed since the last semiannual coupon was paid, so there is an accrued interest, which can be calculated as:

$$\text{Accrued Interest} = \frac{\text{Annual Coupon Payment}}{2} \times \frac{\text{Days since Last Coupon Payment}}{\text{Days Separating Coupon Payment}}$$

$$= \$35 \times (15/182) = \$2.8846$$

The invoice price is the reported price plus accrued interest:

1,000.6250 + 2.8846 = $1,003.5096 ≒ 1,003.51

23. If the yield to maturity is greater than current yield, then the bond offers the prospect of price appreciation as it approaches its maturity date. Therefore, the bond is selling below par value.

24. The coupon rate is below 9%. If coupon divided by price equals 9% and price is less than par, then coupon divided by par is less than 9%.

25. The solution is obtained using Excel:

	A	B	C	D	E
1		5.50% coupon bond,			
2		maturing March 15, 2020			
3			Formula in Column B		
4	Settlement date	2012/2/22	DATE(2012,2,22)		
5	Maturity date	2020/3/15	DATE(2020,3,15)		
6	Annual coupon rate	0.055			
7	Yield to maturity	0.0534			
8	Redemption value (% of face value)	100			
9	Coupon payments per year	2			
10					
11					
12	Flat price (% of par)	101.0333	PRICE(B4,B5,B6,B7,B8,B9)		
13	Days since last coupon	160	COUPDAYBS(B4,B5,2,1)		
14	Days in coupon period	182	COUPDAYS(B4,B5,2,1)		
15	Accrued interest	2.417582418	(B13/B14)*B6*100/2		
16	Invoice price	103.4509	B12+B15		

26. The solution is obtained using Excel:

	A	B	C	D	E	F	G
1					Semiannual		Annual
2					coupons		coupons
3							
4	Settlement date				2012/2/22		2012/2/22
5	Maturity date				2020/3/15		2020/3/15
6	Annual coupon rate				0.055		0.055
7	Bond price				102		102
8	Redemption value (% of face value)				100		100
9	Coupon payments per year				2		1
10							
11	Yield to maturity (decimal)				0.0519268		0.0518889
12							
13							
14	Formula in cell E11:			YIELD(E4,E5,E6,E7,E8,E9)			

27. Using financial calculator, $n = 10$; PV = −900; FV = 1,000; PMT = 140
The stated yield to maturity equals 16.075%.

Based on *expected* coupon payments of $70 annually, the expected yield to maturity is: 8.5258%.

28. The bond is selling at par value. Its yield to maturity equals the coupon rate, 10%. If the first-year coupon is reinvested at an interest rate of r percent, then total proceeds at the end of the second year will be: $[100 \times (1 + r) + 1100]$. Therefore, realized compound yield to maturity will be a function of r as given in the following table:

r	Total proceeds	Realized YTM = $\sqrt{\text{Proceeds}/1{,}000} - 1$
8%	\$1,208	$\sqrt{1{,}208/1{,}000} - 1 = 0.0991 = 9.91\%$
10%	\$1,210	$\sqrt{1{,}210/1{,}000} - 1 = 0.1000 = 10.00\%$
12%	\$1,212	$\sqrt{1{,}210/1{,}000} - 1 = 0.1009 = 10.09\%$

29. April 15 is midway through the semi-annual coupon period. Therefore, the invoice price will be higher than the stated ask price by an amount equal to one-half of the semiannual coupon. The ask price is 101.125 percent of par, so the invoice price is:

    $\$1{,}011.25 + (1/2 \times \$50) = \$1{,}036.25$

30. Factors that might make the ABC debt more attractive to investors, therefore justifying a lower coupon rate and yield to maturity, are:

    - The ABC debt is a larger issue and therefore may sell with greater liquidity.

    - An option to extend the term from 10 years to 20 years is favorable if interest rates ten years from now are lower than today's interest rates. In contrast, if interest rates are rising, the investor can present the bond for payment and reinvest the money for better returns.

    - In the event of trouble, the ABC debt is a more senior claim. It has more underlying security in the form of a first claim against real property.

    - The call feature on the XYZ bonds makes the ABC bonds relatively more attractive since ABC bonds cannot be called from the investor.

    - The XYZ bond has a sinking fund requiring XYZ to retire part of the issue each year. Since most sinking funds give the firm the option to retire this amount at the lower of par or market value, the sinking fund can work to the detriment of bondholders.

31.

    a. The floating-rate note pays a coupon that adjusts to market levels. Therefore, it will not experience dramatic price changes as market yields fluctuate. The fixed rate note therefore will have a greater price range.

    b. Floating rate notes may not sell at par for any of these reasons:

    The yield spread between one-year Treasury bills and other money market instruments of comparable maturity could be wider than it was when the bond was issued.
    The credit standing of the firm may have eroded relative to Treasury securities that have no credit risk. Therefore, the 2% premium would become insufficient to sustain the issue at par.

    The coupon increases are implemented with a lag, i.e., once every year. During a period of rising interest rates, even this brief lag will be reflected in the price of the security.

c. The risk of call is low. Because the bond will almost surely not sell for much above par value (given its adjustable coupon rate), it is unlikely that the bond will ever be called.

d. The fixed-rate note currently sells at only 93% of the call price, so that yield to maturity is above the coupon rate. Call risk is currently low, since yields would have to fall substantially for the firm to use its option to call the bond.

e. The 9% coupon notes currently have a remaining maturity of fifteen years and sell at a yield to maturity of 9.9%. This is the coupon rate that would be needed for a newly issued fifteen-year maturity bond to sell at par.

f. Because the floating rate note pays a *variable stream* of interest payments to maturity, its yield-to-maturity is not a well-defined concept. The cash flows one might want to use to calculate yield to maturity are not yet known. The effective maturity for comparing interest rate risk of floating rate debt securities with other debt securities is better thought of as the next coupon reset date rather than the final maturity date. Therefore, "yield-to-recoupon date" is a more meaningful measure of return.

32.

a. The bond sells for $1,124.7237 based on the 3.5% yield to *maturity*:
[n = 60; i = 3.5; FV = 1,000; PMT = 40]

Therefore, yield to *call* is 3.3679% semiannually, 6.7358% annually:
[n = 10; PV = −1,124.72; FV = 1,100; PMT = 40]

b. If the call price were $1,050, we would set FV = 1,050 and redo part (a) to find that yield to call is 2.9763% semi-annually, 5.9525% annually. With a lower call price, the yield to call is lower.

c. Yield to call is 3.0312% semiannually, 6.0625% annually:
[n = 4; PV = −1,124.7237; FV = 1,100; PMT = 40]

33. The price schedule is as follows:

Year	Remaining Maturity (T)	Constant Yield Value $1{,}000/(1.08)^T$	Imputed interest (Increase in constant yield value)
0 (now)	20 years	$214.55	
1	19	231.71	231.71 – 214.55 = 17.16
2	18	250.25	250.25 – 231.71 = 18.54
19	1	925.93	
20	0	1,000	1,000 – 925.93 = 74.07

34. The bond is issued at a price of $800. Therefore, its yield to maturity is 6.8245%. [n = 10; PV = −800; FV = 1,000; PMT = 40] Using the constant yield method, we can compute that its price in one year (when maturity falls to 9 years) will be (at an unchanged yield) $814.60, representing an increase of $14.60. Total taxable income is: $40 + $14.60 = $54.60.

35.

a. The yield to maturity of the par bond equals its coupon rate, 8.75%. All else equal, the 4% coupon bond would be more attractive because its coupon rate is far below current market yields, and its price is far below the call price. Therefore, if yields fall, capital gains on the bond will not be limited by the call price. In contrast, the 8.75% coupon bond can increase in value to at most $1050, offering a maximum possible gain of only 5%. The disadvantage of the 8.75% coupon bond in terms of vulnerability to a call shows up in its higher *promised* yield to maturity.

b. If an investor expects rates to fall substantially, the 4% bond offers a greater expected return.

c. Implicit call protection is offered in the sense that any likely fall in yields would not be nearly enough to make the firm consider calling the bond. In this sense, the call feature is almost irrelevant.

36. True. Under the expectations hypothesis, there are no risk premia built into bond prices. The only reason for long-term yields to exceed short-term yields is an expectation of higher short-term rates in the future.

37. If the yield curve is upward sloping, we cannot conclude that investors expect short-term interest rates to rise because the rising slope could be due to either expectations of future increases in rates or the demand of investors for a risk premium on long-term bonds. In fact the yield curve can be upward sloping even in the absence of expectations of future increases in rates.

38.

	Zero	8% Coupon	10% Coupon	Formula
a. Current Prices	$463.19	$1,000	$1,134.20	–PV(0.08,10,PMT,1000)
Price one year from now	$500.25	$1,000	$1,124.94	–PV(0.08,9,PMT,1000)
Price Increase	$37.06	$0.00	($9.26)	
Coupon Income	$0.00	$80.00	$100.00	
Income	$37.06	$80.00	$90.74	
b. Holding Period Return	8.00%	8.00%	8.00%	

39. Uncertain. Lower inflation usually leads to lower nominal interest rates. Nevertheless, if the liquidity premium is sufficiently great, long-term yields can exceed short-term yields despite expectations of falling short rates.

40.

a. We summarize the forward rates and current prices in the following table:

Maturity (years)	YTM	Forward rate	Price (for part c)
1	10.0%		$909.09
2	11.0%	12.01%	$811.62
3	12.0%	14.03%	$711.78

Year 1

Price: 1,000/(1 + 10%) = 909.09

Year 2

Price: $1{,}000/(1 + 11\%)^2 = 811.62$

Forward Rate: $(1 + 11\%)^2/(1 + 10\%) - 1 = 0.1201 = 12.01\%$

Year 3

Price: $1000/(1 + 12\%)^3 = 711.78$

Forward Rate: $(1+12\%)^3/(1+11\%)^2 - 1 = 0.1403 = 14.03\%$

b. We obtain next year's prices and yields by discounting each zero's face value at the forward rates derived in part (a):

Maturity (years)	Price		YTM
1	$892.78	[= 1,000/1.1201]	12.01%
2	$782.93	[= 1,000/(1.1201 × 1.1403)]	13.02%

Note that this year's upward sloping yield curve implies, according to the expectations hypothesis, a shift upward in next year's curve.

c. Next year, the two-year zero will be a one-year zero, and it will therefore sell at: $1000/1.1201 = $892.78

Similarly, the current three-year zero will be a two-year zero, and it will sell for: $782.93

Expected total rate of return:

Two-Year Bond: $\dfrac{\$892.78}{\$811.62} - 1 = 0.1000 = 10.00\%$

Three-Year Bond: $\dfrac{\$782.93}{\$711.78} - 1 = 0.1000 = 10.00\%$

41.

a. The forward rate (f_2) is the rate that makes the return from rolling over one-year bonds the same as the return from investing in the two-year maturity bond and holding to maturity:

$(1 + 8\%) \times (1 + f_2) = (1 + 9\%)^2 \Rightarrow f_2 = 0.1001 = 10.01\%$

b. According to the expectations hypothesis, the forward rate equals the expected value of the short-term interest rate next year, so the best guess would be 10.01%.

c. According to the liquidity preference hypothesis, the forward rate exceeds the expected short-term interest rate next year, so the best guess would be less than 10.01%.

42. The top row must be the spot rates. The spot rates are (geometric) averages of the forward rates, and the top row is the average of the bottom row. For example, the spot rate on a two-year investment (12%) is the average of the two forward rates 10% and 14.0364%:

$$(1 + 0.12)^2 = (1 + 0.10) \times (1 + 0.140364) = 1.2544$$

43. Using a financial calculator, PV = 100, $n = 3$, PMT=0, $i = 6.5$.
Price of FV = 120.795.

Using a financial calculator, PV = 100, $n = 4$, PMT=0, $i = 7.0$.
Price or FV = 131.080.

Setting PV = −120.795, FV = 131.080, $n = 1$, PMT= 0.
r = 8.51%.

44.

a. Initial price, $P_0 = 705.46$ [$n = 20$; PMT = 50; FV = 1,000; $i = 8$]
Next year's price, $P_1 = 793.29$ [$n = 19$; PMT = 50; FV = 1,000; $i = 7$]

$$\text{HPR} = \frac{\$50 + (\$793.29 - \$705.46)}{\$705.46} = 0.1954 = 19.54\%$$

b. Using OID tax rules, the cost basis and imputed interest under the constant yield method are obtained by discounting bond payments at the *original* 8% yield to maturity and simply reducing maturity by one year at a time:

P_0 = \$705.46

<u>First Year</u>
Constant yield price, $P_1' = \$711.89$, so imputed taxable interest over the first year is:
\$711.89 − \$705.46 = \$6.43

Coupon received and imputed taxable interest in the year are taxed as the ordinary income: 40% × (\$50 + \$6.43) = \$22.57

Capital gain = Actual price at 7% YTM − Constant yield price = $P_1 - P_1'$

= \$793.29 − \$711.89 = \$81.40

Tax on capital gain = 30% × \$81.40 = \$24.42

Total taxes = \$22.57 + \$24.42 = \$46.99

c. After-tax HPR $= \dfrac{\$50 + (\$793.29 - \$705.46) - \$46.99}{\$705.46}$

$= 0.1288 = 12.88\%$

d. Value of the bond after two years equals \$798.82 [using $n = 18$; $i = 7$]
Total income from the two coupons, including reinvestment income:

(\$50 × 1.03) + \$50 = \$101.50

Total funds after two years: \$798.82 + \$101.50 = \$900.32

Therefore, the \$705.46 investment grows to \$900.32 after two years.

$705.46 \times (1 + r)^2 = 900.32 \Rightarrow r = 0.1297 = 12.97\%$

e.

Coupon received in first year:	\$50.00
Tax on coupon @ 40%	−20.00
Tax on imputed interest (40% × \$6.43)	−2.57
Net cash flow in first year	\$27.43

If you invest the year-1 cash flow at an after-tax rate of:
3% × (1 − 40%) = 1.8%

By year 2, it will grow to: \$27.43 × 1.018 = \$27.92

You sell the bond in the second year for: P_2 = \$718.84, so imputed interest over the second year = \$6.95

Selling price of the bond in the second year:	\$798.82	
Tax on *imputed* interest in second year:	−2.78	[40% × \$6.95]
Coupon received in second year, net of tax:	+30.00	[\$50 × (1 − 40%)]
Capital gains tax on sales price	−23.99	[30% × (\$798.82 − \$718.84)]
Using constant yield value:		
CF from first year's coupon (reinvested):	+ 27.92	[from above]
TOTAL	\$829.97	

Thus, after two years, the initial investment of \$705.46 grows to \$829.97:

$705.46 \times (1 + r)^2 = 829.97 \Rightarrow r = 0.0847 = 8.47\%$

CFA 1

Answer:

a. (3) The yield on the callable bond must compensate the investor for the risk of call.

Choice (1) is wrong because, although the owner of a callable bond receives principal plus a premium in the event of a call, the interest rate at which he can subsequently reinvest will be low. The low interest rate that makes it profitable for the issuer to call the bond makes it a bad deal for the bond's holder.

Choice (2) is wrong because a bond is more apt to be called when interest rates are low. There will be an interest saving for the issuer only if rates are low.

b. (3)

c. (2)

d. (3)

CFA 2

Answer:

a. The maturity of each bond is 10 years, and we assume that coupons are paid semiannually. Since both bonds are selling at par value, the current yield to maturity for each bond is equal to its coupon rate.

If the yield declines by 1% to 5% (2.5% semiannual yield), the Sentinal bond will increase in value to 107.79 [n=20; i = 2.5; FV = 100; PMT = 3]. The price of the Colina bond will increase, but only to the call price of 102. The present value of scheduled payments is greater than 102, but the call price puts a ceiling on the actual bond price.

b. If rates are expected to fall, the Sentinal bond is more attractive: Since it is not subject to being called, its potential capital gains are higher. If rates are expected to rise, Colina is a better investment. Its higher coupon (which presumably is compensation to investors for the call feature of the bond) will provide a higher rate of return than that of the Sentinal bond.

c. An increase in the volatility of rates increases the value of the firm's option to call back the Colina bond. If rates go down, the firm can call the bond, which puts a cap on possible capital gains. So, higher volatility makes the option to call back the bond more valuable to the issuer. This makes the Colina bond less attractive to the investor.

CFA 3

Answer

Market conversion value = Value if converted into stock

= 20.83 × \$28 = \$583.24

Conversion premium = Bond value − Market conversion value

= \$775 − \$583.24 = \$191.76

CFA 4

Answer:

a. The call provision requires the firm to offer a higher coupon (or higher promised yield to maturity) on the bond in order to compensate the investor for the firm's option to call back the bond at a specified call price if interest rates fall sufficiently. Investors are willing to grant this valuable option to the issuer, but only for a price that reflects the possibility that the bond will be called. That price is the higher promised yield at which they are willing to buy the bond.

b. The call option reduces the expected life of the bond. If interest rates fall substantially so that the likelihood of a call increases, investors will treat the bond as if it will "mature" and be paid off at the call date, not at the stated maturity date. On the other hand if rates rise, the bond must be paid off at the maturity date, not later. This asymmetry means that the expected life of the bond will be less than the stated maturity.

c. The advantage of a callable bond is the higher coupon (and higher promised yield to maturity) when the bond is issued. If the bond is never called, then an investor will earn a higher realized compound yield on a callable bond issued at par than on a non-callable bond issued at par on the same date. The disadvantage of the callable bond is the risk of call. If rates fall and the bond is called, then the investor receives the call price and will have to reinvest the proceeds at interest rates that are lower than the yield to maturity at which the bond was originally issued. In this event, the firm's savings in interest payments are the investor's loss.

CFA 5

Answer:

a.

(1) Current yield = Coupon/Price = \$70/\$960 = 0.0729 = 7.29%

(2) YTM = 3.993% semiannually or 7.986% annual bond equivalent yield
[n = 10; PV = −960; FV = 1000; PMT = 35]
Then compute the interest rate.

(3) Realized compound yield is 4.166% (semiannually), or 8.332% annual bond equivalent yield. To obtain this value, first calculate the future value of reinvested coupons. There will be six payments of \$35 each, reinvested semiannually at a per period rate of 3%:
[PV = 0; PMT = \$35; n = 6; i = 3] Compute FV = \$226.39

The bond will be selling at par value of \$1,000 in three years, since coupon is forecast to equal yield to maturity. Therefore, total proceeds in three years will be \$1,226.39. To find realized compound yield on a semiannual basis (i.e., for six half-year periods), we solve:

$$\$960 \times (1 + r_{realized})^6 = \$1,226.39 \Rightarrow r_{realized} = 4.166\% \text{ (semiannual)}$$

b. Shortcomings of each measure:

(1) Current yield does not account for capital gains or losses on bonds bought at prices other than par value. It also does not account for reinvestment income on coupon payments.

(2) Yield to maturity assumes that the bond is held to maturity and that all coupon income can be reinvested at a rate equal to the yield to maturity.

(3) Realized compound yield (horizon yield) is affected by the forecast of reinvestment rates, holding period, and yield of the bond at the end of the investor's holding period.

CHAPTER 11
MANAGING BOND PORTFOLIOS

1. Duration can be thought of as a weighted average of the 'maturities' of the cash flows paid to holders of the perpetuity, where the weight for each cash flow is equal to the present value of that cash flow divided by the total present value of all cash flows. For cash flows in the distant future, present value approaches zero (i.e., the weight becomes very small) so that these distant cash flows have little impact, and eventually, virtually no impact on the weighted average.

2. A low coupon, long maturity bond will have the highest duration and will, therefore, produce the largest price change when interest rates change.

3. An intermarket spread swap should work. The trade would be to long the corporate bonds and short the treasuries. A relative gain will be realized when the rate spreads return to normal.

4. Change in Price = − (Modified Duration × Change in YTM) × Price

$$= -\frac{\text{Macaulay's Duration}}{1+\text{YTM}} \times \text{Change in YTM} \times \text{Price}$$

Given the current bond price is \$1,050, yield to maturity is 6%, and the increase in YTM and new price, we can calculate D:

$$\$1{,}025 - \$1{,}050 = -\frac{\text{Macaulay's Duration}}{1+0.06} \times 0.0025 \times \$1{,}050 \Rightarrow D = 10.0952$$

5. d. None of the above.

6. The increase will be larger than the decrease in price.

7. While it is true that short-term rates are more volatile than long-term rates, the longer duration of the longer-term bonds makes their rates of return more volatile. The higher duration magnifies the sensitivity to interest-rate savings. Thus, it can be true that *rates* of short-term bonds are more volatile, but the *prices* of long-term bonds are more volatile.

8. When YTM = 6%, the duration is 2.8334.

(1) Time until Payment (Years)	(2) Payment	(3) Payment Discounted at 6%	(4) Weight	(5) Column (1) × Column (4)
1	60	56.60	0.0566	0.0566
2	60	53.40	0.0534	0.1068
3	1060	890.00	0.8900	2.6700
Column Sum:		1000.00	1.0000	2.8334

When YTM = 10%, the duration is 2.8238

(1) Time until Payment (Years)	(2) Payment	(3) Payment Discounted at 10%	(4) Weight	(5) Column (1) × Column (4)
1	60	54.55	0.0606	0.0606
2	60	49.59	0.0551	0.1101
3	1060	796.39	0.8844	2.6531
	Column Sum:	900.53	1.0000	2.8238

When the yield to maturity increases, the duration decreases.

9. Using Equation 11.2, the percentage change in the bond price is:

$$\frac{\Delta P}{P} = -\text{Duration} \times \frac{\Delta y}{1+y} = -7.194 \times \frac{0.0050}{1.10} = -0.0327 \text{ or a 3.27\% decline}$$

10. The computation of duration is as follows:
Interest Rate (YTM) is 10%.

(1) Time until Payment (Years)	(2) Payment (in millions of dollars)	(3) Payment Discounted At 10%	(4) Weight	(5) Column (1) × Column (4)
1	1	0.9091	0.2744	0.2744
2	2	1.6529	0.4989	0.9977
3	1	0.7513	0.2267	0.6803
	Column Sum:	3.3133	1.0000	1.9524

Duration = 1.9524 years

11. The duration of the perpetuity is: (1 + y)/y = 1.10/0.10 = 11 years
Let w be the weight of the zero-coupon bond. Then we find w by solving:
$(w \times 1) + [(1 - w) \times 11] = 1.9523 \Rightarrow w = 9.048/10 = 0.9048$
Therefore, the portfolio should be 90.48% invested in the zero and 9.52% in the perpetuity.

12. Using Equation 11.2, the percentage change in the bond price will be:

$$\frac{\Delta P}{P} = -\text{Duration} \times \frac{\Delta y}{1+y} = -5.0 \times \frac{-0.0010}{1.08} = 0.00463 \text{ or a 0.463\% increase.}$$

13.

a. Bond B has a higher yield to maturity than bond A since its coupon payments and maturity are equal to those of A, while its price is lower. (Perhaps the yield is higher because of differences in credit risk.) Therefore, the duration of Bond B must be shorter. Homer and Liebowitz (1972) had demonstrated that the sensitivity of a bond's price to a change in its yield is inversely related to the yield to maturity at which the bond currently is selling. Thus, with a lower YTM, Bond A has higher duration and is more sensitive to the interest rate change.

b. Bond A has a lower yield and a lower coupon, both of which cause it to have a longer duration than that of Bond B. Moreover, Bond A cannot be called. Therefore, the maturity of Bond A is at least as long as that of Bond B, which implies that the duration of Bond A is at least as long as that of Bond B.

14. Choose the longer-duration bond to benefit from a rate decrease.

a. The Aaa-rated bond has the lower yield to maturity and therefore the longer duration.

b. The lower-coupon bond has the longer duration *and* more de facto call protection.

c. The lower coupon bond has the longer duration.

15.

a. The present value of the obligation is $17,832.65 and the duration is 1.4808 years, as shown in the following table:

Computation of duration, interest rate = 8%

(1) Time until Payment (Years)	(2) Payment	(3) Payment Discounted at 8%	(4) Weight	(5) Column (1) × Column (4)
1	10,000	9,259.26	0.5192	0.51923
2	10,000	8,573.39	0.4808	0.96154
	Column Sum:	17,832.65	1.0000	1.48077

b. To immunize the obligation, invest in a zero-coupon bond maturing in 1.4808 years. Since the present value of the zero-coupon bond must be $17,832.65, the face value (i.e., the future redemption value) must be:

$$\$17,832.65 \times (1.08)^{1.4808} = \$19,985.26$$

c. If the interest rate increases to 9%, the zero-coupon bond would fall in value to:

$$\frac{\$19,985.26}{(1.09)^{1.4808}} = \$17,590.92$$

The present value of the tuition obligation would fall to $17,591.11, so that the net position changes by $0.19.

If the interest rate falls to 7%, the zero-coupon bond would rise in value to:

$$\frac{\$19,985.26}{(1.07)^{1.4808}} = \$18,079.99$$

The present value of the tuition obligation would increase to \$18,080.18, so that the net position changes by \$0.19.

The reason the net position changes at all is that, as the interest rate changes, so does the duration of the stream of tuition payments.

16.

a. PV of obligation = \$2 million/0.16 = \$12.5 million

Duration of obligation = 1.16/0.16 = 7.25 years

Call w the weight on the five-year maturity bond (with duration of 4 years). Then:

$(w \times 4) + [(1 - w) \times 11] = 7.25 \Rightarrow w = 0.5357$

Therefore:

0.5357 × \$12.5 = \$6.7 million in the 5-year bond, and

0.4643 × \$12.5 = \$5.8 million in the 20-year bond.

b. The price of the 20-year bond is:

[60 × Annuity factor(16%, 20)] + [1000 × PV factor(16%, 20)] = \$407.1

Therefore, the bond sells for 0.4071 times its par value, so that:

Market value = Par value × 0.4071

\$5.8 million = Par value × 0.4071 ⇒ Par value = \$14.247 million

Another way to see this is to note that each bond with par value \$1000 sells for \$407.1. If total market value is \$5.8 million, then you need to buy:

\$5,800,000/407.1 = 14,247 bonds

Therefore, total par value is \$14,247,000.

17. *a.* Shorten his portfolio duration to decrease the sensitivity to the expected rate increase.

18. Change in price = – (Modified duration × Change in YTM) × Price
= – 3.5851 × 0.01 × \$100
= – \$3.5851

⇒ The price will decrease by \$3.59.

19.

a. The duration of the perpetuity is: 1.05/0.05 = 21 years
Let w be the weight of the zero-coupon bond, so that we find w by solving:

$(w \times 5) + [(1 - w) \times 21] = 10 \Rightarrow w = 11/16 = 0.6875$

Therefore, the portfolio will be 11/16 invested in the zero-coupon bond and 5/16 in the perpetuity.

b. The zero-coupon bond will then have a duration of 4 years while the perpetuity will still have a 21-year duration. To have a portfolio with duration equal to nine years, which is now the duration of the obligation, we again solve for w:

$$(w \times 4) + [(1 - w) \times 21] = 9 \Rightarrow w = 12/17 = 0.7059$$

So the proportion invested in the zero increases to 12/17 and the proportion in the perpetuity falls to 5/17.

20. Macaulay Duration and Modified Duration are calculated using Excel as follows:

Inputs		Formula in column B
Settlement date	5/27/2012	=DATE(2012,5,27)
Maturity date	11/15/2021	=DATE(2021,11,15)
Coupon rate	0.07	0.07
Yield to maturity	0.08	0.08
Coupons per year	2	2
Outputs		
Macaulay Duration	6.9659	=DURATION(B2,B3,B4,B5,B6)
Modified Duration	6.6980	=MDURATION(B2,B3,B4,B5,B6)

21. Macaulay Duration and Modified Duration are calculated using Excel as follows:

Inputs		Formula in column B
Settlement date	5/27/2012	=DATE(2012,5,27)
Maturity date	11/15/2021	=DATE(2021,11,15)
Coupon rate	0.07	0.07
Yield to maturity	0.08	0.08
Coupons per year	1	1
Outputs		
Macaulay Duration	6.8844	=DURATION(B2,B3,B4,B5,B6)
Modified Duration	6.3745	=MDURATION(B2,B3,B4,B5,B6)

Generally, we would expect duration to increase when the frequency of payment decreases from two payments per year to one payment per year because more of the bond's payments are made further in to the future when payments are made annually. However, in this example, duration decreases as a result of the timing of the settlement date relative to the maturity date and the interest payment dates. For annual payments, the first payment is $70 paid on November 15, 2012. For semi-annual payments, the first $70 is paid as follows: $35 on November 15, 2012 and $35 on May 15, 2013, so the weighted average "maturity" of these payments is longer than the "maturity" of the $70 payment on November 15, 2012 for the annual payment bond.

22.

a. The duration of the perpetuity is: 1.10/0.10 = 11 years
The present value of the payments is: $1 million/0.10 = $10 million

Let w be the weight of the five-year zero-coupon bond and therefore (1 – w) is the weight of the twenty-year zero-coupon bond. Then we find w by solving:

$(w \times 5) + [(1 - w) \times 20] = 11 \Rightarrow w = 9/15 = 0.60$

So, 60% of the portfolio will be invested in the five-year zero-coupon bond and 40% in the twenty-year zero-coupon bond.

Therefore, the market value of the five-year zero is:
$10 million × 0.60 = $6 million

Similarly, the market value of the twenty-year zero is:
$10 million × 0.40 = $4 million

b. Face value of the five-year zero-coupon bond is:
$\$6 \text{ million} \times (1.10)^5 = \$9{,}663{,}060.00$

Face value of the twenty-year zero-coupon bond is:
$\$4 \text{ million} \times (1.10)^{20} = \$26{,}909{,}999.80$

23. Convexity is calculated using the Excel spreadsheet below:

		Time (t)	Cash flow	PV(CF)	t + t^2	(t + t^2) x PV(CF)
Coupon	6	1	6	5.556	2	11.111
YTM	0.08	2	6	5.144	6	30.864
Maturity	7	3	6	4.763	12	57.156
Price	$89.59	4	6	4.41	20	88.204
		5	6	4.083	30	122.505
		6	6	3.781	42	158.803
		7	106	61.85	56	3463.599
		8	0	0	72	0
		9	0	0	90	0
		10	0	0	110	0
		Sum:		89.58726		3932.242
			Convexity:			37.631057

24.
a. Interest rate = 12%

	Time until Payment (Years)	Payment	Payment Discounted at 12%	Weight	Time × Weight
8% coupon	1	80	71.429	0.0790	0.0790
	2	80	63.776	0.0706	0.1411
	3	1080	768.723	0.8504	2.5513
		Sum:	903.927	1.0000	2.7714

Zero-coupon	1	0	0.000	0.0000	0.0000
	2	0	0.000	0.0000	0.0000
	3	1000	711.780	1.0000	3.0000
		Sum:	711.780	1.0000	3.0000

At a higher discount rate, the weights of the later payments of the coupon bond fall and those of the earlier payments rise. So duration falls. For the zero, the weight of the payment in three years remains at 1.0, and duration therefore remains at 3 years.

b. Continue to use a yield to maturity of 12%:

	Time until Payment (Years)	Payment	Payment Discounted at 12%	Weight	Time × Weight
12% coupon	1	120	107.143	0.1071	0.1071
	2	120	95.663	0.0957	0.1913
	3	1120	797.194	0.7972	2.3916
		Sum:	1000.000	1.0000	2.6901

The weights of the earlier payments are higher when the coupon increases. Therefore, duration falls.

25.

a.

	A	B	C	D	E	F	G
1			Time (t)	Cash flow	PV(CF)	t + t^2	(t + t^2) x PV(CF)
2	Coupon	80	1	80	72.727273	2	145.4545455
3	YTM	0.1	2	80	66.115702	6	396.6942149
4	Maturity	3	3	1080	811.420	12	9737.040
5	Price	$950.263		Sum	950.263		10279.189
6							
7				Convexity:	8.939838	=G5/(E5*(1+B2)^2)	

b.

	A	B	C	D	E	F	G
1			Time (t)	Cash flow	PV(CF)	t + t^2	(t + t^2) x PV(CF)
2	YTM	0.1	1	0	0	2	0
3	Maturity	3	2	0	0	6	0
4	Price	$751.315	3	1000	751.315	12	9015.778
5				Sum	751.315		9015.778
6							
7				Convexity:	9.917355	=G5/(E5*(1+B2)^2)	

26. Using a financial calculator, we find that the price of the bond is:

For yield to maturity of 7%: $1,620.45

For yield to maturity of 8%: $1,450.31

For yield to maturity of 9%: $1,308.21

Using the duration rule, assuming yield to maturity falls to 7%:

$$\text{Predicted price change} = -\text{Duration} \times \frac{\Delta y}{1+y} \times P_0$$

$$= -11.54 \times \frac{-0.01}{1.08} \times \$1{,}450.31 = \$154.97$$

Therefore: Predicted price = $154.97 + $1,450.31 = $1,605.28

The actual price at a 7% yield to maturity is $1,620.45. Therefore:

$$\%\ \text{error} = \frac{\$1{,}620.45 - \$1{,}605.28}{\$1{,}620.45} = 0.0094 = 0.94\%$$

Using the duration rule, assuming yield to maturity increases to 9%:

$$\text{Predicted price change} = -\text{Duration} \times \frac{\Delta y}{1+y} \times P_0$$

$$= -11.54 \times \frac{+0.01}{1.08} \times \$1{,}450.31 = -\$154.97$$

Therefore: Predicted price = –$154.97 + $1,450.31 = $1,295.34

The actual price at a 9% yield to maturity is $1,308.21. Therefore:

$$\%\ \text{error} = \frac{\$1{,}308.21 - \$1{,}295.34}{\$1{,}308.21} = 0.0098 = 0.98\%$$

Using the duration-with-convexity rule, assuming yield to maturity falls to 7%:

Predicted price change

$$= \left[-\text{Duration} \times \frac{\Delta y}{1+y} + \left(0.5 \times \text{Convexity} \times (\Delta y)^2\right)\right] \times P_0$$

$$= \left[\left(-11.54 \times \frac{-0.01}{1.08}\right) + \left(0.5 \times 192.4 \times (-0.01)^2\right)\right] \times \$1{,}450.31$$

= $168.92

Therefore: Predicted price = $168.92 + $1,450.31 = $1,619.23

The actual price at a 7% yield to maturity is $1,620.45. Therefore:

$$\%\ \text{error} = \frac{\$1{,}620.45 - \$1{,}619.23}{\$1{,}620.45} = 0.00075 = 0.075\%$$

<u>Using the duration-with-convexity rule, assuming yield to maturity rises to 9%:</u>

Predicted price change

$$= \left[-\text{Duration} \times \frac{\Delta y}{1+y} + \left(0.5 \times \text{Convexity} \times (\Delta y)^2\right)\right] \times P_0$$

$$= \left[\left(-11.54 \times \frac{+0.01}{1.08}\right) + \left(0.5 \times 192.4 \times (-0.01)^2\right)\right] \times \$1{,}450.31$$

$$= -\$141.02$$

Therefore: Predicted price = −\$141.02 + \$1,450.31 = \$1,309.29

The actual price at a 9% yield to maturity is \$1,308.21. Therefore:

$$\%\ \text{error} = \frac{\$1{,}309.29 - \$1{,}308.21}{\$1{,}308.21} = 0.00083 = 0.083\%$$

Conclusion: The duration-with-convexity rule provides more accurate approximations to the actual change in price. In this example, the percentage error using convexity with duration is less than one-tenth the error using duration only to estimate the price change.

27. You should buy the three-year bond because it will offer a 9% holding-period return over the next year, which is greater than the return on either of the other bonds, as shown below:

Maturity	One year	Two years	Three years
YTM at beginning of year	7.00%	8.00%	9.00%
Beginning of year price	\$1,009.35	\$1,000.00	\$974.69
End of year price (at 9% YTM)	\$1,000.00	\$990.83	\$982.41
Capital gain	−\$ 9.35	−\$ 9.17	\$7.72
Coupon	\$80.00	\$80.00	\$80.00
One year total \$ return	\$70.65	\$70.83	\$87.72
One year total rate of return	7.00%	7.08%	9.00%

28. The maturity of the 30-year bond will fall to 25 years, and the yield is forecast to be 8%. Therefore, the price forecast for the bond is:

\$893.25 [n = 25; i = 8; FV = 1,000; PMT = 70]

At a 6% interest rate, the five coupon payments will accumulate to \$394.60 (FV) after five years. [n =5; i = 6; PV = 0; PMT = 70]

Therefore, total proceeds will be:

\$394.60 + \$893.25 = \$1,287.85

The five-year return is therefore: (\$1,287.85/867.42) − 1 = 1.48469 − 1 = 48.469%

The annual rate of return is: $(1.48469)^{(1/5)} - 1 = 0.0822 = 8.22\%$

The maturity of the 20-year bond will fall to 15 years, and its yield is forecast to be 7.5%. Therefore, the price forecast for the bond is:

$911.73 [n = 15; i = 7.5; FV = 1000; PMT = 65]

At a 6% interest rate, the five coupon payments will accumulate to $366.41 after five years. [n=15; i = 6; PV = 0; PMT = 65]

Therefore, total proceeds will be:

$366.41 + $911.73 = $1,278.14

The five-year return is therefore: ($1,278.14/$879.50) − 1 = 1.45326 − 1 = 45.326%
The annual rate of return is: $1.45326^{(1/5)} - 1 = 0.0776 = 7.76\%$

Conclusion: The 30-year bond offers the higher expected return.

29.

a. Using a financial calculator, we find that the price of the zero-coupon bond (with $1000 face value) is:
For yield to maturity of 8%: $374.84
For yield to maturity of 9%: $333.28

The price of the 6% coupon bond is:
For yield to maturity of 8%: $774.84
For yield to maturity of 9%: $691.79

Zero Coupon Bond

$$\text{Actual \% loss} = \frac{\$333.28 - \$374.84}{\$374.84} = -0.1109\text{, an 11.09\% loss}$$

The percentage loss predicted by the duration-with-convexity rule is:

$$\text{Predicted \% loss} = [(-11.81) \times 0.01] + [0.5 \times 150.3 \times (0.01)^2]$$
$$= -0.1106\text{, an 11.06\% loss}$$

Coupon Bond

$$\text{Actual \% loss} = \frac{\$691.79 - \$774.84}{\$774.84} = -0.1072\text{, a 10.72\% loss}$$

The percentage loss predicted by the duration-with-convexity rule is:

$$\text{Predicted \% loss} = [(-11.79) \times 0.01] + [0.5 \times 231.2 \times (0.01)^2]$$
$$= -0.1063\text{, a 10.63\% loss}$$

b. Now assume yield to maturity falls to 7%. The price of the zero increases to $422.04, and the price of the coupon bond increases to $875.91.

Zero Coupon Bond

$$\text{Actual \% gain} = \frac{\$422.04 - \$374.84}{\$374.84} = 0.1259\text{, a 12.59\% gain}$$

The percentage gain predicted by the duration-with-convexity rule is:

$$\text{Predicted \% gain} = [(-11.81) \times (-0.01)] + [0.5 \times 150.3 \times (-0.01)^2]$$

$$= 0.1256\text{, a 12.56\% gain}$$

Coupon Bond

$$\text{Actual \% gain} = \frac{\$875.91 - \$774.84}{\$774.84} = 0.1304\text{, a 13.04\% gain}$$

The percentage gain predicted by the duration-with-convexity rule is:

$$\text{Predicted \% gain} = [(-11.79) \times (-0.01)] + [0.5 \times 231.2 \times (-0.01)^2]$$

$$= 0.1295\text{, a 12.95\% gain}$$

c. The 6% coupon bond (which has higher convexity) outperforms the zero regardless of whether rates rise or fall. This is a general property which can be understood by first noting from the duration-with-convexity formula that the duration effect resulting from the change in rates is the same for the two bonds because their durations are approximately equal. However, the convexity effect, which is always positive, always favors the higher convexity bond. Thus, if the yields on the bonds always change by equal amounts, as we have assumed in this example, the higher convexity bond always outperforms a lower convexity bond with the same duration and initial yield to maturity.

d. This situation cannot persist. No one would be willing to buy the lower convexity bond if it always underperforms the other bond. The price of the lower convexity bond will fall and its yield to maturity will rise. Thus, the lower convexity bond will sell at a higher initial yield to maturity. That higher yield is compensation for the lower convexity. If rates change only slightly, the higher yield-lower convexity bond will perform better; if rates change by a greater amount, the lower yield-higher convexity bond will do better.

CFA 1

Answer:

C: Highest maturity, zero coupon
D: Highest maturity, next-lowest coupon
A: Highest maturity, same coupon as remaining bonds (Bond B and E)
B: Lower yield to maturity than bond E
E: Highest coupon, shortest maturity, highest yield of all bonds

CFA 2

Answer:

a. $\text{Modified duration} = \dfrac{\text{Macaulay duration}}{1 + \text{YTM}}$

If the Macaulay duration is 10 years and the yield to maturity is 8%, then the modified duration is: 10/1.08 = 9.26 years

b. For option-free coupon bonds, modified duration is better than maturity as a measure of the bond's sensitivity to changes in interest rates. Maturity considers only the final cash flow, while modified duration includes other factors such as the size and timing of coupon payments and the level of interest rates (yield to maturity). Modified duration, unlike maturity, tells us the approximate proportional change in the bond price for a given change in yield to maturity.

c. i. Modified duration increases as the coupon decreases.

ii. Modified duration decreases as maturity decreases.

CFA 3

Answer:

a. *Scenario (i)*: Strong economic recovery with rising inflation expectations. Interest rates and bond yields will most likely rise, and the prices of both bonds will fall. The probability that the callable bond will be called declines, so that it will behave more like the non-callable bond. (Notice that they have similar durations when priced to maturity.) The slightly lower duration of the callable bond will result in somewhat better performance in the high interest rate scenario.

Scenario (ii): Economic recession with reduced inflation expectations. Interest rates and bond yields will most likely fall. The callable bond is likely to be called. The relevant duration calculation for the callable bond is now its modified duration to call. Price appreciation is limited as indicated by the lower duration. The non-callable bond, on the other hand, continues to have the same modified duration and hence has greater price appreciation.

b. If yield to maturity (YTM) on Bond B falls by 75 basis points:

$$\text{Projected \% change in price} = -\,(\text{Modified duration}) \times (\text{Change in YTM})$$

$$= (-6.80) \times (-0.75\%) = 5.1\%$$

So the price will rise to approximately \$105.10 from its current level of \$100.

c. For Bond A (the callable bond), bond life and therefore bond cash flows are uncertain. If one ignores the call feature and analyzes the bond on a "to maturity" basis, all calculations for yield and duration are distorted. Durations are too long and yields are too high. On the other hand, if one treats the premium bond selling above the call price on a "to call" basis, the duration is unrealistically short and yields too low.

The most effective approach is to use an option valuation approach. The callable bond can be decomposed into two separate securities: a non-callable bond and an option.

Price of callable bond = Price of non-callable bond − Price of option

Since the option to call the bond always has a positive value, the price of the callable bond is always less than the price of the non-callable security.

CFA 4

Answer:

a. The Aa bond initially has the higher yield to maturity (yield spread of 40 b.p. versus 31 b.p.), but the Aa bond is expected to have a widening spread relative to Treasuries. This will reduce rate of return. The Aaa spread is expected to be stable. Calculate comparative returns as follows:

<u>Incremental return over Treasuries:</u>
Incremental yield spread − (Change in spread × duration)
Aaa bond: 31 bp − (0 × 3.1) = 31 bp
Aa bond: 40 bp − (10 bp × 3.1) = 9 bp
So choose the Aaa bond.

b. Other variables that one should consider:

- Potential changes in issue-specific credit quality: If the credit quality of the bonds changes, spreads relative to Treasuries will also change.
- Changes in relative yield spreads for a given bond rating: If quality spreads in the general bond market change because of changes in required risk premiums, the yield spreads of the bonds will change even if there is no change in the assessment of the credit quality of these *particular* bonds.
- Maturity effect: As bonds near maturity, the effect of credit quality on spreads can also change. This can affect bonds of different initial credit quality differently.

CFA 5

Answer:

$\Delta P/P = -D^* \, \Delta y$

<u>For Strategy I:</u>
5-year maturity: $\Delta P/P = -4.83 \times (-0.75\%) = 3.6225\%$
25-year maturity: $\Delta P/P = -23.81 \times 0.50\% = -11.9050\%$
Strategy I: $\Delta P/P = (0.5 \times 3.6225\%) + [0.5 \times (-11.9050\%)] = -4.1413\%$

<u>For Strategy II:</u>
15-year maturity: $\Delta P/P = -14.35 \times 0.25\% = -3.5875\%$

CFA 6

Answer:

a. For an option-free bond, the effective duration and modified duration are approximately the same. The duration of the bond described in Table 22A is calculated as follows:

Modified Duration = − ΔP/(P × Δy)

= − (99.29 − 100.71)/[100 × (0.001− (−0.001))]

= 7.1

b. The total percentage price change for the bond described in Table 22A is estimated as follows:

Percentage price change using D* = −7.90 × (−0.02) × 100 = 15.80%

Convexity adjustment = 1.66%

Total estimated percentage price change = 15.80% + 1.66% = 17.46%

CFA 7

Answer:

a. i. Effective duration = (116.887 − 100.00)/(2 × 100 × 0.01) = 15.26

ii. Effective duration = (50/98.667) × 15.26 + (48.667/98.667) × 2.15 = 8.79

b. The statement would only be correct if the portfolio consisted of only zero coupon bonds.

CFA 8

Answer:

a. The two risks are price risk and reinvestment rate risk. The former refers to bond price volatility as interest rates fluctuate, the latter to uncertainty in the rate at which coupon income can be reinvested.

b. Immunization is the process of structuring a bond portfolio in such a manner that the value of the portfolio (including proceeds reinvested) will reach a given target level regardless of future changes in interest rates. This is accomplished by matching both the values and durations of the assets and liabilities of the plan. This may be viewed as a low-risk bond management strategy.

c. Duration matching is superior to maturity matching because bonds of equal duration — not those of equal maturity — are equally sensitive to interest rate fluctuations.

CFA 9

Answer:

The economic climate is one of impending interest rate increases. Hence, we will want to shorten portfolio duration.

a. Choose the short maturity (2017) bond.

b. The Arizona bond likely has lower duration. Coupons are about equal, but the Arizona yield is higher.

c. Choose the 9⅜ % coupon bond. Maturities are about equal, but the coupon is much higher, resulting in lower duration.

d. The duration of the Shell bond will be lower if the effect of the higher yield to maturity and earlier start of sinking fund redemption dominates the slightly lower coupon rate.

e. The floating rate bond has a duration that approximates the adjustment period, which is only six months.

CFA 10

Answer:

a. (4) A low coupon and a long maturity
b. (4) Zero, long
c. (4) All the above
d. (2) Great price volatility

CFA 11

Answer:

a. A manager who believes that the level of interest rates will change should engage in a rate anticipation swap, lengthening duration if rates are expected to fall, and shortening duration if rates are expected to rise.

b. A change in yield spreads across sectors would call for an inter-market spread swap, in which the manager buys bonds in the sector for which yields are expected to fall and sells bonds in the sector for which yields are expected to rise.

c. A belief that the yield spread on a particular instrument will change calls for a substitution swap in which that security is sold if its relative yield is expected to rise or is bought if its yield is expected to fall compared to other similar bonds.

CFA 12

Answer:

a. This swap would have been made if the investor anticipated a decline in long-term interest rates and an increase in long-term bond prices. The deeper discount, lower coupon 2⅜% bond would provide more opportunity for capital gains, greater call protection, and greater protection against declining reinvestment rates at a cost of only a modest drop in yield.

b. This swap was probably done by an investor who believed the 24 basis point yield spread between the two bonds was too narrow. The investor anticipated that, if the spread widened to a more normal level, either a capital gain would be experienced on the Treasury note or a capital loss would be avoided on the Phone bond, or both. This swap might also have been done by an investor who anticipated a decline in interest rates, and who also wanted to maintain high current coupon income and have the better call protection of the Treasury note. The Treasury note would have much greater potential for price appreciation, in contrast to the Phone bond which would be restricted by its call price. Furthermore, if intermediate-term interest rates were to rise, the price decline of the higher quality, higher coupon Treasury note would likely be "cushioned" and the reinvestment return from the higher coupons would likely be greater.

c. This swap would have been made if the investor were bearish on the bond market. The zero coupon note would be extremely vulnerable to an increase in interest rates since the yield to maturity, determined by the discount at the time of purchase, is locked in. This is in contrast to the floating rate note, for which interest is adjusted periodically to reflect current returns on debt instruments. The funds received in interest income on the floating rate notes could be used at a later time to purchase long-term bonds at more attractive yields.

d. These two bonds are similar in most respects other than quality and yield. An investor who believed the yield spread between Government and Al bonds was too narrow would have made the swap either to take a capital gain on the Government bond or to avoid a capital loss on the Al bond. The increase in call protection after the swap would not be a factor except under the most bullish interest rate scenarios. The swap does, however, extend maturity another 8 years, and yield to maturity sacrifice is 169 basis points.

e. The principal differences between these two bonds are the convertible feature of the Z mart bond, and, for the Lucky Duck debentures, the yield and coupon advantage, and the longer maturity. The swap would have been made if the investor believed some combination of the following:

First, that the appreciation potential of the Z mart convertible, based primarily on the intrinsic value of Z mart common stock, was no longer as attractive as it had been.

Second, that the yields on long-term bonds were at a cyclical high, causing bond portfolio managers who could take A2-risk bonds to reach for high yields and long maturities, either to lock them in or take a capital gain when rates subsequently declined.

Third, while waiting for rates to decline, the investor will enjoy an increase in coupon income. Basically, the investor is swapping an equity-equivalent for a long- term corporate bond.

CHAPTER 12
MACROECONOMIC AND INDUSTRY ANALYSIS

1. A top-down approach to security valuation begins with an analysis of the global and domestic economy. Analysts who follow a top-down approach then narrow their attention to an industry or sector likely to perform well, given the expected performance of the broader economy. Finally, the analysis focuses on specific companies within an industry or sector that has been identified as likely to perform well. A bottom-up approach typically emphasizes fundamental analysis of individual company stocks and is largely based on the belief that undervalued stocks will perform well regardless of the prospects for the industry or the broader economy. The major advantage of the top-down approach is that it provides a structured approach to incorporating the impact of economic and financial variables, at every level, into analysis of a company's stock. One would expect, for example, that prospects for a particular industry are highly dependent on broader economic variables. Similarly, the performance of an individual company's stock is likely to be greatly affected by the prospects for the industry in which the company operates.

2. The yield curve, by definition, incorporates future interest rates. As such, it reflects future expectations and is a leading indicator.

3. c. A defensive firm. Defensive firms and industries have below-average sensitivity to the state of the economy.

4. It would be considered a supply shock which affects production capacity and costs.

5.
   a. Financial leverage increases the sensitivity of profits in the business cycle since the interest payments have to be made regardless of the business cycle. Companies would thus become more sensitive to the business cycle while increasing their financial leverage.

   b. Firms with high fixed costs are said to have high operating leverage. As small swings in business conditions can have large impacts on profitability, they are more sensitive to the business cycle.

6. d. Asset play. Some of the valuable assets of the company are not currently reflected in the present value.

7. A peak is the transition from the end of an expansion to the start of a contraction. A trough occurs at the bottom of a recession just as the economy enters a recovery. Contraction is the period from peak to trough. Expansion is the period from trough to peak.

8. a. Monetary policy is expansive and fiscal policy is expansive. This is consistent with a steeply upward-sloping yield curve because, while the expansionary policies stimulate the economy and decrease the short-term rate, high inflation in the future is expected which forces up the yield in longer maturity.

9. a. A redistributive tax system is a demand-side management approach.

10. Companies tend to pay very low, if any, dividends early in their business life cycle since these firms need to reinvest as much capital as possible in order to grow.

11. $1+\text{Real Interest Rate}=\dfrac{1+\text{Nominal Interest Rate}}{1+\text{Inflation Rate}}$

Given nominal interest rate, R, is 5% and inflation rate, *i*, is 3%, we can solve for the real interest rate, *r*:

$$1+r=\frac{1.05}{1.03}=1.0194 \Rightarrow r=1.94\%$$

12. $\text{DOL}=1+\dfrac{\text{Fixed Costs}}{\text{Profits}}=1+\dfrac{7}{4}=2.75$

13. This exercise is left to the student.

14. Expansionary (i.e., looser) monetary policy to lower interest rates would help to stimulate investment and expenditures on consumer durables. Expansionary fiscal policy (i.e., lower taxes, higher government spending, increased welfare transfers) would directly stimulate aggregate demand.

15. A depreciating dollar makes imported cars more expensive and American cars cheaper to foreign consumers. This should benefit the U.S. auto industry.

16.

a. Gold Mining. Gold is traditionally viewed as a hedge against inflation. Expansionary monetary policy may lead to increased inflation, and could thus enhance the value of gold mining stocks.

b. Construction. Expansionary monetary policy will lead to lower interest rates which ought to stimulate housing demand. The construction industry should benefit.

17.

a. The robotics process entails higher fixed costs and lower variable (labor) costs. Therefore, this firm will perform better in a boom and worse in a recession. For example, costs will rise less rapidly than revenue when sales volume expands during a boom.

b. Because its profits are more sensitive to the business cycle, the robotics firm will have the higher beta.

18. Supply side economists believe that a reduction in income tax rates will make workers more willing to work at current or even slightly lower (gross-of-tax) wages. Such an effect ought to mitigate cost pressures on the inflation rate and thus the price level.

19.

Deep recession	Health care (non-cyclical)
Superheated economy	Steel production (cyclical)
Healthy expansion	Housing construction (cyclical, but interest rate sensitive)
Stagflation	Gold mining (counter cyclical)

20.

a. General Autos. Pharmaceutical purchases are less discretionary than automobile purchases.

b. Friendly Airlines. Travel expenditures are more sensitive to the business cycle than movie consumption.

21.

a. Oil well equipment	Decline (environmental pressures, decline in easily-developed oil fields)
b. Computer hardware	Consolidation stage
c. Computer software	Consolidation stage
d. Genetic engineering	Start-up stage
e. Railroads	Relative decline

22. The index of consumer expectations is a useful leading economic indicator because, if consumers are optimistic about the future, then they are more willing to spend money, especially on consumer durables. This spending will increase aggregate demand and stimulate the economy.

23. Labor cost per unit of output is a lagging indicator because wages typically start rising well into an economic expansion. At the beginning of an expansion, there is considerable slack in the economy and output can expand without employers bidding up the price of inputs or the wages of employees. By the time wages start increasing due to high demand for labor, the boom period has already progressed considerably.

24.

a. Because of the very short average maturity (30 days), the rate of return on the money market fund will be affected only slightly by changes in interest rates. The fund might be a good place to "park" cash if you forecast an increase in interest rates, especially given the high liquidity of money market funds. The $5,000 can be reinvested in longer-term assets after rates increase.

b. If you are relatively neutral on rates, the one-year CD might be a reasonable "middle-ground" choice. The CD provides a higher return than the money market fund, unless rates rise considerably. On the other hand, the CD has far less interest rate risk (that is, a much lower duration) than the 20-year bond, and therefore less exposure to interest rate increases.

c. The long-term bond is the best choice for an investor who wants to speculate on a decrease in rates.

25. The expiration of the patent means that General Weedkillers will soon face considerably greater competition from its competitors. We would expect prices and profit margins to fall, and total industry sales to increase somewhat as prices decline. The industry will probably enter the consolidation stage in which producers are forced to compete more extensively on the basis of price.

26. Equity prices are positively correlated with job creation or longer work weeks, as each new dollar earned means more will be spent. High confidence presages well for spending and stock prices.

27. a. Stock prices are one of the leading indicators. One possible explanation is that stock prices anticipate future interest rates, corporate earnings and dividends. Another possible explanation is that stock prices react to changes in the other leading economic indicators, such as changes in the money supply or the spread between long-term and short-term interest rates.

28. a. Industrial production is a coincident indicator; the others are leading.

29. a. Foreign exchange rates can significantly affect the competitiveness and profitability for a given industry. For industries that derive a significant proportion of sales via exports, an appreciating currency is usually bad news because it makes the industry less competitive overseas. Here, the appreciating French currency makes French imports more expensive in England.

30. Determinants of buyer power include buyer concentration, buyer volume, buyer information, available substitutes, switching costs, brand identity, and product differences. Point 1 addresses available substitutes, Point 2 addresses buyer information, and Point 4 addresses buyer volume and buyer concentration. Point 3, which addresses the number of competitors in the industry and Point 5, new entrants, may be factual statements but do not support the conclusion that consumers have strong bargaining power.

31. a. Product differentiation can be based on the product itself, the method of delivery, or the marketing approach.

A firm with a strategic planning process not guided by their generic competitive strategy usually makes one or more of the following mistakes:

1. The strategic plan is a list of unrelated action items that does not lead to a sustainable competitive advantage.
2. Price and cost forecasts are based on current market conditions and fail to take into account how industry structure will influence future long-term industry profitability.

3. Business units are placed into categories such as build, hold, and harvest; with businesses failing to realize that these are not business strategies but rather the means to achieve the strategy.
4. The firm focuses on market share as a measure of competitive position, failing to realize that market share is the result and not the cause of a sustainable competitive position.

Smith's observations 2 and 3 describe two of these mistakes and therefore do not support the conclusion that the North Winery's strategic planning process is guided and informed by their generic competitive strategy.

32.

Sales (mil)	2	1
Price per unit	200	200
Var Cost per unit	-140	-140
Revenue	400	200
Variable cost	-280	-140
Fixed cost	-30	-30
EBT	90	30
Taxes	-27	-9
Net Income	63	21

Percentage change in sales	100%
Percentage chagne in profits	200%

DOL = 2.00

If the economy enters a recession, the firm will have $21 million after-tax profit.

CFA 1

Answer:

a. Relevant data items from the table that support the conclusion that the retail auto parts industry as a whole is in the maturity phase of the industry life cycle are:
   - The population of 18 to 29-year olds, a major customer base for the industry, is gradually declining.
   - The number of households with income less than $40,000, another important consumer base, is not expanding.
   - The number of cars 5 to 15 years old, an important end market, has experienced low annual growth (and actual declines in some years), so that the number of units potentially in need of parts is not growing.
   - Automotive aftermarket industry retail sales have been growing slowly for several years.

- Consumer expenditures on automotive parts and accessories have grown slowly for several years.
- Average operating margins of all retail auto parts companies have steadily declined.

b. Relevant items of data from the table that support the conclusion that Wigwam Autoparts Heaven, Inc. (WAH) and its major competitors are in the consolidation stage of their life cycle are:

- Sales of retail auto parts companies with 100 or more stores have been growing rapidly and at an increasing rate.
- Market share of retail auto parts stores with 100 or more stores has been increasing, but is still less than 20 percent, leaving room for much more growth.
- Average operating margins for retail auto parts companies with 100 or more stores are high and rising.

Because of industry fragmentation (i.e., most of the market share is distributed among many companies with only a few stores), the retail auto parts industry apparently is undergoing marketing innovation and consolidation. The industry is moving toward the "category killer" format, in which a few major companies control large market shares through proliferation of outlets. The evidence suggests that a new "industry within an industry" is emerging in the form of the "category killer" large chain-store company. This industry subgroup is in its consolidation stage (i.e., rapid growth with high operating profit margins and emerging market leaders) despite the fact that the industry is in the maturity stage of its life cycle.

CFA 2

Answer:

a. The concept of an industrial life cycle refers to the tendency of most industries to go through various stages of growth. The rate of growth, the competitive environment, profit margins and pricing strategies tend to shift as an industry moves from one stage to the next, although it is difficult to pinpoint exactly when one stage has ended and the next begun.

The start-up stage is characterized by perceptions of a large potential market and by high optimism for potential profits. In this stage, however, there is usually a high failure rate. In the second stage, often called rapid growth or consolidation, growth is high and accelerating, markets broaden, unit costs decline, and quality improves. In this stage, industry leaders begin to emerge. The third stage, usually called the maturity stage, is characterized by decelerating growth caused by such things as maturing markets and/or competitive inroads by other products. Finally, an industry reaches a stage of relative decline, in which sales slow or even decline.

Product pricing, profitability, and industry competitive structure often vary by phase. Thus, for example, the first phase usually encompasses high product prices, high costs (R&D, marketing, etc.) and a (temporary) monopolistic industry structure. In phase two (consolidation stage), new entrants begin to appear and costs fall rapidly due to the learning curve. Prices generally do not fall as rapidly, however, allowing profit margins to increase. In phase three (maturity stage), growth begins to slow as the product or service begins to saturate the market, and margins are eroded by significant price reductions. In the final stage, cumulative industry production is so high that production costs have stopped declining, profit margins are thin (assuming competition exists), and the fate of the industry depends on the extent of replacement demand and the existence of substitute products/services.

b. The passenger car business in the United States has probably entered the final stage in the industrial life cycle because normalized growth is quite low. The information processing business, on the other hand, is undoubtedly earlier in the cycle. Depending on whether or not growth is still accelerating, it is either in the second or third stage.

c. Cars: In the final phases of the life cycle, demand tends to be price sensitive. Thus, Universal can not raise prices without losing volume. Moreover, given the industry's maturity, cost structures are likely to be similar for all competitors, and any price cuts can be matched immediately. Thus, Universal's car business is boxed in: Product pricing is determined by the market, and the company is a "price-taker."

Idata: Idata should have much more pricing flexibility given that it is in an earlier phase of the industrial life cycle. Demand is growing faster than supply, and, depending on the presence and/or actions of an industry leader, Idata may price high in order to maximize current profits and generate cash for product development, or price low in an effort to gain market share.

CFA 3

Answer:

a. A basic premise of the business cycle approach to investing is that stock prices anticipate fluctuations in the business cycle. For example, there is evidence that stock prices tend to move about six months ahead of the economy. In fact, stock prices are a leading indicator for the economy.

Over the course of a business cycle, this approach to investing would work roughly as follows. As the top of a business cycle is perceived to be approaching, stocks purchased should not be vulnerable to a recession. When a downturn is perceived to be at hand, stock holdings should be reduced, with proceeds invested in fixed-income securities. Once the recession has matured to some extent, and interest rates fall, bond prices will rise. As it is perceived that the recession is about to end, profits should be taken in the bonds and proceeds reinvested in stocks, particularly stocks with high beta that are in cyclical industries.

Abnormal returns will generally be earned only if these asset allocation switches are timed better than those of other investors. Switches made after the turning points may not lead to excess returns.

b. Based on the business cycle approach to investment timing, the ideal time to invest in a cyclical stock like a passenger car company would be just before the end of a recession. If the recovery is already underway, Adams's recommendation would be too late. The equities market generally anticipates changes in the economic cycle. Therefore, since the "recovery is underway," the price of Universal Auto should already reflect the anticipated improvements in the economy.

CFA 4

Answer:

a.

- The industry-wide ROE is leveling off, indicating that the industry may be approaching a later stage of the life cycle.
- Average P/E ratios are declining, suggesting that investors are becoming less optimistic about growth prospects.
- Dividend payout is increasing, suggesting that the firm sees less reason to reinvest earnings in the firm. There may be fewer growth opportunities in the industry.
- Industry dividend yield is also increasing, even though market dividend yield is decreasing.

b.

- Industry growth rate is still forecast at 10 – 15%, higher than would be true of a mature industry.
- Non-U.S. markets are still untapped, and some firms are now entering these markets.
- Mail order sale segment is growing at 40% a year.
- Niche markets are continuing to develop.
- New manufacturers continue to enter the market.

CFA 5

Answer:

a. (4) Government deficits are planned during the economic recessions, and surpluses are utilized to restrain inflationary booms.

b. (2) Higher marginal tax rates promote economic inefficiency and thereby retard aggregate output because they encourage investors to undertake low productivity projects with substantial tax-shelter benefits.

CHAPTER 13
EQUITY VALUATION

1. Theoretically, dividend discount models can be used to value the stock of rapidly growing companies that do not currently pay dividends; in this scenario, we would be valuing expected dividends in the relatively more distant future. However, as a practical matter, such estimates of payments to be made in the more distant future are notoriously inaccurate, rendering dividend discount models problematic for valuation of such companies; free cash flow models are more likely to be appropriate. At the other extreme, one would be more likely to choose a dividend discount model to value a mature firm paying a relatively stable dividend.

2. It is most important to use multi-stage dividend discount models when valuing companies with temporarily high growth rates. These companies tend to be companies in the early phases of their life cycles, when they have numerous opportunities for reinvestment, resulting in relatively rapid growth and relatively low dividends (or, in many cases, no dividends at all). As these firms mature, attractive investment opportunities are less numerous so that growth rates slow.

3. The intrinsic value of a share of stock is the individual investor's assessment of the true worth of the stock. The market capitalization rate is the market consensus for the required rate of return for the stock. If the intrinsic value of the stock is equal to its price, then the market capitalization rate is equal to the expected rate of return. On the other hand, if the individual investor believes the stock is underpriced (i.e., intrinsic value > price), then that investor's expected rate of return is greater than the market capitalization rate.

4. Intrinsic value $= V_0 = \dfrac{D_1}{1+k} + \dfrac{D_2}{(1+k)^2} + \ldots + \dfrac{D_H + P_H}{(1+k)^H}$

$$= \frac{\$1 \times 1.2}{1+0.085} + \frac{\$1 \times 1.2^2}{(1+0.085)^2} + \frac{\$1 \times 1.2^2 \times 1.04}{(0.085 - 0.04) \times (1+0.085)^2}$$

$$= \$30.60$$

5. Intrinsic value $= V_0 = \dfrac{D_0 \times (1+g)}{k - g}$:

$$\$32.03 = \frac{\$1.22 \times 1.05}{k - 0.05} \Rightarrow k = 0.089994 \text{ or } 8.9994\%$$

6. Intrinsic value $= V_0 = \dfrac{D_0 \times (1+g)}{k - g}$:

$$\$35 = \frac{\$1 \times 1.05}{k - 0.05} \Rightarrow k = 0.08 \text{ or } 8\%$$

7. $\text{Price} = \$41 = \frac{E_1}{k} + PVGO = \frac{\$3.64}{0.09} + PVGO \Rightarrow PVGO = \$0.56$

8. Market value of the firm

 = Market value of assets − Market value of debts

 = (\$10 million + \$90 million) − \$50 million = \$50 million

 Book value of the firm

 = Book value of assets − Book value of debts

 = (\$10 million + \$60 million) − \$40 million = \$30 million

 Market-to-book ratio = 50 / 30 = 1.6667

9. $g = ROE \times b = 0.10 \times 0.6 = 0.06$ or 6%

 $$P/E = \frac{1-b}{k-g} = \frac{1-0.6}{0.08-0.06} = 20$$

10. Market capitalization rate $= k = r_f + \beta\,[E(r_M) - r_f]$

 $= 0.04 + 0.75\,(0.12 - 0.04) = 0.10$

 $$\text{Intrinsic value} = V_0 = \frac{D_1}{k-g} = \frac{\$4}{0.10-0.04} = \$66.67$$

11. Given EPS = \$6, ROE = 15%, plowback ratio = 0.6, and k = 10%, we first calculate the price with the constant dividend growth model:

 $$P_0 = \frac{D_1}{k-g} = \frac{EPS \times (1-b)}{k - ROE \times b} = \frac{\$6 \times (1-0.6)}{0.10 - 0.15 \times 0.6} = \frac{\$2.4}{0.10-0.09} = \$240$$

 Then, knowing that the price is equal to the price with no growth plus the present value of the growth opportunity, we can solve the following equation:

 $$\text{Price} = \$240 = \frac{E_1}{k} + PVGO = \frac{\$6}{0.10} + PVGO \Rightarrow PVGO = \$240 - \$60 = \$180$$

12. $FCFF = EBIT(1 - t_c) + \text{Depreciation} - \text{Capital expenditures} - \text{Increase in NWC}$

 $= \$300 \times (1 - 0.35) + \$20 - \$60 - \$30 = \$125$

13. $FCFE_1 = FCFF - \text{Interest expenses}(1 - t_c) + \text{Increases in net debt}$

 $= \$205 - \$22 \times (1 - 0.35) + \$3 = \$193.70$ (million)

 $$\text{Market value of equity} = \frac{FCFE_1}{k-g} = \frac{\$193.7}{0.12-0.03} = \$2{,}152.22 \text{ (million)}$$

14. Cost of equity = r_f + E(Risk premium) = 7% + 4% = 11%

Because the dividends are expected to be constant every year, the price can be calculated as the no-growth-value per share:

$$P_0 = \frac{D}{k_e} = \frac{\$2.10}{0.11} = \$19.09$$

15. $k = r_f + \beta\,[E(r_M) - r_f] = 0.05 + 1.5 \times (0.10 - 0.05) = 0.125$ or 12.5%

Therefore:

$$P_0 = \frac{D_1}{k - g} = \frac{\$2.5}{0.125 - 0.04} = \$29.41$$

16.

a. False. Higher beta means that the risk of the firm is higher and the discount rate applied to value cash flows is higher. For any expected path of earnings and cash flows, the present value of the cash flows, and therefore, the price of the firm will be lower when risk is higher. Thus the ratio of price to earnings will be lower.

b. True. Higher ROE means more valuable growth opportunities.

c. Uncertain. The answer depends on a comparison of the expected rate of return on reinvested earnings with the market capitalization rate. If the expected rate of return on the firm's projects is higher than the market capitalization rate, then P/E will increase as the plowback ratio increases.

17.

a. Using the constant-growth DDM, $P_0 = \frac{D_1}{k - g}$:

$$\$50 = \frac{\$2}{0.16 - g} \Rightarrow g = 0.12 \text{ or } 12\%$$

b. $P_0 = \frac{D_1}{k - g} = \frac{\$2}{0.16 - 0.05} = \$18.18$

The price falls in response to the more pessimistic forecast of dividend growth. The forecast for *current* earnings, however, is unchanged. Therefore, the P/E ratio decreases. The lower P/E ratio is evidence of the diminished optimism concerning the firm's growth prospects.

18. ROE = 20%, b = 0.3, EPS = $2, k = 12%

a. P/E Ratio

We can calculate the P/E ratio by dividing the current price by the projected earnings:

$$P_0 = \frac{D_1}{k - g} = \frac{EPS \times (1 - b)}{k - (ROE \times b)} = \frac{\$2 \times (1 - 0.3)}{0.12 - 0.20 \times 0.3} = \frac{\$1.4}{0.12 - 0.06} = \$23.33$$

P/E = $23.33/$2 = 11.67

Or we can use Equation 13.8 in the chapter:

$$\frac{P_0}{E_1} = \frac{1 - b}{k - (ROE \times b)} = \frac{1 - 0.3}{0.12 - 0.20 \times 0.3} = 11.67$$

b. Present Value of Growth Opportunities (PVGO)

$g = ROE \times b = 0.20 \times 0.3 = 0.6$

$$PVGO = P_0 - \frac{E_1}{k} = \frac{D_1}{k - g} - \frac{E_1}{k} = \frac{\$1.4}{0.12 - 0.06} - \frac{\$2}{0.12} = \$6.67$$

c. Impacts of Reducing Plowback Ratio

$g = ROE \times b = 0.20 \times 0.2 = 0.04 = 4\%$

$D_1 = EPS \times (1 - b) = \$2 \times (1 - 0.2) = \$1.6$

$$P_0 = \frac{D_1}{k - g} = \frac{\$1.6}{0.12 - 0.04} = \$20$$

P/E = $20/$2 = 10.0

$$PVGO = P_0 - \frac{E_1}{k} = \$20.00 - \frac{\$2}{0.12} = \$3.33$$

19. ROE = 16%, b = 0.5, EPS = $2, k = 12%

a. $P_0 = \frac{D_1}{k - g} = \frac{EPS \times (1 - b)}{k - (ROE \times b)} = \frac{\$2 \times (1 - 0.5)}{0.12 - 0.16 \times 0.5} = \frac{\$1}{0.12 - 0.08} = \$25$

b. $P_3 = \frac{EPS \times (1 - b) \times (1 + g)^3}{k - g} = P_0 \times (1 + g)^3 = \$25 \times (1.08)^3 = \$31.49$

20.

a. $k = r_f + \beta\,[E(r_M) - r_f] = 0.06 + 1.25 \times (0.14 - 0.06) = 0.16$ or 16%

$g = ROE \times b = 0.09 \times (2/3) = 0.06$ or 6%

$D_1 = E_0 \times (1 + g) \times (1 - b) = \$3 \times 1.06 \times (1/3) = \$1.06$

$$P_0 = \frac{D_1}{k - g} = \frac{\$1.06}{0.16 - 0.06} = \$10.60$$

b. Leading P_0/E_1 = \$10.60/\$3.18 = 3.33

Trailing P_0/E_0 = \$10.60/\$3.00 = 3.53

c. $PVGO = P_0 - \frac{E_1}{k} = \$10.60 - \frac{\$3.18}{0.16} = -\$9.28$

The low P/E ratios and negative PVGO are due to a poor ROE (9%) that is less than the market capitalization rate (16%).

d. Now, you revise the plowback ratio in the calculation so that b = 1/3:

$g = ROE \times b = 0.09 \times 1/3 = 0.03$ or 3%

$D_1 = E_0 \times (1 + g) \times (1 - b) = 3 \times 1.03 \times (2/3) = \$2.06$

Intrinsic value = $V_0 = \frac{D_1}{k - g} = \frac{\$2.06}{0.16 - 0.03} = \$15.85$

V_0 increases because the firm pays out more earnings instead of reinvesting earnings at a poor ROE. This information is not yet known to the rest of the market.

21. FI Corporation

a. $P_0 = \frac{D_1}{k - g} = \frac{\$8}{0.10 - 0.05} = \$160.00$

b. The dividend payout ratio is 8/12 = 2/3, so the plowback ratio is b = (1/3). The implied value of ROE on future investments is found by solving as follows:

$g = b \times ROE$

$0.05 = (1/3) \times ROE \Rightarrow ROE = 15\%$

c. $PVGO = P_0 - \frac{E_1}{k} = \$160.00 - \frac{\$12}{0.10} = \$40.00$

22. Nogro Corporation

a. $D_1 = E_1 \times (1 - b) = \$2 \times 0.5 = \$1$

$g = b \times ROE = 0.5 \times 0.20 = 0.10$ or 10%

Therefore:

$k = \frac{D_1}{P_0} + g = \frac{\$1}{\$10} + 0.10 = 0.20$ or 20%

b. Since k = ROE, the NPV of future investment opportunities is zero:

$PVGO = P_0 - \frac{E_1}{k} = \$10 - \frac{\$2}{0.20} = \$0$

c. Since k = ROE, the stock price would be unaffected if Nogro were to cut its dividend payout ratio to 25%. The additional earnings that would be reinvested would earn the ROE (20%).

Again, if Nogro eliminated the dividend, this would have no impact on Nogro's stock price since the NPV of the additional investments would be zero.

23. Xyrong Corporation

a. $k = r_f + \beta\,[E(r_M) - r_f] = 0.08 + 1.2 \times (0.15 - 0.08) = 0.164$ or 16.4%

$g = b \times ROE = 0.6 \times 0.20 = 0.12$ r 12%

$$V_0 = \frac{D_0 \times (1+g)}{k - g} = \frac{\$4 \times (1 + 0.12\%)}{0.164 - 0.12} = \$101.82$$

b. $P_1 = V_1 = V_0 \times (1 + g) = \$101.82 \times (1 + 0.12) = \$114.04$

$$E(r) = \frac{D_1 + P_1 - P_0}{P_0} = \frac{\$4.48 + \$114.04 - \$100}{\$100} = 0.1852 = 18.52\%$$

24.

Before-tax cash flow from operations	\$2,100,000
Depreciation	210,000
Taxable income	1,890,000
Taxes (@ 35%)	661,500
After-tax unleveraged income	1,228,500
After-tax cash flow from operations	
(After-tax unleveraged income + depreciation)	1,438,500
New investment (20% of cash flow from operations)	420,000
Free cash flow	
(After-tax cash flow from operations − new investment)	\$1,018,500

The value of the firm (i.e., debt plus equity) is:

$$V_0 = \frac{FCFF_1}{k - g} = \frac{\$1{,}018{,}500}{0.12 - 0.05} = \$14{,}550{,}000$$

Since the value of the debt is \$4 million, the value of the equity is \$10,550,000.

25. Use this spreadsheet for all answers

Inputs		Year	Dividend	Div growth	Term value	Investor CF
beta	1.05	2009	0.90			0.90
mkt_prem	0.085	2010	0.98			0.98
rf	0.035	2011	1.07			1.07
k_equity	0.12425	2012	1.15			1.15
plowback	0.7	2013	1.25	0.0851		1.25
ROE	0.11	2014	1.35	0.0843		1.35
term_gwth	0.077	2015	1.47	0.0835		1.47
		2016	1.59	0.0827		1.59
		2017	1.72	0.0819		1.72
		2018	1.86	0.0811		1.86
		2019	2.01	0.0803		2.01
		2020	2.16	0.0794		2.16
		2021	2.34	0.0786		2.34
		2022	2.52	0.0778		2.52
		2023	2.71	0.0770		2.71
		2024	2.92	0.0770	66.54	69.46
					Price =	$20.07

a. Price = $20.62

b. Price = $18.95

c. Price = $20.07

26. The solutions derived from Spreadsheet 13.2 are as follows:

a.

Intrinsic val	Equity val	Intrin/share
91,375	63,875	35.49
66,778	66,778	37.10

b.

Intrinsic val	Equity val	Intrin/share
89,419	61,919	34.40
65,720	65,720	36.51

c.

Intrinsic val	Equity val	Intrin/share
85,872	58,372	32.43
62,905	62,905	34.95

27.

a. $g = ROE \times b = 0.20 \times 0.5 = 0.10$ or 10%

$$P_0 = \frac{D_0 \times (1+g)}{k - g} = \frac{\$0.5 \times (1+0.10)}{0.15 - 0.10} = \$11$$

b.

Time	EPS	Dividend	BVPS	Comment
0	\$1.0000	\$0.5000	\$5.5000	Book Value Per Share is \$5.5.
1	\$1.1000	\$0.5500	\$6.0500	g = 10%, plowback = 0.50
2	\$1.2100	\$0.7260	\$6.5340	EPS has grown by 10% based on last year's earnings plowback and ROE; this year's earnings plowback ratio now falls to 0.40 and payout ratio = 0.60
3	\$0.9801	\$0.5881	\$6.9260	ROE has decrease to 15%, along with the payout ratio of 0.6 gives the new growth rate of 15% × (1 − 0.6) = 6% from next year.

c. $P_0 = \$11$ and $P_1 = P_0 \times (1 + g) = \$12.10$

(Because the market is unaware of the changed competitive situation, it believes the stock price should grow at 10% per year.)

$P_2 = \dfrac{D_3}{k - g} = \dfrac{\$0.5881}{0.15 - 0.06} = \$6.5340$ *after* the market becomes aware of the changed competitive situation. Notice that after the market aware of the ROE decreases to the required rate of return and there is no future growth opportunities, the price becomes its no-growth value per share: $P_2 = \dfrac{E_3}{k}$; $P_3 = \dfrac{E_4}{k}$

$P_3 = P_2 \times (1 + g) = \$6.5340 \times 1.06$

$$= \frac{E_3 \times (1+g)}{k} = \frac{\$0.9801 \times (1+0.06)}{0.15 - 0.06} = \$6.9260$$ (The new growth rate is 6%.)

Year	Return
1	$\dfrac{(\$12.10 - \$11) + \$0.55}{\$11} = 0.150 = 15.0\%$
2	$\dfrac{(\$6.534 - \$12.10) + \$0.726}{\$12.10} = -0.4 = -40.0\%$
3	$\dfrac{(\$6.9260 - \$6.534) + \$0.5881}{\$6.534} = 0.150 = 15.0\%$

Moral: In "normal periods" when there is no special information, the stock return = k = 15%. When special information arrives, all the abnormal returns accrue *in that period*, as one would expect in an efficient market.

CFA 1

Answer:

a. This director is confused. In the context of the constant growth model, it is true that price is higher when dividends are higher *holding everything else (including dividend growth) constant*. But everything else will not be constant. If the firm raises the dividend payout rate, then the growth rate (*g*) will fall, and stock price will not necessarily rise. In fact, if ROE > *k*, price will fall.

b. i. An increase in dividend payout reduces the sustainable growth rate as fewer funds are reinvested in the firm.

ii. The sustainable growth rate is (ROE × plowback), which falls as the plowback ratio falls. The increased dividend payout rate reduces the growth rate of book value for the same reason—fewer funds are reinvested in the firm.

CFA 2

Answer:

a. It is true that NewSoft sells at higher multiples of earnings and book value than Capital. But this difference may be justified by NewSoft's higher expected growth rate of earnings and dividends. NewSoft is in a growing market with abundant profit and growth opportunities. Capital is in a mature industry with fewer growth prospects. Both the price-earnings and price-book ratios reflect the prospect of growth opportunities, indicating that the ratios for these firms do not necessarily imply mispricing.

b. The most important weakness of the constant-growth dividend discount model in this application is that it assumes a perpetual constant growth rate of dividends. While dividends may be on a steady growth path for Capital, which is a more mature firm, that is far less likely to be a realistic assumption for NewSoft.

c. NewSoft should be valued using a multi-stage DDM, which allows for rapid growth in the early years, but also recognizes that growth must ultimately slow to a more sustainable rate.

CFA 3

Answer:

a. The industry's estimated P/E can be computed using the following model:

P_0/E_1 = payout ratio/(r – g)

However, since r and g are not explicitly given, they must be computed using the following formulas:

g_{ind} = ROE × retention rate = 0.25 × 0.40 = 0.10

r_{ind} = government bond yield + (industry beta × equity risk premium)
= 0.06 + (1.2 × 0.05) = 0.12

Therefore:

$P_0/E_1 = 0.60/(0.12 - 0.10) = 30.0$

b. i. Forecast growth in real GDP would cause P/E ratios to be generally higher for Country A. Higher expected growth in GDP implies higher earnings growth and a higher P/E.

ii. Government bond yield would cause P/E ratios to be generally higher for Country B. A lower government bond yield implies a lower risk-free rate and therefore a higher P/E.

iii. Equity risk premium would cause P/E ratios to be generally higher for Country B. A lower equity risk premium implies a lower required return and a higher P/E.

CFA 4

Answer:

a. $k = r_f + \beta\,[E(r_M) - r_f] = 0.045 + 1.15 \times (0.145 - 0.045) = 0.16$ or 16%

b.

Year	Dividends	
2010	\$1.72	
2011	$\$1.72 \times 1.12$	= \$1.93
2012	$\$1.72 \times 1.12^2$	= \$2.16
2013	$\$1.72 \times 1.12^3$	= \$2.42
2014	$\$1.72 \times 1.12^3 \times 1.09$	= \$2.63

Present value of dividends paid in years 2011 to 2013:

Year	PV of Dividends
2011	$\$1.93/1.16 = \$1.66$
2012	$\$2.16/1.16^2 = \$1.61$
2013	$\$2.42/1.16^3 = \underline{\$1.55}$
Total:	\$4.82

$$P_{2013} = \frac{D_{2014}}{k - g} = \frac{\$2.63}{0.16 - 0.09} = \$37.57$$

PV (in 2010) of $P_{2013} = \$37.57/(1.16^3) = \$24.07$

Intrinsic value of stock = \$4.82 + \$24.07 = \$28.89

c. The table presented in the problem indicates that QuickBrush is selling below intrinsic value, while we have just shown that SmileWhite is selling somewhat above the estimated intrinsic value. Based on this analysis, QuickBrush offers the potential for considerable abnormal returns, while SmileWhite offers slightly below-market risk-adjusted returns.

d. Strengths of two-stage DDM compared to constant growth DDM:

- The two-stage model allows for separate valuation of two distinct periods in a company's future. This approach can accommodate life cycle effects. It also can avoid the difficulties posed when the initial growth rate is higher than the discount rate.

- The two-stage model allows for an initial period of above-sustainable growth. It allows the analyst to make use of her expectations as to when growth may shift to a more sustainable level.

- A weakness of all DDMs is that they are all very sensitive to input values. Small changes in *k* or *g* can imply large changes in estimated intrinsic value. These inputs are difficult to measure.

CFA 5

Answer:

a. The value of a share of Rio National equity using the Gordon growth model and the capital asset pricing model is $22.40, as shown below.

Calculate the required rate of return using the capital asset pricing model:

$$k = r_f + \beta\,[E(r_M) - r_f] = 0.04 + 1.8 \times (0.09 - 0.04) = 0.13 \text{ or } 13\%$$

Calculate the share value using the Gordon growth model:

$$P_0 = \frac{D_0 \times (1+g)}{k-g} = \frac{\$0.20 \times (1+0.12)}{0.13 - 0.12} = \$22.40$$

b. The sustainable growth rate of Rio National is 9.97%, calculated as follows:

$$g = \text{ROE} \times b = \text{ROE} \times \text{Retention Rate} = \text{ROE} \times (1 - \text{Payout Ratio})$$

$$= \left(1 - \frac{\text{Dividends}}{\text{Net Income}}\right) \times \frac{\text{Net Income}}{\text{Beginning Equity}}$$

$$= \left(1 - \frac{\$3.20}{\$30.16}\right) \times \frac{\$30.16}{\$270.35} = 0.0997 = 9.97\%$$

CFA 6

Answer:

a. To obtain free cash flow to equity (FCFE), the two adjustments that Shaar should make to cash flow from operations (CFO) are:

i. Subtract investment in fixed capital: CFO does not take into account the investing activities in long-term assets, particularly plant and equipment. The cash flows corresponding to those necessary expenditures are not available to equity holders and should be subtracted from CFO.

ii. Add net borrowing: CFO does not take into account the amount of capital supplied to the firm by lenders (e.g., bondholders). The new borrowings, net of debt repayment, are cash flows available to equity holders and should be added to CFO to obtain FCFE.

b. *Note 1*: Rio National had \$75 million in capital expenditures during the year.
Adjustment: Negative \$75 million
The cash flows required for those capital expenditures (−\$75 million) are no longer available to the equity holders and should be subtracted from net income to obtain FCFE.

Note 2: A piece of equipment that was originally purchased for \$10 million was sold for \$7 million at year-end, when it had a net book value of \$3 million. Equipment sales are unusual for Rio National.
Adjustment: Positive \$3 million
In calculating FCFE, only cash flow investments in fixed capital should be considered. The \$7 million sale price of equipment is a cash inflow now available to equity holders and should be added to net income. However, the gain over book value that was realized when selling the equipment (\$4 million) is already included in net income. Because the total sale is cash, not just the gain, the \$3 million net book value must be added to net income. Therefore, the adjustment calculation is:

\$7 million in cash received − \$4 million of gain recorded in net income = \$3 million additional cash received that must be added to net income to obtain FCFE.

Note 3: The decrease in long-term debt represents an unscheduled principal repayment; there was no new borrowing during the year.
Adjustment: Negative \$5 million
The unscheduled debt repayment cash flow (−\$5 million) is an amount no longer available to equity holders and should be subtracted from net income to determine FCFE.

Note 4: On 1 January 2012, the company received cash from issuing 400,000 shares of common equity at a price of \$25.00 per share.
No adjustment
Transactions between the firm and its shareholders do not affect FCFE. To calculate FCFE, therefore, no adjustment to net income is required with respect to the issuance of new shares.

Note 5: A new appraisal during the year increased the estimated market value of land held for investment by \$2 million, which was not recognized in 2012 income.
No adjustment
The increased market value of the land did not generate any cash flow and was not reflected in net income. To calculate FCFE, therefore, no adjustment to net income is required.

c. Free cash flow to equity (FCFE) is calculated as follows:

FCFE = NI + NCC − FCINV − WCINV + Net borrowing
where NCC = non-cash charges
FCINV = investment in fixed capital
WCINV = investment in working capital

	Million $	Explanation
NI =	$30.16	From Table 13.6
NCC =	+$67.17	$71.17 (depreciation and amortization from Table 13.6) −$4.00* (gain on sale from Note 2)
FCINV =	−$68.00	$75.00 (capital expenditures from Note 1) −$7.00* (cash on sale from Note 2)
WCINV =	−$24.00	−$3.00 (increase in accounts receivable from Table 13.5) + −$20.00 (increase in inventory from Table 13.5) + −$1.00 (decrease in accounts payable from Table 13.5)
Net Borrowing =	+(−$5.00)	−$5.00 (decrease in long-term debt from Table 13.5)
FCFE =	$0.33	

*Supplemental Note 2 in Table 13.7 affects both NCC and FCINV.

CFA 7

Answer:
Rio National's equity is relatively undervalued compared to the industry on a P/E-to-growth (PEG) basis. Rio National's PEG ratio of 1.33 is below the industry PEG ratio of 1.66. The lower PEG ratio is attractive because it implies that the growth rate at Rio National is available at a relatively lower price than is the case for the industry. The PEG ratios for Rio National and the industry are calculated below:

<u>Rio National</u>

Current price = $25.00

Normalized earnings per share = $1.71

Price-to-earnings ratio = $25/$1.71 = 14.62

Growth rate (as a percentage) = 11

PEG ratio = 14.62/11 = 1.33

<u>Industry</u>

Price-to-earnings ratio = 19.90

Growth rate (as a percentage) = 12

PEG ratio = 19.90/12 = 1.66

CFA 8

Answer:

Using a two-stage dividend discount model, the current value of a share of Sundanci is calculated as follows:

$$V_0 = \frac{D_1}{(1+k)^1} + \frac{D_2}{(1+k)^2} + \frac{\frac{D_3}{(k-g)}}{(1+k)^2}$$

$$= \frac{\$0.3770}{1.14^1} + \frac{\$0.4976}{1.14^2} + \frac{\frac{\$0.5623}{(0.14-0.13)}}{1.14^2} = \$43.98$$

where:

$E_0 = \$0.952$

$D_0 = \$0.286$

$E_1 = E_0 \times (1.32)^1 = \$0.952 \times 1.32 = \$1.2566$

$D_1 = E_1 \times 0.30 = \$1.2566 \times 0.30 = \$0.3770$

$E_2 = E_0 \times (1.32)^2 = \$0.952 \times (1.32)^2 = \$1.6588$

$D_2 = E_2 \times 0.30 = \$1.6588 \times 0.30 = \$0.4976$

$E_3 = E_0 \times (1.32)^2 \times 1.13 = \$0.952 \times (1.32)^3 \times 1.13 = \$1.8744$

$D_3 = E_3 \times 0.30 = \$1.8744 \times 0.30 = \$0.5623$

CFA 9

Answer:

a. Free cash flow to equity (FCFE) is defined as the cash flow remaining after meeting all financial obligations (including debt payment) and after covering capital expenditure and working capital needs. The FCFE is a measure of how much the firm can afford to pay out as dividends, but in a given year may be more or less than the amount actually paid out.

Sundanci's FCFE for the year 2013 is computed as follows:

FCFE =

Earnings after tax + Depreciation expense – Capital expenditures – Increase in NWC

= \$80 million + \$23 million – \$38 million – \$41 million = \$24 million

FCFE per share = FCFE/Number of shares outstanding

= \$24 million/84 million shares = \$0.286

At the given dividend payout ratio, Sundanci's FCFE per share equals dividends per share.

b. The FCFE model requires forecasts of FCFE for the high growth years (2014 and 2015) plus a forecast for the first year of stable growth (2016) in order to allow for an estimate of the terminal value in 2015 based on perpetual growth. Because all of the components of FCFE are expected to grow at the same rate, the values can be obtained by projecting the FCFE at the common rate. (Alternatively, the components of FCFE can be projected and aggregated for each year.)

The following table shows the process for estimating Sundanci's current value on a per share basis:

Free Cash Flow to Equity					
Base Assumptions					
Shares outstanding: 84 millions					
Required return on equity (r): 14%					
	Actual 2013		Projected 2014	Projected 2015	Projected 2016
Growth rate (g)			27%	27%	13%
	Total	Per share			
Earnings after tax	$80	$0.952	$1.2090	$1.5355	$1.7351
Plus: Depreciation expense	$23	$0.274	$0.3480	$0.4419	$0.4994
Less: Capital expenditures	$38	$0.452	$0.5740	$0.7290	$0.8238
Less: Increase in net working capital	$41	$0.488	$0.6198	$0.7871	$0.8894
Equals: FCFE	$24	$0.286	$0.3632	$0.4613	$0.5213
Terminal value				$52.1300*	
Total cash flows to equity			$0.3632	$52.5913**	
Discounted value			$0.3186***	$40.4673***	
Current value per share				$40.7859****	

* Projected 2012 Terminal value = (Projected 2013 FCFE)/(r – g)

** Projected 2012 Total cash flows to equity

= Projected 2012 FCFE + Projected 2012 Terminal value

*** Discounted values obtained using r = 14%

**** Current value per share

= Sum of Discounted Projected 2011 and 2012 Total cash flows to equity

c. i. The following limitations of the dividend discount model (DDM) are addressed by the FCFE model. The DDM uses a strict definition of cash flows to equity, i.e. the expected dividends on the common stock. In fact, taken to its extreme, the DDM cannot be used to estimate the value of a stock that pays no dividends. The FCFE model expands the definition of cash flows to include the balance of residual cash flows after all financial obligations and investment needs have been met. Thus the FCFE model explicitly recognizes the firm's investment and financing policies as well as its dividend policy. In instances of a change of corporate control, and therefore the possibility of changing dividend policy, the FCFE model provides a better estimate of value. The DDM is biased toward finding low PIE ratio stocks with high dividend yields to be undervalued and conversely, high PIE ratio stocks with low dividend yields to be overvalued. It is considered a conservative model in that it tends to identify fewer undervalued firms as market prices rise relative to fundamentals. The DDM does not allow for the potential tax disadvantage of high dividends relative to the capital gains achievable from retention of earnings.

ii. The following limitations of the DDM are not addressed by the FCFE model. Both two-stage valuation models allow for two distinct phases of growth, an initial finite period where the growth rate is abnormal, followed by a stable growth period that is expected to last indefinitely. These two-stage models share the same limitations with respect to the growth assumptions. First, there is the difficulty of defining the duration of the extraordinary growth period. For example, a longer period of high growth will lead to a higher valuation, and there is the temptation to assume an unrealistically long period of extraordinary growth. Second, the assumption of a sudden shift form high growth to lower, stable growth is unrealistic. The transformation is more likely to occur gradually, over a period of time. Given that the assumed total horizon does not shift (i.e., is infinite), the timing of the shift form high to stable growth is a critical determinant of the valuation estimate. Third, because the value is quite sensitive to the steady-state growth assumption, over- or under-estimating this rate can lead to large errors in value. The two models share other limitations as well, notably difficulties inaccurately forecasting required rates of return, in dealing with the distortions that result from substantial and/or volatile debt ratios, and in accurately valuing assets that do not generate any cash flows.

CFA 11

Answer:

a. The formula for calculating a price earnings ratio (P/E) for a stable growth firm is the dividend payout ratio divided by the difference between the required rate of return and the growth rate of dividends. If the P/E is calculated based on trailing earnings (year 0), the payout ratio is increased by the growth rate. If the P/E is calculated based on next year's earnings (year 1), the numerator is the payout ratio.

P/E on trailing earnings:

$P/E = [\text{Payout ratio} \times (1 + g)]/(r - g) = [0.30 \times 1.13]/(0.14 - 0.13) = 33.9$

P/E on next year's earnings:

$P/E = \text{Payout ratio}/(r - g) = 0.30/(0.14 - 0.13) = 30.0$

b. The P/E ratio is a decreasing function of riskiness; as risk increases the P/E ratio decreases. Increases in the riskiness of Sundanci stock would be expected to lower the P/E ratio.

The P/E ratio is an increasing function of the growth rate of the firm; the higher the expected growth the higher the P/E ratio. Sundanci would command a higher P/E if analysts increase the expected growth rate.

The P/E ratio is a decreasing function of the market risk premium. An increased market risk premium would increase the required rate of return, lowering the price of a stock relative to its earnings. A higher market risk premium would be expected to lower Sundanci's P/E ratio.

CHAPTER 14
FINANCIAL STATEMENT ANALYSIS

1.

a. Inventory turnover ratio in 2012

$$= \frac{\text{Cost of Goods Sold}}{\text{Average Inventories}} = \frac{\$2,850}{(\$490 + \$480)/2} = 5.876$$

b. Debt to equity ratio in 2012

$$= \frac{\text{Debt}}{\text{Equity}} = \frac{\$3,340}{\$960} = 3.479$$

c. Cash flow from operating activities in 2012

Net income	$ 410,000
Adjustments to Net Income	
+ Depreciation	280,000
Change in AR	30,000
Change in inventory	(10,000)
Change in AP	(110,000)
CF from Operations	$ 600,000

d. Average collection period

$$= \frac{\text{Average Accounts Receivables}}{\text{Annual Sales}} \times 365 = \frac{(\$660 + \$690)/2}{\$5,500} \times 365 = 44.795$$

e. Asset turnover ratio

$$= \frac{\text{Sales}}{\text{Average Total Assets}} = \frac{\$5,500}{(\$4,300 + \$4,010)/2} = 1.324$$

f. Interest coverage ratio

$$= \frac{\text{EBIT}}{\text{Interest Expense}} = \frac{\$870}{\$130} = 6.692$$

g. Operating profit margin

$$= \frac{\text{EBIT}}{\text{Sales}} = \frac{\$870}{\$5,500} = .158 = 15.8\%$$

h. Return on equity

$$= \frac{\text{Net Income}}{\text{Average Shareholder's Equity}} = \frac{\$410}{(\$960 + \$810)/2} = .463 = 46.3\%$$

i. P/E ratio
Unable to calculate as market price is not provided.

j. Compound leverage ratio

$$= \frac{\text{Pretax Profit}}{\text{EBIT}} \times \frac{\text{Average Assets}}{\text{Average Equity}} = \frac{\$740}{\$870} \times \frac{(\$4{,}300 + \$4{,}010)/2}{(\$960 + \$810)/2} = 3.993$$

k. Net cash provided by operating activities. See answer to part c.

2.

a.

Purchase of Bus	$	(33,000)
Sale of old equipment		72,000
Cash from Investments	$	39,000

b.

Cash dividend	$	(80,000)
Repurchase of stock		(55,000)
Cash from financing	$	(135,000)

c.

Cash dividend	$	(80,000)
Purchase of bus		(33,000)
Interest paid on debt		(25,000)
Sales of old equipment		72,000
Repurchase of stock		(55,000)
Cash payments to suppliers		(95,000)
Cash collections from customers		300,000
Total cash flow	$	84,000

3. ROA = (EBIT/Sales) × (Sales/Average Total Assets) = Return on Sales × ATO

The only way that Crusty Pie can have a return on sales higher than the industry average and an ROA equal to the industry average is for its ATO to be lower than the industry average.

4. ABC's asset turnover must be above the industry average.

5. This transaction would increase the current ratio. The transaction reduces both current assets and current liabilities by the same amount, but the reduction has a larger proportionate impact on current liabilities than on current assets. Therefore, the current ratio would increase.

   This transaction would increase the asset turnover ratio. Sales should remain unaffected, but assets are reduced.

6. c. Inventory increases due to a new (internally developed) product line.

7. c. Interest paid to bondholders.

8.
   a. Lower bad debt expense will result in higher operating income.

   b. Lower bad debt expense will have no effect on operating cash flow until Galaxy actually collects receivables.

9. a. Certain GAAP rules can be exploited by companies in order to achieve specific goals, while still remaining within the letter of the law. Aggressive assumptions, such as lengthening the depreciable life of an asset (which are utilized to boost earnings), result in a lower quality of earnings.

10. a. Off balance-sheet financing through the use of operating leases is acceptable when used appropriately. However, companies can use them too aggressively in order to reduce their perceived leverage. A comparison among industry peers and their practices may indicate improper use of accounting methods.

11. a. A warning sign of accounting manipulation is abnormal inventory growth as compared to sales growth. By overstating inventory, the cost of goods sold is lower, leading to higher profitability.

12. ROE = Net Profit Margin × Total Asset Turnover × Leverage Ratio

$$= \frac{\text{Net Profit}}{\text{Sales}} \times \frac{\text{Sales}}{\text{Average Assets}} \times \frac{\text{Average Assets}}{\text{Average Equity}} = .055 \times 2.0 \times 2.2 = .242 = 24.2\%$$

13. Use Equation 14.1 to solve for operating ROA:

$$\text{ROE} = (1 - \text{Tax rate})\left[\text{ROA} + (\text{ROA} - \text{Interest rate})\frac{\text{Debt}}{\text{Equity}}\right]$$

$$.03 = (1 - .35) \times [\text{ROA} + (\text{ROA} - .06) \times .5] \Rightarrow \text{ROA} = .05 = 5\%$$

14. ROE = Tax Burden × Interest Burden × Margin × Turnover × Leverage

$$= .75 \times .6 \times .1 \times 2.4 \times 1.25 = .135 = 13.5\%$$

15.

Value of Common Stock	20,000 × \$20 =	\$ 400,000
Retained Earnings		5,000,000
Addition to Retained Earnings		70,000
Book Value		\$5,470,000

Book value per share = \$5,470,000/20,000 = \$273.50

16.

a. Economic Value Added = (ROC − Cost of Capital) × Total Assets
Acme: (.17 − .09) × (\$100 + \$50) = \$12 million
Apex: (.15 − .10) × (\$450 + \$150) = \$30 million

Apex has higher economic value added.

b. Economic value added per dollar of invested capital:
Acme: (.17 − .09) × \$1 = \$ .08
Apex: (.15 − .10) × \$1 = \$ .05

Acme has higher economic value added per dollar of invested capital.

CFA 1

Answer:
Since ROE is a function of net profit and equity, it is possible to maintain a stable ROE while net profits decline, so long as equity also declines proportionally.

CFA 2

Answer:
c. Old plant and equipment is likely to have a low net book value, making the ratio of "net sales to average net fixed assets" higher.

CFA 3

Answer:
SmileWhite has the higher quality of earnings for several reasons:

i. SmileWhite amortizes its goodwill over a shorter period than does QuickBrush. SmileWhite therefore presents more conservative earnings because it has greater goodwill amortization expense.

ii. SmileWhite depreciates its property, plant and equipment using an accelerated method. This results in earlier recognition of depreciation expense, so that income is more conservatively stated.

iii. SmileWhite's bad debt allowance, as a percent of receivables, is greater. SmileWhite therefore recognizes higher bad-debt expense than does QuickBrush. If the actual collection experience for the two firms is comparable, then SmileWhite has the more conservative recognition policy.

CFA 4

Answer:

a. $\text{Quick Ratio} = \dfrac{\text{Cash + receivables}}{\text{Current liabilities}} = \dfrac{\$325 + \$3{,}599}{\$3{,}945} = .99$

b. $\text{ROA} = \dfrac{\text{EBIT}}{\text{Assets}} = \dfrac{\text{Net income before tax + interest expense}}{\text{Average assets}}$

$= \dfrac{\$2{,}259 + \$78}{(\$8{,}058 + \$4{,}792)/2} = .364 = 36.4\%$

c. Preferred Dividends = $0.1 \times \$25 \times 18{,}000 = \$45{,}000$

Common Equity in 2013 = $829 + $575 + $1,949 = $3,353 thousand

Common Equity in 2012 = $550 + $450 + $1,368 = $2,368 thousand

$\text{ROE} = \dfrac{\text{Net income} - \text{Preferred dividends}}{\text{Average common equity}} = \dfrac{\$1{,}265 - \$45}{(\$3{,}353 + \$2{,}368)/2} = .426 = 42.6\%$

d. $\text{Earnings Per Share} = \dfrac{\$1{,}265 - \$45}{(829 + 550)/2} = \$1.77$

e. $\text{Profit Margin} = \dfrac{\text{EBIT}}{\text{Sales}} = \dfrac{\$2{,}259 + \$78}{\$12{,}065} = .194 = 19.4\%$

f. $\text{Times Interest Earned} = \dfrac{\text{EBIT}}{\text{Interest expense}} = \dfrac{\$2{,}259 + \$78}{\$78} = 30.0$

g. $\text{Inventory Turnover} = \dfrac{\text{Cost of goods sold}}{\text{Average inventory}} = \dfrac{\$8{,}048}{(\$1{,}415 + \$2{,}423)/2} = 4.2$

h. $\text{Leverage ratio} = \dfrac{\text{Average Assets}}{\text{Average Equity}} = \dfrac{(\$4{,}792 + \$8{,}058)/2}{(\$2{,}868 + \$3{,}803)/2} = 1.9$

CFA 5

Answer:

a. QuickBrush has had higher sales and earnings growth (per share) than SmileWhite. Margins are also higher. But this does not necessarily mean that QuickBrush is a better investment. SmileWhite has a higher ROE, which has been stable, while QuickBrush's ROE has been declining. We can use DuPont analysis to identify the source of the difference in ROE:

Component	Definition	QuickBrush	SmileWhite
Tax burden	Net profit/Pretax profit	67.44%	65.99%
Interest burden	Pretax profit/EBIT	1.00	0.9545
Profit margin	EBIT/Sales	8.51%	6.46%
Asset turnover	Sales/Average Assets	1.8259	3.6286
Leverage	Average Assets/Average Equity	1.5071	1.5386
ROE	Net profit/Average Equity	15.8%	22.7%

While tax burden, interest burden, and leverage are similar, profit margin and asset turnover differ. Although SmileWhite has a lower profit margin, it has far higher asset turnover.

Sustainable Growth = ROE × Plowback Ratio

	ROE	Plowback ratio	Sustainable growth rate	Ludlow's estimate
QuickBrush	15.8%	1.00	15.8%	30.0%
SmileWhite	22.7%	.344	7.8%	10.0%

Ludlow has overestimated the sustainable growth rate for each company. QuickBrush has little ability to increase its sustainable growth because plowback already equals 100%. SmileWhite could increase its sustainable growth by increasing its plowback ratio.

b. QuickBrush's recent EPS growth has been achieved by increasing book value per share, not by achieving greater profits per dollar of equity. Since EPS is equal to (Book value per share × ROE), a firm can increase EPS even if ROE is declining; this is the case for QuickBrush. QuickBrush's book value per share has more than doubled in the last two years.

Book value per share can increase either by retaining earnings or by issuing new stock at a market price greater than book value. QuickBrush has been retaining all earnings, but the increase in the number of outstanding shares indicates that it has also issued a substantial amount of stock.

CFA 6

Answer:

a. $$\text{ROE} = \frac{\text{Net profit}}{\text{Equity}} = \frac{\text{Net profit}}{\text{Pretax profit}} \times \frac{\text{Pretax profit}}{\text{EBIT}} \times \frac{\text{EBIT}}{\text{Sales}} \times \frac{\text{Sales}}{\text{Assets}} \times \frac{\text{Assets}}{\text{Equity}}$$

$$= \text{Tax burden} \times \text{Interest burden} \times \text{Profit margin} \times \text{Asset turnover} \times \text{Leverage}$$

$$\text{Tax burden} = \frac{\textit{Net profit}}{\text{Pretax Profit}} = \frac{\$510}{\$805} = .6335$$

$$\text{Interest burden} = \frac{\text{Pretax } \textit{profit}}{\text{EBIT}} = \frac{\$805}{\$830} = .9699$$

$$\text{Profit margin} = \frac{\text{EBIT}}{\text{Sales}} = \frac{\$830}{\$5,140} = .1615$$

$$\text{Asset turnover} = \frac{\text{Sales}}{\text{Average Total Assets}} = \frac{\$5,140}{(\$3,100 + \$2,950)/2} = 1.6992$$

$$\text{Leverage} = \frac{\text{Average Total Assets}}{\text{Average Total Equity}} = \frac{(\$3,100 + \$2,950)/2}{(\$2,200 + \$2,100)/2} = 1.4070$$

b. ROE = .6335 × .9699 × .1615 × 1.6992 × 1.4070 = .2372 = 23.72%

c. $g = \text{ROE} \times \text{plowback} = .2372 \times \frac{\$1.96 - \$.60}{\$1.96} = .1646 = 16.46\%$

CFA 8

Answer:

	2010	2013
$\text{Operating margin} = \frac{\text{Operating income} - \text{Depreciation}}{\text{Sales}}$	$\frac{\$38 - \$3}{\$542} = 6.45\%$	$\frac{\$76 - \$9}{\$979} = 6.84\%$
$\text{Asset turnover} = \frac{\text{Sales}}{\text{Total Assets}}$	$\frac{\$542}{\$245} = 2.2122$	$\frac{\$979}{\$291} = 3.3643$
$\text{Interest Burden} = \frac{\text{Pretax income}}{\text{Operating income} - \text{Depreciation}}$	$\frac{\$32}{\$38 - \$3} = 0.9143$	$\frac{\$67}{\$76 - \$9} = 1.00$
$\text{Financial Leverage} = \frac{\textit{Total Assets}}{\textit{Shareholders' Equity}}$	$\frac{\$245}{\$159} = 1.5409$	$\frac{\$291}{\$220} = 1.3227$
$\text{Income tax rate} = \frac{\text{Income taxes}}{\text{Pretax income}}$	$\frac{\$13}{\$32} = 40.63\%$	$\frac{\$37}{\$67} = 55.22\%$

* As ROE can be defined as either (Net Income/Average Equity) or (Net Income/Year-end Equity), here we use the latter definition for this problem.

a. Using the DuPont formula:

ROE (2010) = (1 − .4063) × .9143 × .0645 × 2.2122 × 1.5409 = .119 = 11.9%

ROE (2013) = (1 − .5522) × 1.0 × .0684 × 3.3643 × 1.3227 = .136 = 13.6%

i. Asset turnover measures the ability of a company to minimize the level of assets (current or fixed) to support its level of sales. The asset turnover increased substantially over the period, thus contributing to an increase in the ROE.

ii. Financial leverage measures the amount of financing, not including equity, but including short and long-term debt, that the firm uses. Financial leverage declined over the period, thus adversely affecting the ROE. Since asset turnover increased substantially more than financial leverage declined, the net effect was an increase in ROE.

CHAPTER 15
OPTIONS MARKETS

1. Options provide numerous opportunities to modify the risk profile of a portfolio. The simplest example of an option strategy that increases risk is investing in an 'all options' portfolio of at-the-money options (as illustrated in the text). The leverage provided by options makes this strategy very risky and potentially very profitable. An example of a risk-reducing options strategy is a protective put strategy. Here, the investor buys a put on an existing stock or portfolio, with exercise price of the put near or somewhat less than the market value of the underlying asset. This strategy protects the value of the portfolio because the minimum value of the stock-plus-put strategy is the exercise price of the put.

2. Options at the money have the highest time premium and thus the highest potential for gain. Since the highest potential gain is at the money, the logical conclusion is that they will have the highest volume. A common phrase used by traders is "avoid the cheaps and the deeps." Cheap options are those with very little time premium. Deep options are those that are way out of or in the money. None of these provide profit opportunities.

3. Each contract is for 100 shares: $7.25 × 100 = $725

4.

	Cost	Payoff	Profit
Call option, X = 160	15.00	5.00	-10.00
Put option, X = 160	9.40	0.00	-9.40
Call option, X = 165	11.70	0.00	-11.70
Put option, X = 165	10.85	0.00	-10.85
Call option, X = 170	8.93	0.00	-8.93
Put option, X = 170	13.00	5.00	-8.00

5. If the stock price drops to zero, you will make $160 − $2.62 per stock, or $157.38. Given 100 units per contract, the total potential profit is $15,738.

6. The price has to be at least as much as the sum of the exercise price and the premium of the option to breakeven: $40 + $4.50 = $45.50

7.
   a. Maximum loss happens when the stock price is the same to the strike price upon expiration. Both the call and the put expire worthless, and the investor's outlay for the purchase of both options is lost: $4.25 + $5.00 = $9.25

   b. Loss: Final value − Original investment

   $= (S_T - X) - (C + P) = \$8 - \$9.25 = -\$1.25$

c. There are two break even prices:

i. $S_T > X$

$(S_T - X) - (C + P) = (S_T - 50) - \$9.25 = \$0 \Rightarrow S_T = \$59.25$

ii. $S_T < X$

$(X - S_T) - (C + P) = (50 - S_T) - \$9.25 = \$0 \Rightarrow S_T = \$40.75$

8. Option *c* is the only correct statement.
   a. The value of the short position in the put is −$4 if the stock price is $76.
   b. The value of the long position in the put is $4 if the stock price is $76.
   d. The value of the short position in the put is zero for stock prices equaling or exceeding $80, the exercise price.

9.
   a. i. A long straddle produces gains if prices move up or down and limited losses if prices do not move. A short straddle produces significant losses if prices move significantly up or down. A bullish spread produces limited gains if prices move up.

   b. i. Long put positions gain when stock prices fall and produce very limited losses if prices instead rise. Short calls also gain when stock prices fall but create losses if prices instead rise. The other two positions will not protect the portfolio should prices fall.

10. The initial outlay of this position is $38, the purchase price of the stock, and the payoff of such position will be between two boundaries, $35 and $40. The maximum profit will thus be: $40 − $38 = $2, and the maximum loss will be: $35 − $38 = −$3.

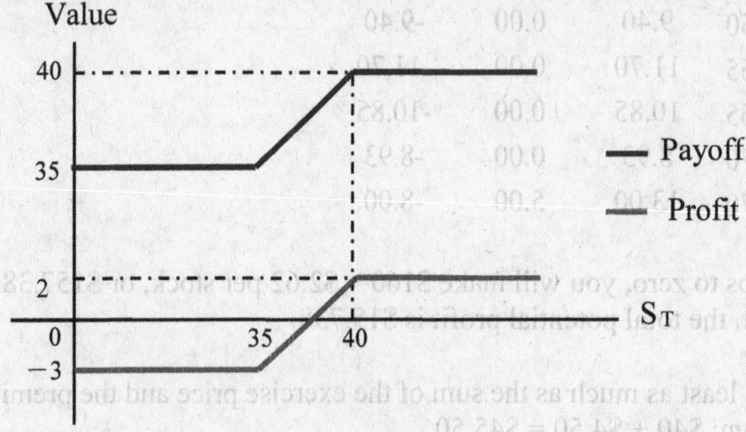

11. The collar involves purchasing a put for $3 and selling a call for $2. The initial outlay is $1.

    a. $S_T = \$30$

    Value at expiration = Value of call + Value of put + Value of stock

    = $0 + ($35 − $30) + $30 = $35

Given 5,000 shares, the total net proceeds will be:

(Final Value − Original Investment) × # of shares

= ($35 − $1) × 5,000 = $170,000

Net proceeds without using collar = S_T × # of shares

= $30 × 5,000 = $150,000

b. S_T = $40

Value at expiration = Value of call + Value of put + Value of stock

= 0 + 0 + $40 = $40

Given 5,000 shares, the total net proceeds will be:

(Final value − Original investment) × # of shares

= ($40 − $1) × 5,000 = $195,000

Net proceeds without using collar = S_T × # of shares

= $40 × 5,000 = $200,000

c. S_T = $50

Value at expiration = Value of call + Value of put + Value of stock

= ($45 − $50) + 0 + $50 =$45

Given 5,000 shares, the total net proceeds will be:

(Final value − Original investment) × # of shares

= ($45 − $1) × 5,000 = $220,000

Net proceeds without using collar = S_T × # of shares

= $50 × 5,000 = $250,000

With the initial outlay of $1, the collar locks the net proceeds per share in between the lower bound of $34 and the upper bound of $44. Given 5,000 shares, the total net proceeds will be between $170,000 and $220,000 when the position is closed. If we simply continued to hold the shares without using the collar, the upside potential is not limited but the downside is not protected.

12. In terms of dollar returns:

	Price of Stock Six Months from Now			
Stock price:	$80	$100	$110	$120
a. All stocks (100 shares)	8,000	10,000	11,000	12,000
b. All options (1,000 shares)	0	0	10,000	20,000
c. Bills + 100 options	9,360	9,360	10,360	11,360

In terms of rate of return, based on a $10,000 investment:

	Price of Stock Six Months from Now			
Stock price:	$80	$100	$110	$120
a. All stocks (100 shares)	−20%	0%	10%	20%
b. All options (1,000 shares)	−100%	−100%	0%	100%
c. Bills + 100 options	−6.4%	−6.4%	3.6%	13.6%

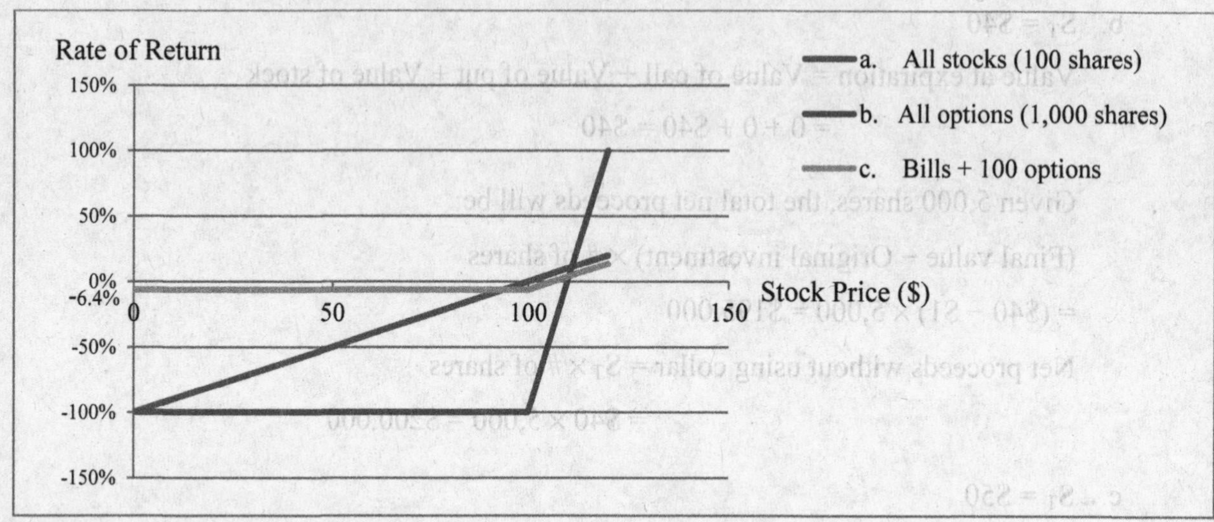

13.

a. Purchase a straddle, i.e., both a put and a call on the stock. The total cost of the straddle would be: $10 + $7 = $17

b. Since the straddle costs $17, this is the amount by which the stock would have to move in either direction for the profit on either the call or the put to cover the investment cost (not including time value of money considerations).

14.

a. Sell a straddle, i.e., sell a call *and* a put to realize premium income of:

$4 + $7 = $11

b. If the stock ends up at $50, both of the options will be worthless and the profit will be $11. This is the maximum possible profit since, at any other stock price, you will have to pay off on either the call or the put. The stock price can move by $11 (your initial revenue from writing the two at-the-money options) in either direction before your profits become negative.

c. Buy the call, sell (write) the put, lend the present value of $50. The payoff is as follows:

Position	Initial Outlay	Final Payoff $S_T < X$	$S_T > X$
Long call	C = 7	0	$S_T - 50$
Short put	−P = −4	$-(50 - S_T)$	0
Lending	$50/(1 + r)^{(1/4)}$	50	50
Total	$7 - 4 + [50/(1 + r)^{(1/4)}]$	S_T	S_T

The initial outlay equals: (the present value of $50) + $3
In either scenario, you end up with the same payoff as you would if you bought the stock itself.

15.

a. By writing covered call options, Jones receives premium income of $30,000. If, in January, the price of the stock is less than or equal to $45, he will keep the stock plus the premium income. Since the stock will be called away from him if its price exceeds $45 per share, the *most* he can have is:

$450,000 + $30,000 = $480,000

(We are ignoring interest earned on the premium income from writing the option over this short time period.) The payoff structure is:

Stock Price	Portfolio Value
Less than $45	(10,000 times stock price) + $30,000
Greater than $45	$450,000 + $30,000 = $480,000

This strategy offers some premium income but leaves the investor with substantial downside risk. At the extreme, if the stock price falls to zero, Jones would be left with only $30,000. This strategy also puts a cap on the final value at $480,000, but this is more than sufficient for the down payment of the house.

b. By buying put options with a $35 strike price, Jones will be paying $30,000 in premiums in order to insure a minimum level for the final value of his position. That minimum value is: ($35 × 10,000) − $30,000 = $320,000

This strategy allows for upside gain, but exposes Jones to the possibility of a moderate loss equal to the cost of the puts. The payoff structure is:

Stock Price	Portfolio Value
Less than $35	$350,000 − $30,000 = $320,000
Greater than $35	(10,000 times stock price) − $30,000

c. The net cost of the collar is zero. The value of the portfolio will be as follows:

Stock Price	Portfolio Value
Less than \$35	\$350,000
Between \$35 and \$45	10,000 times stock price
Greater than \$45	\$450,000

If the stock price is less than or equal to \$35, then the collar preserves the \$350,000 in principal. If the price exceeds \$45, then Jones gains up to a cap of \$450,000. In between \$35 and \$45, his proceeds equal 10,000 times the stock price.

The best strategy in this case is (c) since it satisfies the two requirements of preserving the \$350,000 in principal while offering a chance of getting \$450,000. Strategy (a) should be ruled out because it leaves Jones exposed to the risk of substantial loss of principal.

Our ranking is: (1) c (2) b (3) a

16.

a. Butterfly Spread

Position	$S_T < X_1$	$X_1 < S_T < X_2$	$X_2 < S_T < X_3$	$X_3 < S_T$
Long call (X_1)	0	$S_T - X_1$	$S_T - X_1$	$S_T - X_1$
Short 2 calls (X_2)	0	0	$-2(S_T - X_2)$	$-2(S_T - X_2)$
Long call (X_3)	0	0	0	$S_T - X_3$
Total	0	$S_T - X_1$	$2X_2 - X_1 - S_T$	$(X_2 - X_1) - (X_3 - X_2) = 0$

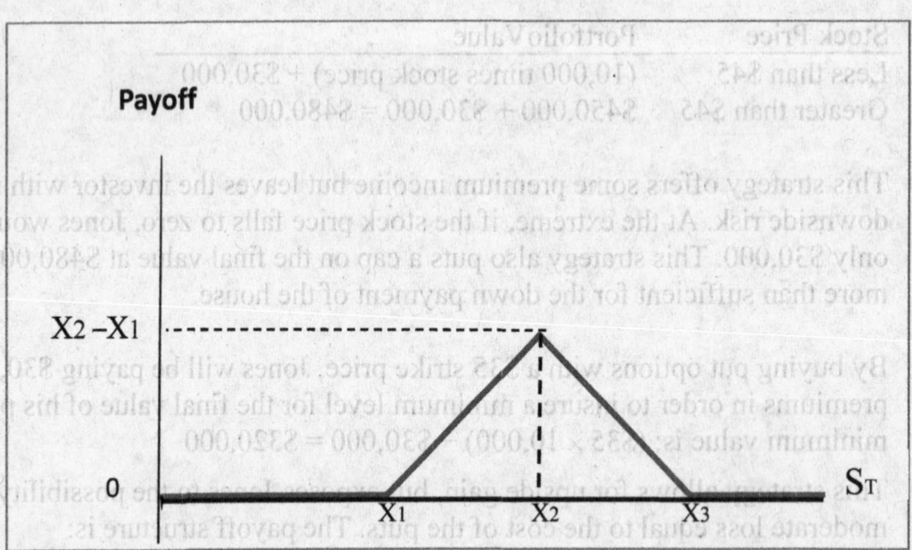

b. Vertical combination

Position	$S_T < X_1$	$X_1 < S_T < X_2$	$S_T > X_2$
Long call (X_2)	0	0	$S_T - X_2$
Long put (X_1)	$X_1 - S_T$	0	0
Total	$X_1 - S_T$	0	$S_T - X_2$

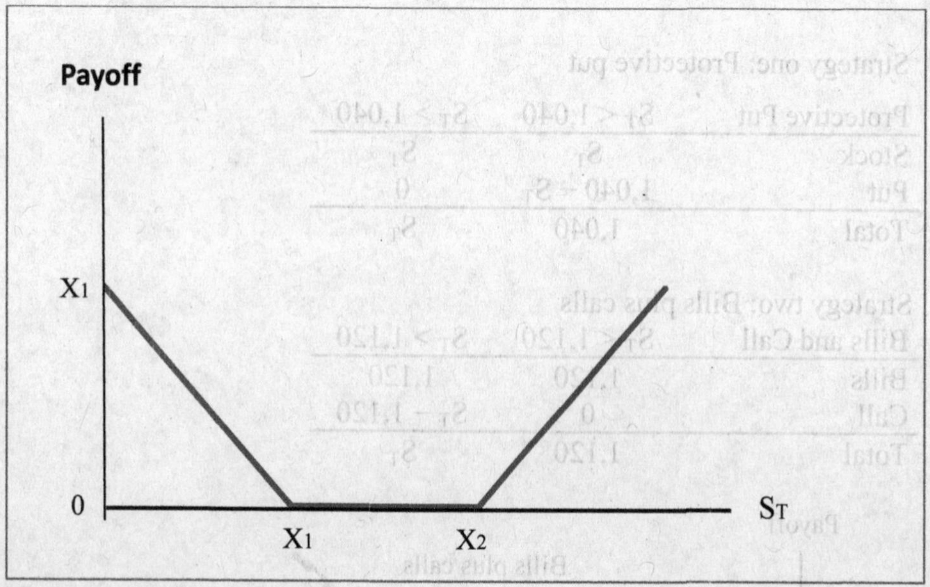

17. Bearish spread

Position	$S_T < X_1$	$X_1 < S_T < X_2$	$S_T > X_2$
Long call (X_2)	0	0	$S_T - X_2$
Short call (X_1)	0	$-(S_T - X_1)$	$-(S_T - X_1)$
Total	0	$X_1 - S_T$	$X_1 - X_2$

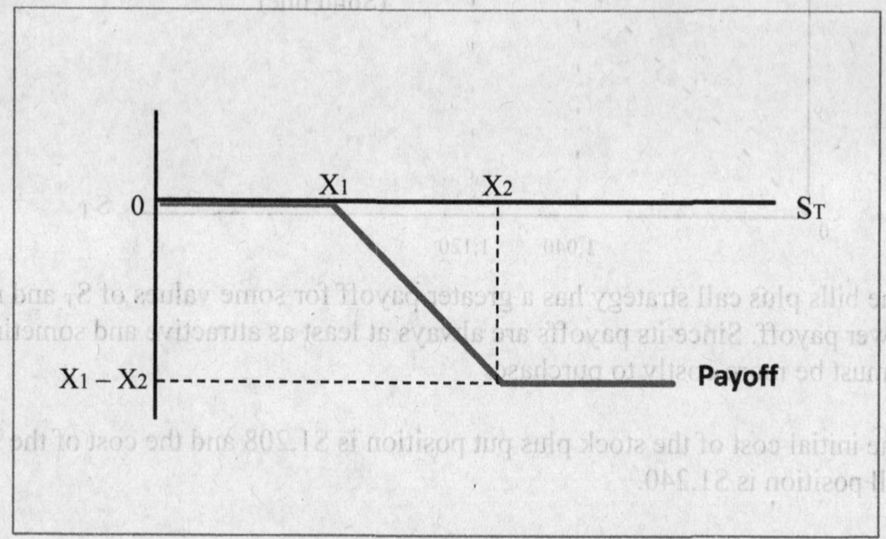

In the bullish spread, the payoff either increases or is unaffected by stock price increases. In the bearish spread, the payoff either increases or is unaffected by stock price *decreases*.

18.

a. Strategy one: Protective put

Protective Put	$S_T < 1{,}040$	$S_T > 1{,}040$
Stock	S_T	S_T
Put	$1{,}040 - S_T$	0
Total	1,040	S_T

Strategy two: Bills plus calls

Bills and Call	$S_T < 1{,}120$	$S_T > 1{,}120$
Bills	1,120	1,120
Call	0	$S_T - 1{,}120$
Total	1,120	S_T

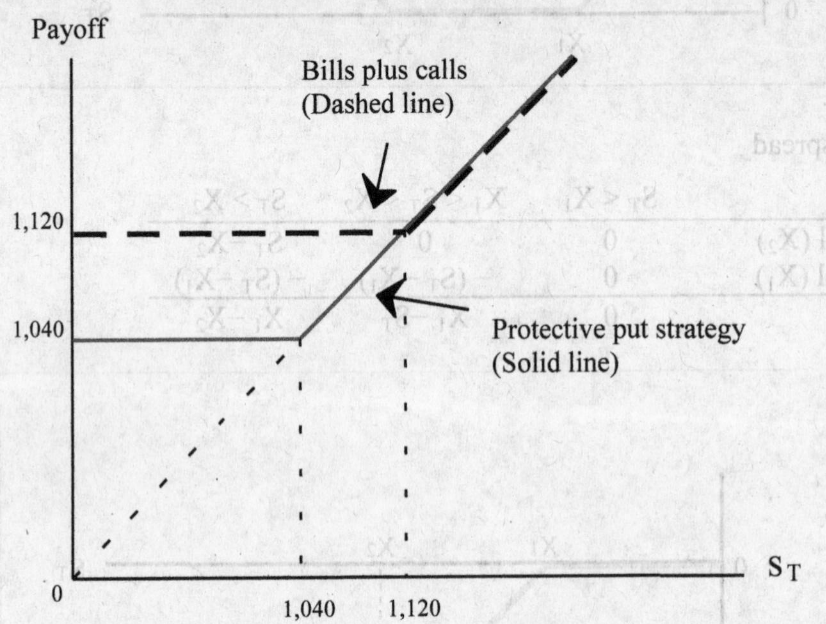

b. The bills plus call strategy has a greater payoff for some values of S_T and never a lower payoff. Since its payoffs are always at least as attractive and sometimes greater, it must be more costly to purchase.

c. The initial cost of the stock plus put position is $1,208 and the cost of the bills plus call position is $1,240.

Strategy one: Protective put

Position	$S_T = 0$	$S_T = 1{,}040$	$S_T = 1{,}120$	$S_T = 1{,}200$	$S_T = 1{,}280$
Stock	0	1,040	1,120	1,200	1,280
+ Put	1,040	0	0	0	0
Payoff	1,040	1,040	1,120	1,200	1,280
Profit	−168	−168	−88	−8	+72

*Profit = Payoff − Initial Outlay = Payoff − $1,208

Strategy two: Bills plus calls

Position	$S_T = 0$	$S_T = 1,040$	$S_T = 1,120$	$S_T = 1,200$	$S_T = 1,280$
Bill	1,120	1,120	1,120	1,120	1,120
+ Call	0	0	0	80	160
Payoff	1,120	1,120	1,120	1,200	1,280
Profit	−120	−120	−120	−40	+40

*Profit = Payoff − Initial Outlay = Payoff − $1,240

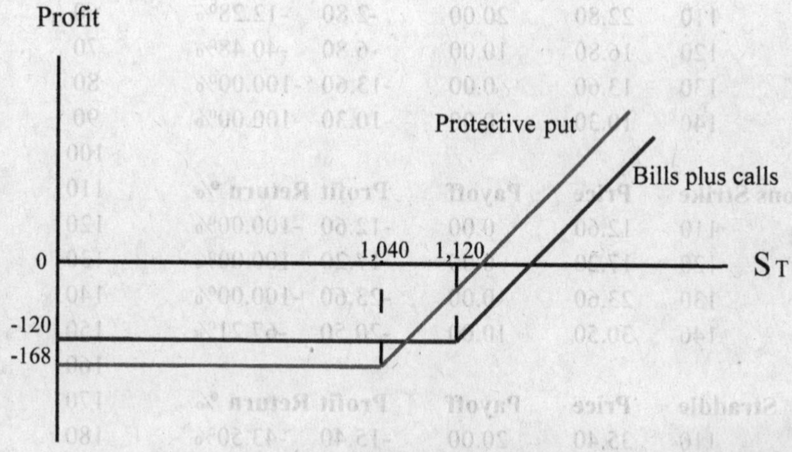

d. The stock and put strategy is riskier. It does worse when the market is down, and better when the market is up. Therefore, its beta is higher.

19. The Excel spreadsheet for both parts (a) and (b) is shown on the next page, and the profit diagrams are on the following page.

a. & b.

Stock Prices

Beginning Market Price	116.5
Ending Market Price	130

Buying Options:

Call Options Strike	Price	Payoff	Profit	Return %
110	22.80	20.00	-2.80	-12.28%
120	16.80	10.00	-6.80	-40.48%
130	13.60	0.00	-13.60	-100.00%
140	10.30	0.00	-10.30	-100.00%

Put Options Strike	Price	Payoff	Profit	Return %
110	12.60	0.00	-12.60	-100.00%
120	17.20	0.00	-17.20	-100.00%
130	23.60	0.00	-23.60	-100.00%
140	30.50	10.00	-20.50	-67.21%

Straddle	Price	Payoff	Profit	Return %
110	35.40	20.00	-15.40	-43.50%
120	34.00	10.00	-24.00	-70.59%
130	37.20	0.00	-37.20	-100.00%
140	40.80	10.00	-30.80	-75.49%

	X 130 Straddle
Ending	Profit
Stock Price	-37.20
50	42.8
60	32.8
70	22.8
80	12.8
90	2.8
100	-7.2
110	-17.2
120	-27.2
130	-37.2
140	-27.2
150	-17.2
160	-7.2
170	2.8
180	12.8
190	22.8
200	32.8
210	42.8

Selling Options:

Call Options Strike	Price	Payoff	Profit	Return %
110	22.80	-20	2.80	12.28%
120	16.80	-10	6.80	40.48%
130	13.60	0	13.60	100.00%
140	10.30	0	10.30	100.00%

Put Options Strike	Price	Payoff	Profit	Return %
110	12.60	0	12.60	100.00%
120	17.20	0	17.20	100.00%
130	23.60	0	23.60	100.00%
140	30.50	10	40.50	132.79%

Money Spread	Price	Payoff	Profit
Bullish Spread			
Purchase 120 Call	16.80	10	-6.80
Sell 130 Call	13.60	0	13.60
Combined Profit		10.00	6.80

	Bullish
Ending	Spread
Stock Price	6.80
50	-3.2
60	-3.2
70	-3.2
80	-3.2
90	-3.2
100	-3.2
110	-3.2
120	-3.2
130	6.80
140	6.80
150	6.80
160	6.80
170	6.80
180	6.80
190	6.80
200	6.80
210	6.80

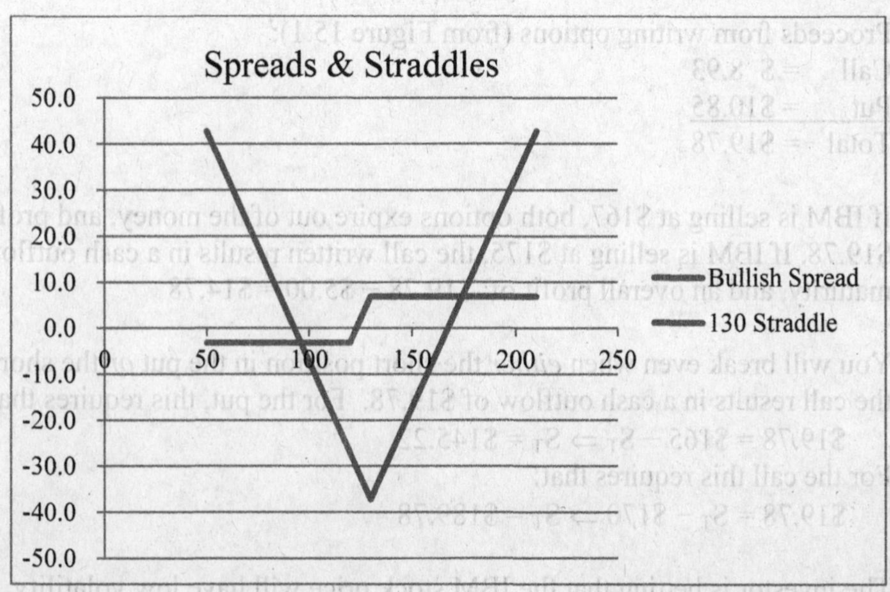

20. The bondholders have, in effect, made a loan which requires repayment of B dollars, where B is the face value of bonds. If, however, the value of the firm (V) is less than B, then the loan is satisfied by the bondholders taking over the firm. In this way, the bondholders are forced to "pay" B (in the sense that the loan is cancelled) in return for an asset worth only V. It is as though the bondholders wrote a put on an asset worth V, with exercise price B. Alternatively, one can view the bondholders as giving to the equity holders the right to reclaim the firm by paying off the B dollar debt. The bondholders have issued a call to the equity holders.

21. The executive receives a bonus if the stock price exceeds a certain value, and receives nothing otherwise. This is the same as the payoff to a call option.

22.

a.

Position	$S_T < 165$	$165 < S_T < 170$	$S_T > 170$
Short call	0	0	$-(S_T - 170)$
Short put	$-(165 - S_T)$	0	0
Total	$S_T - 165$	0	$170 - S_T$

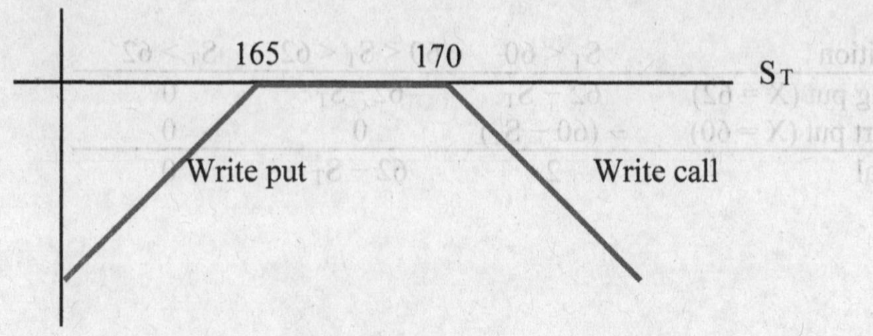

b. Proceeds from writing options (from Figure 15.1):

Call	= \$ 8.93
Put	= \$10.85
Total	= \$19.78

If IBM is selling at \$167, both options expire out of the money, and profit equals \$19.78. If IBM is selling at \$175, the call written results in a cash outflow of \$5 at maturity, and an overall profit of: \$19.78 – \$5.00 = \$14.78

c. You will break even when *either* the short position in the put *or* the short position in the call results in a cash outflow of \$19.78. For the put, this requires that:

$\$19.78 = \$165 - S_T \Rightarrow S_T = \$145.22$

For the call this requires that:

$\$19.78 = S_T - \$170 \Rightarrow S_T = \$189.78$

d. The investor is betting that the IBM stock price will have low volatility.

23.

a.

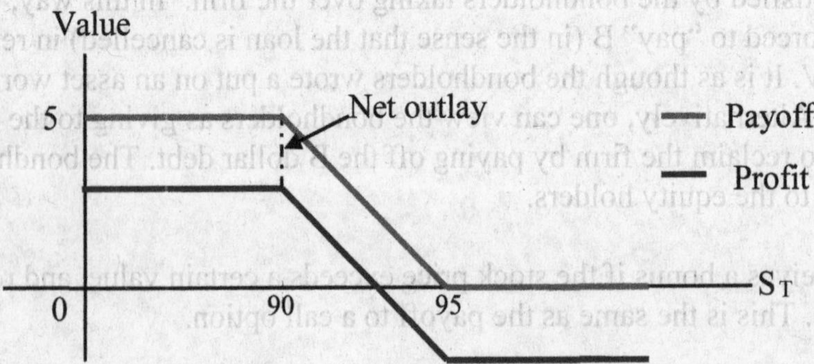

b. The put with the higher exercise price must cost more. Therefore, the net outlay to establish the portfolio is positive.

24. Buy the X = 62 put (which should cost more than it does) and write the X = 60 put. Since the options have the same price, the net outlay is zero. The proceeds at maturity will be between 0 and 2 and will never be negative.

Position	$S_T < 60$	$60 < S_T < 62$	$S_T > 62$
Long put (X = 62)	$62 - S_T$	$62 - S_T$	0
Short put (X = 60)	$-(60 - S_T)$	0	0
Total	2	$62 - S_T$	0

Payoff = Profit, because net outlay is 0.

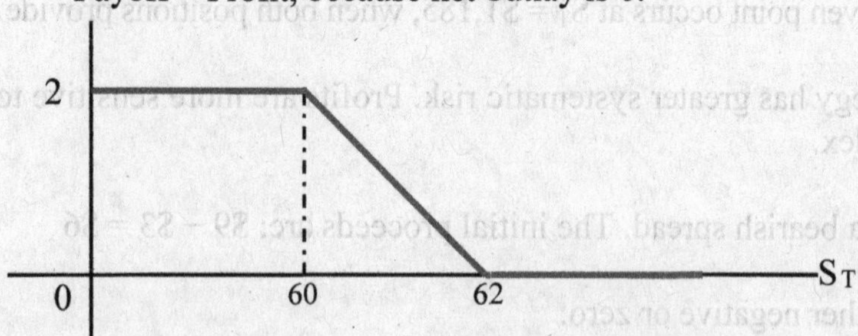

25. The following payoff table shows that the portfolio is riskless with time-T value equal to \$10. Therefore, the risk-free rate is: (\$10/\$9.50) − 1 = .0526 = 5.26%

Position	$S_T < 10$	$S_T > 10$
Buy stock	S_T	S_T
Short call	0	$-(S_T - 10)$
Long put	$10 - S_T$	0
Total	10	10

26.

a.

Joe's strategy		Final Payoff	
Position	Initial Outlay	$S_T < 1200$	$S_T > 1200$
Stock index	1,200	S_T	S_T
Long put (X = 1,200)	60	$1{,}200 - S_T$	0
Total	1,260	1,200	S_T
Profit = payoff − 1,260		−60	$S_T - 1{,}260$

Sally's strategy		Final Payoff	
Position	Initial Outlay	$S_T < 1{,}170$	$S_T > 1{,}170$
Stock index	1,200	S_T	S_T
Long put (X = 1,170)	45	$1{,}170 - S_T$	0
Total	1,260	1,170	S_T
Profit = payoff − 1,245		−75	$S_T - 1{,}245$

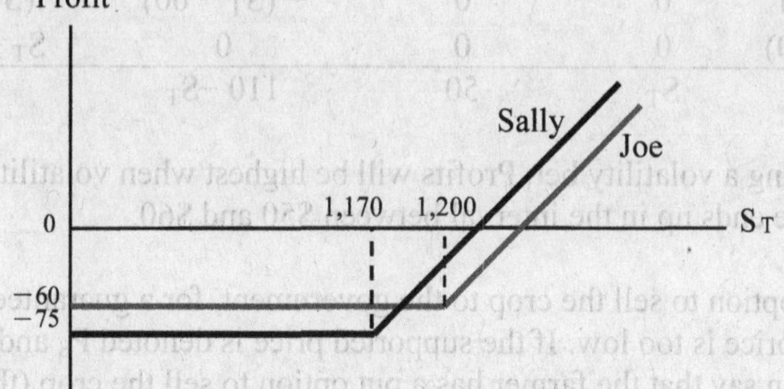

b. Sally does better when the stock price is high, but worse when the stock price is low. (The break-even point occurs at S_T = \$1,185, when both positions provide losses of \$60.)

c. Sally's strategy has greater systematic risk. Profits are more sensitive to the value of the stock index.

27. This strategy is a bearish spread. The initial proceeds are: \$9 – \$3 = \$6

The payoff is either negative or zero:

Position	$S_T < 50$	$50 < S_T < 60$	$S_T > 60$
Long call (X = 60)	0	0	$S_T - 60$
Short call (X = 50)	0	$-(S_T - 50)$	$-(S_T - 50)$
Total	0	$-(S_T - 50)$	−10

Breakeven occurs when the payoff offsets the initial proceeds of \$6, which occurs at a stock price of S_T = \$56.

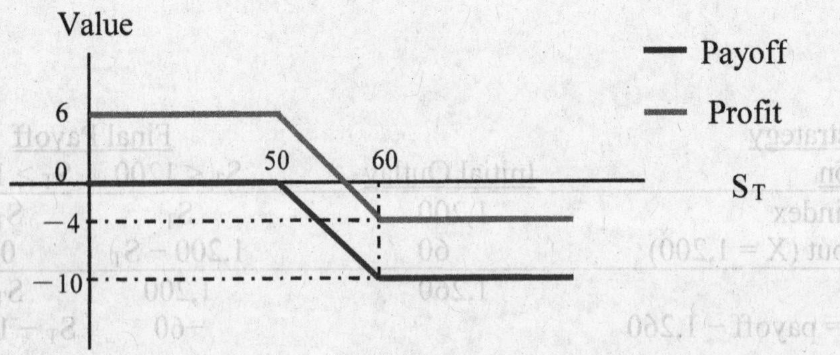

28. Buy a share of stock, write a call with X = 50, write a call with X = 60, and buy a call with X = 110.

Position	$S_T < 50$	$50 < S_T < 60$	$60 < S_T < 110$	$S_T > 110$
Buy stock	S_T	S_T	S_T	S_T
Short call (X = 50)	0	$-(S_T - 50)$	$-(S_T - 50)$	$-(S_T - 50)$
Short call (X = 60)	0	0	$-(S_T - 60)$	$-(S_T - 60)$
Long call (X = 110)	0	0	0	$S_T - 110$
Total	S_T	50	$110 - S_T$	0

The investor is making a volatility bet. Profits will be highest when volatility is low, such that if the stock price ends up in the interval between \$50 and \$60.

29. The farmer has the option to sell the crop to the government, for a guaranteed minimum price, if the market price is too low. If the supported price is denoted P_S and the market price P_M, then we can say that the farmer has a put option to sell the crop (the asset) at an exercise price of P_S even if the market price of the underlying asset (P_M) is less than P_S.

CFA 1

Answer:

Option *c* is false. This is the description of the payoff to a put, not a call.

CFA 2

Answer:

a. Donie should choose the long strangle strategy. A long strangle option strategy consists of buying a put and a call with the same expiration date and the same underlying asset, but different exercise prices. In a strangle strategy, the call has an exercise price above the stock price and the put has an exercise price below the stock price. An investor who buys (goes long) a strangle expects that the price of the underlying asset (TRT Materials in this case) will either move substantially below the exercise price on the put or above the exercise price on the call. With respect to TRT, the long strangle investor buys both the put option and the call option for a total cost of $9.00, and will experience a profit if the stock price moves more than $9.00 above the call exercise price or more than $9.00 below the put exercise price. This strategy would enable Donie's client to profit from a large movement in the stock price, either up or down, in reaction to the expected court decision.

b. i. The maximum possible loss per share is $9.00, which is the total cost of the two options ($5.00 + $4.00).

ii. The maximum possible gain is unlimited if the stock price keeps moving up and outside the breakeven range of prices.

iii. The breakeven prices are $46.00 and $69.00. The put will just cover costs if the stock price finishes $9.00 below the put exercise price ($55 − $9 = $46), and the call will just cover costs if the stock price finishes $9.00 above the call exercise price ($60 + $9 = $69).

CFA 3

Answer:

a. If an investor buys a call option and writes a put option on a T-bond, then, at maturity, the total payoff to the position is (S_T − X), where S_T is the price of the T-bond at the maturity date (time T) and X is the exercise price of the options. This is equivalent to the profit on a forward or futures position with futures price X. If you choose an exercise price (X) equal to the current T-bond futures price, then the profit on the portfolio replicates that of market-traded futures.

b. Such a position would increase the portfolio duration, just as adding a T-bond futures contract increases duration. As interest rates fall, the portfolio increases in value, so that duration is longer than it was before the synthetic futures position was established.

c. Futures can be bought and sold very cheaply and quickly. They give the manager flexibility to pursue strategies or particular bonds that seem attractively priced without worrying about the impact of these actions on portfolio duration. The futures can be used to make adjustments to duration necessitated by other portfolio actions.

CFA 4

Answer:

a. Conversion value of a convertible bond is the value of the security if it is converted immediately. That is:

Conversion value = market price of common stock × conversion ratio

= \$40 × 22 = \$880

b. Market conversion price is the price that an investor effectively pays for the common stock if the convertible bond is purchased:

Market conversion price = market price of the convertible bond/conversion ratio

= \$1,050/22 = \$47.73

CFA 5

Answer:

a. i. The current market conversion price is computed as follows:
Market conversion price = market price of the convertible bond/conversion ratio

= \$980/25 = \$39.20

ii. The expected one-year return for the Ytel convertible bond is:
Expected return = [(end of year price + coupon)/current price] − 1

= [(\$1,125 + \$40)/\$980] − 1 = 0.1888 = 18.88%

iii. The expected one-year return for the Ytel common equity is:
Expected return = [(end of year price + dividend)/current price] − 1

= (\$45/\$35) − 1 = 0.2857 = 28.57%

b. The two components of a convertible bond's value are:

- The straight bond value, which is the convertible bond's value as a bond, and;
- The option value, which is the value associated with the potential conversion into equity.

i. In response to the increase in Ytel's common equity price, the straight bond value should stay the same and the option value should increase.

The increase in equity price does not affect the straight bond value component of the Ytel convertible. The increase in equity price increases the option value component significantly, because the call option becomes deep "in the money" when the $51 per share equity price is compared to the convertible's conversion price of: $1,000/25 = $40 per share.

ii. In response to the increase in interest rates, the straight bond value should decrease and the option value should increase.

The increase in interest rates decreases the straight bond value component (bond values decline as interest rates increase) of the convertible bond and increases the value of the equity call option component (call option values increase as interest rates increase). This increase may be small or even unnoticeable when compared to the change in the option value resulting from the increase in the equity price.

CHAPTER 16
OPTION VALUATION

1. Intrinsic value = $S_0 - X$ = \$55 − \$50 = \$5.00

   Time value = C − Intrinsic value = \$6.50 − \$5.00 = \$1.50

2. Using put-call parity: Put = $C - S_0 + PV(X) + PV(Dividends)$

   $= \$2.25 - \$33 + \$35/(1 + .04)^{3/12} + 0 = \$3.91$

3. Using put-call parity: Put = $C - S_0 + PV(X) + PV(Dividends)$

   $\$2.50 = \$3.00 - S_0 + \$75/(1 + .08) + 0 \Rightarrow S_0 = \$69.94$

4. Put values also increase as the volatility of the underlying stock increases. We see this from the parity relationship as follows:

   $C = P + S_0 - PV(X) - PV(Dividends)$

   Given a value of S and a risk-free interest rate, if C increases because of an increase in volatility, so must P in order to keep the parity equation in balance.

   Numerical example:
   Suppose you have a put with exercise price 100, and that the stock price can take on one of three values: 90, 100, 110. The payoff to the put for each stock price is:

Stock price	90	100	110
Put value	10	0	0

   Now suppose the stock price can take on one of three alternate values also centered around 100, but with less volatility: 95, 100, 105. The payoff to the put for each stock price is:

Stock price	95	100	105
Put value	5	0	0

   The payoff to the put in the low volatility example has one-half the expected value of the payoff in the high volatility example.

5.
   a. (1) Put A must be written on the lower-priced stock. Otherwise, given the lower volatility of stock A, put A would sell for less than put B.

   b. (2) Put B must be written on the stock with lower price. This would explain its higher value.

c. (2) Call B. Despite the higher price of stock B, call B is cheaper than call A. This can be explained by a lower time to maturity.

d. (2) Call B. This would explain its higher price.

e. (3) Not enough information. The call with the lower exercise price sells for more than the call with the higher exercise price. The values given are consistent with either stock having higher volatility.

6. $H = \dfrac{C_u - C_d}{uS_0 - dS_0}$

uS0 – dS0 = 120 – 90 = 30

X	Cu – Cd	Hedge Ratio
120	0 – 0	0/30=0.000
110	10 – 0	10/30=0.333
100	20 – 0	20/30=0.666
90	30 – 0	30/30=1.00

Note that, as the option becomes progressively more in the money, its hedge ratio increases to a maximum of 1.0.

7. We first calculate $d_1 = \dfrac{\ln(S_0/X) + (r - \delta + \sigma^2/2)T}{\sigma\sqrt{T}}$, and then find $N(d_1)$, which is the Black Scholes hedge ratio for the call. We can observe from the following that when the stock price increases, $N(d_1)$ increases as well.

X	50
r	3%
σ	20%
T	1

S	d_1	$N(d_1)$
45	-0.2768	0.3910
50	0.2500	0.5987
55	0.7266	0.7662
		=normsdist(d1)

8.

a. When S_T = \$130, then P = 0.
When S_T = \$80, then P = \$30.

The hedge ratio is: $H = \dfrac{P_u - P_d}{uS_0 - dS_0} = \dfrac{0 - 30}{130 - 80} = -.6$

b.

Riskless Portfolio	$S_T = 80$	$S_T = 130$
3 shares	240	390
5 puts	150	0
Total	390	390

Present value = \$390/1.10 = \$354.545

c. Portfolio cost = 3S + 5P = \$300 + 5P = \$354.545

Therefore 5P = \$54.545 ⇒ P = \$54.545/5 = \$10.91

9. The hedge ratio for the call is: $H = \dfrac{C_u - C_d}{uS_0 - dS_0} = \dfrac{20 - 0}{130 - 80} = .4$

Riskless Portfolio	S =80	S = 130
2 shares	160	260
Short 5 calls	0	−100
Total	160	160

Present value = \$160/1.10 = \$145.455

Portfolio cost = 2S − 5C = 200 − 5C = \$145.455 ⇒ C = \$10.91

Put-call parity relationship: $P = C - S_0 + PV(X)$

\$10.91 = \$10.91 − \$100 + (\$110/1.10) = \$10.91

10. a. A delta-neutral portfolio is perfectly hedged against small price changes in the underlying asset. This is true both for price increases and decreases. That is, the portfolio value will not change significantly if the asset price changes by a small amount. However, large changes in the underlying asset will cause the hedge to become imperfect. This means that overall portfolio value can change by a significant amount if the price change in the underlying asset is large.

11. a. Delta is the change in the option price for a given instantaneous change in the stock price. The change is equal to the slope of the option price diagram.

12. The best estimate for the change in price of the option is: Change in asset price × delta = (−\$6) × (− .65) = \$3.90. The option price is estimated to increase by \$3.90.

13. The number of call options necessary to delta hedge is $\dfrac{51,750}{0.69} = 75,000$ options or 750 options contracts, each covering 100 shares. Since these are call options, the options should be sold short.

14. The number of calls needed to create a delta-neutral hedge is inversely proportional to the delta. The delta decreases when stock price decreases. Therefore the number of calls necessary would increase if the stock price falls.

15. A delta-neutral portfolio can be created with any of the following combinations: long stock and short calls, long stock and long puts, short stock and long calls, and short stock and short puts.

16. $d_1 = \dfrac{\ln(S_0/X) + (r - \delta + \sigma^2/2)T}{\sigma\sqrt{T}} = \dfrac{\ln(50/50) + (.03 - 0 + .5^2/2) \times .5}{.5 \times \sqrt{.5}} = 0.2192$

$N(d_1) = 0.5868$

$d_2 = d_1 - \sigma\sqrt{T} = -0.1344$

$N(d_2) = 0.4466$

$C = S_0\, e^{-\delta T} N(d_1) - Xe^{-rT}\, N(d_2) = \$7.34$

17. $P = Xe^{-rT}\,[1 - N(d_2)] - S_0\, e^{-\delta T}\,[1 - N(d_1)] = \$6.60$

This value is from our Black-Scholes spreadsheet, but note that we could have derived the value from put-call parity:

$P = C - S_0 + PV(X) = \$7.34 - \$50 + \$49.26 = \$6.60$

18. Use the Black-Scholes spreadsheet and change the input for each of the followings:

a. Time to expiration = 3 months = .25 year ⇒ C falls to \$5.14
b. Standard deviation = 25% per year ⇒ C falls to \$3.88
c. Exercise price = \$55 ⇒ C falls to \$5.40
d. Stock price = \$55 ⇒ C rises to \$10.54
e. Interest rate = 5% ⇒ C rises to \$7.56

19. A straddle is a call and a put. The Black-Scholes value is:

$$C + P = S_0 e^{-\delta T}\, N(d_1) - Xe^{-rT}\, N(d_2) + Xe^{-rT}\,[1 - N(d_2)] - S_0 e^{-\delta T}\,[1 - N(d_1)]$$

$$= S_0 e^{-\delta T}\,[2\,N(d_1) - 1] + Xe^{-rT}\,[1 - 2N(d_2)]$$

On the Excel spreadsheet (Spreadsheet 16.1 in the text), the valuation formula is:

E6 + E7 = B5 × EXP(−B7 × B3) × (2 × E4 − 1) + B6 × EXP(−B4 × B3) × (1 − 2 × E5)

20. The call price will decrease by less than \$1. The change in the call price would be \$1 only if: (i) there were a 100% probability that the call would be exercised; and (ii) the interest rates were zero.

21. Holding firm-specific risk constant, higher beta implies higher total stock volatility. Therefore, the value of the put option increases as beta increases.

22. Holding beta constant, the stock with high firm-specific risk has higher total volatility. Therefore, the option on the stock with a lot of firm-specific risk is worth more.

23. The call option with a high exercise price has a lower hedge ratio. Both d1 and N(d1) are lower when X is higher. Holding else equal, as the call option is less in the money, the hedge ratio is also lower.

24. The call option is more sensitive to changes in interest rates. The option elasticity exceeds 1.0. In other words, the option is effectively a levered investment and is more sensitive to interest rate changes.

25. The call option's implied volatility has increased. If this were not the case, then the call price would have fallen.

26. The put option's implied volatility has increased. If this were not the case, then the put price would have fallen.

27. As the stock price becomes infinitely large, the hedge ratio of the call option [N(d1)] approaches one. As S increases, the probability of exercise approaches 1.0 [i.e., N(d1) approaches 1.0].

28. The hedge ratio of a put option with a very small exercise price is zero. As X decreases, exercise of the put becomes less and less likely, so the probability of exercise approaches zero. The put's hedge ratio [N(d1) −1] approaches zero as N(d1) approaches 1.0.

29. The hedge ratio of the straddle is the sum of the hedge ratios for the two options: $.4 + (-.6) = -.2$

30.

a. The spreadsheet appears as follows:

INPUTS		OUTPUTS		FORMULA FOR OUTPUT IN COLUMN E
Standard deviation (annual)	0.3213	d1	0.0089	(LN(B5/B6)+(B4-B7+.5*B2^2)*B3)/(B2*SQRT(B3))
Maturity (in years)	0.5	d2	-0.2183	E2-B2*SQRT(B3)
Risk-free rate (annual)	0.05	N(d1)	0.5036	NORMSDIST(E2)
Stock Price	100	N(d2)	0.4136	NORMSDIST(E3)
Exercise price	105	B/S call value	8.0000	B5*EXP(-B7*B3)*E4 - B6*EXP(-B4*B3)*E5
Dividend yield (annual)	0	B/S put value	10.4075	B6*EXP(-B4*B3)*(1-E5) - B5*EXP(-B7*B3)*(1-E4)

The implied standard deviation is .3213.

b. The spreadsheet below shows the standard deviation has increased to: .3568

INPUTS		OUTPUTS		FORMULA FOR OUTPUT IN COLUMN E
Standard deviation (annual)	0.3568	d1	0.0318	(LN(B5/B6)+(B4-B7+.5*B2^2)*B3)/(B2*SQRT(B3))
Maturity (in years)	0.5	d2	-0.2204	E2-B2*SQRT(B3)
Risk-free rate (annual)	0.05	N(d1)	0.5127	NORMSDIST(E2)
Stock Price	100	N(d2)	0.4128	NORMSDIST(E3)
Exercise price	105	B/S call value	9.0000	B5*EXP(-B7*B3)*E4 - B6*EXP(-B4*B3)*E5
Dividend yield (annual)	0	B/S put value	11.4075	B6*EXP(-B4*B3)*(1-E5) - B5*EXP(-B7*B3)*(1-E4)

Implied volatility has increased because the value of an option increases with greater volatility.

c. Implied volatility increases to .4087 when maturity decreases to four months. The shorter maturity decreases the value of the option; therefore, in order for the option price to remain unchanged at $8, implied volatility must increase.

INPUTS		OUTPUTS		FORMULA FOR OUTPUT IN COLUMN E
Standard deviation (annual)	0.4087	d1	-0.0182	(LN(B5/B6)+(B4-B7+.5*B2^2)*B3)/(B2*SQRT(B3))
Maturity (in years)	0.3333	d2	-0.2541	E2-B2*SQRT(B3)
Risk-free rate (annual)	0.05	N(d1)	0.4927	NORMSDIST(E2)
Stock Price	100	N(d2)	0.3997	NORMSDIST(E3)
Exercise price	105	B/S call value	8.0000	B5*EXP(-B7*B3)*E4 - B6*EXP(-B4*B3)*E5
Dividend yield (annual)	0	B/S put value	11.2645	B6*EXP(-B4*B3)*(1-E5) - B5*EXP(-B7*B3)*(1-E4)

d. Implied volatility decreases to .2406 when exercise price decreases to $100. The decrease in exercise price increases the value of the call, so that in order for the option price to remain at $8, implied volatility decreases.

INPUTS		OUTPUTS		FORMULA FOR OUTPUT IN COLUMN E
Standard deviation (annual)	0.2406	d1	0.2320	(LN(B5/B6)+(B4-B7+.5*B2^2)*B3)/(B2*SQRT(B3))
Maturity (in years)	0.5	d2	0.0619	E2-B2*SQRT(B3)
Risk-free rate (annual)	0.05	N(d1)	0.5917	NORMSDIST(E2)
Stock Price	100	N(d2)	0.5247	NORMSDIST(E3)
Exercise price	100	B/S call value	8.0010	B5*EXP(-B7*B3)*E4 - B6*EXP(-B4*B3)*E5
Dividend yield (annual)	0	B/S put value	5.5320	B6*EXP(-B4*B3)*(1-E5) - B5*EXP(-B7*B3)*(1-E4)

e. The decrease in stock price decreases the value of the call. In order for the option price to remain at $8, implied volatility increases to .3566.

INPUTS		OUTPUTS		FORMULA FOR OUTPUT IN COLUMN E
Standard deviation (annual)	0.3566	d1	-0.0484	(LN(B5/B6)+(B4-B7+.5*B2^2)*B3)/(B2*SQRT(B3))
Maturity (in years)	0.5	d2	-0.3006	E2-B2*SQRT(B3)
Risk-free rate (annual)	0.05	N(d1)	0.4807	NORMSDIST(E2)
Stock Price	98	N(d2)	0.3819	NORMSDIST(E3)
Exercise price	105	B/S call value	8.0000	B5*EXP(-B7*B3)*E4 - B6*EXP(-B4*B3)*E5
Dividend yield (annual)	0	B/S put value	12.4075	B6*EXP(-B4*B3)*(1-E5) - B5*EXP(-B7*B3)*(1-E4)

31. A put is more in the money, and has a hedge ratio closer to −1, when its exercise price is higher:

Put	X	Delta
A	10	−.1
B	20	−.5
C	30	−.9

32.

a,

Position	$S_T < X$	$S_T > X$
Stock	$S_T + D$	$S_T + D$
Put	$X - S_T$	0
Total	$X + D$	$S_T + D$

b. The total value for each of the two strategies is the same, regardless of the stock price (S_T).

Position	$S_T < X$	$S_T > X$
Call	0	$S_T - X$
Zeroes	X + D	X + D
Total	X + D	$S_T + D$

c. The cost of the stock-plus-put portfolio is (S_0 + P). The cost of the call-plus-zero portfolio is: [C + PV(X + D)]. Therefore:

$$S_0 + P = C + PV(X + D)$$

33.

a. The delta of the collar is calculated as follows:

	Delta
Stock	1.0
Short call	$-N(d_1) = -.35$
Long put	$N(d_1) - 1 = -.40$
Total	.25

If the stock price increases by \$1, the value of the collar increases by \$ .25. The stock will be worth \$1 more, the loss on the short put is \$ .40, and the call written is a *liability* that increases by \$ .35.

b. If S becomes very large, then the delta of the collar approaches zero. Both N(d1) terms approach 1 so that the delta for the short call position approaches −1.0 and the delta for the long put position approaches zero. Intuitively, for very large stock prices, the value of the portfolio is simply the (present value of the) exercise price of the call, and is unaffected by small changes in the stock price.

As S approaches zero, the delta of the collar also approaches zero. Both N(d1) terms approach 0 so that the delta for the short call position approaches zero and the delta for the long put position approaches −1.0. For very small stock prices, the value of the portfolio is simply the (present value of the) exercise price of the put, and is unaffected by small changes in the stock price.

34.

a. Choice A: Calls have higher elasticity than shares. For equal *dollar* investments, the capital gain potential for calls is higher than for stocks.

b. Choice B: Calls have hedge ratios less than 1.0. For equal numbers of *shares* controlled, the dollar exposure of the calls is less than that of the stocks, and the profit potential is less.

35. Step 1: Calculate the option values at expiration. The two possible stock prices are: $S^+ =$ \$120 and $S^- =$ \$80. Therefore, since the exercise price is \$100, the corresponding two possible call values are: $C_u =$ \$20 and $C_d =$ \$0.

Step 2: Calculate the hedge ratio: $(C_u - C_d)/(uS_0 - dS_0) = (20 - 0)/(120 - 80) = .5$

Step 3: Form a riskless portfolio made up of one share of stock and two written calls. The cost of the riskless portfolio is: $(S_0 - 2C_0) = 100 - 2C_0$ and the certain end-of-year value is \$80.

Step 4: Calculate the present value of \$80 with a one-year interest rate of 10%: \$80/1.1 = \$72.73

Step 5: Set the value of the hedged position equal to the present value of the certain payoff: $\$100 - 2C_0 = \$72.73$

Step 6: Solve for the value of the call: $C_0 = \$13.64$
Notice that we never use the probabilities of a stock price increase or decrease. These are not needed to value the call option.

36. Step 1: Calculate the option values at expiration. The two possible stock prices are: $S^+ =$ \$130 and $S^- =$ \$70. Therefore, since the exercise price is \$100, the corresponding two possible call values are: $C_u =$ \$30 and $C_d =$ \$0.

Step 2: Calculate the hedge ratio: $(C_u - C_d)/(uS_0 - dS_0) = (30 - 0)/(130 - 70) = .5$

Step 3: Form a riskless portfolio made up of one share of stock and two written calls. The cost of the riskless portfolio is: $(S_0 - 2C_0) = 100 - 2C_0$ and the certain end-of-year value is \$70.

Step 4: Calculate the present value of \$70 with a one-year interest rate of 10% = \$63.64

Step 5: Set the value of the hedged position equal to the present value of the certain payoff: $\$100 - 2C_0 = \$63.64$

Step 6: Solve for the value of the call: $C_0 = \$18.18$
The value of the call is now greater than the value of the call in the lower-volatility scenario.

37. We start by finding the value of P_u. From this point, the put can fall to an expiration-date value of $P_{uu} =$ \$0 (since at this point the stock price is $uuS_0 =$ \$121) or rise to a final value of $P_{ud} =$ \$5.50 (since at this point the stock price is $udS_0 =$ \$104.50, which is less than the \$110 exercise price). Therefore, the hedge ratio at this point is:

$$H = \frac{P_{uu} - P_{ud}}{uuS_0 - udS_0} = \frac{\$0 - \$5.50}{\$121 - \$104.50} = -\frac{1}{3}$$

Thus, the following portfolio will be worth \$121 at option expiration regardless of the ultimate stock price:

Riskless portfolio	udS_0 = \$104.50	uuS_0 = \$121
Buy 1 share at price uS_0 = \$110	\$104.50	\$121.00
Buy 3 puts at price P_u	16.50	0.00
Total	\$ 121.00	\$121.00

The portfolio must have a current market value equal to the present value of \$121:

$$110 + 3P_u = \$121/1.05 = \$115.238 \Rightarrow P_u = \$1.746$$

Next we find the value of P_d. From this point (at which dS_0 = \$95), the put can fall to an expiration-date value of P_{du} = \$5.50 (since at this point the stock price is duS_0 = \$104.50) or rise to a value of P_{dd} = \$19.75 (since at this point, the stock price is ddS_0 = \$90.25). Therefore, the hedge ratio at this point is –1.0, which reflects the fact that the put will necessarily expire in the money if the stock price falls to \$95 in the first period:

$$H = \frac{P_{du} - P_{dd}}{duS_0 - ddS_0} = \frac{\$5.50 - \$19.75}{\$104.50 - \$90.25} = -1.0$$

Thus, the following portfolio will be worth \$110 at option expiration regardless of the ultimate stock price:

Riskless portfolio	ddS_0 = \$90.25	duS_0 = \$104.50
Buy 1 share at price dS_0 = \$95	\$ 90.25	\$104.50
Buy 1 put at price P_d	19.75	5.50
Total	\$110.00	\$110.00

The portfolio must have a current market value equal to the present value of \$110:

$$95 + P_d = \$110/1.05 = \$104.762 \Rightarrow P_d = \$9.762$$

Finally, we solve for P using the values of P_u and P_d. From its initial value, the put can rise to a value of P_d = \$9.762 (at this point, the stock price is dS_0 = \$95) or fall to a value of P_u = \$1.746 (at this point, the stock price is uS_0 = \$110). Therefore, the hedge ratio at this point is:

$$H = \frac{P_u - P_d}{uS_0 - dS_0} = \frac{\$1.746 - \$9.762}{\$110 - \$95} = -0.5344$$

Thus, the following portfolio will be worth $60.53 at option expiration regardless of the ultimate stock price:

Riskless portfolio	dS_0 = $95	uS_0 = $110
Buy 0.5344 share at price S = $100	$50.768	$58.784
Buy 1 put at price P	9.762	1.746
Total	$60.530	$60.530

The portfolio must have a market value equal to the present value of $60.53:

$$\$53.44 + P = \$60.53/1.05 = \$57.648 \Rightarrow P = \$4.208$$

Finally, we check put-call parity. Recall from Example 15.1 and Concept Check #4 that C = $4.434. Put-call parity requires that:

$$P = C + PV(X) - S$$

$$\$4.208 = \$4.434 + (\$110/1.05^2) - \$100$$

Except for minor rounding error, put-call parity is satisfied.

38.

S_0 = 100 (current value of portfolio)

X = 100 (floor promised to clients, 0% return)

σ = .25 (volatility)

r = .05 (risk-free rate)

T = 4 years (horizon of program)

a. The put delta is: $N(d_1) - 1 = 0.7422 - 1 = -.2578$
Place 25.78% of the portfolio in bills, 74.22% in equity ($74.22 million).

b. At the new portfolio value, the put delta becomes − .2779, so that the amount held in bills should be: ($97 million × .2779) = $26.96 million. The manager must sell $1.18 million of equity and use the proceeds to buy bills.

39.

a.

Stock price	110	90
Put payoff	0	10

The hedge ratio is: $H = \dfrac{P_u - P_d}{uS_0 - dS_0} = -10/20 = -.5$

A portfolio comprised of one share and two puts provides a guaranteed payoff of 110, with present value: $110/1.05 = $104.76

Therefore:

$$S + 2P = \$104.76$$

$$\$100 + 2P = \$104.76 \Rightarrow P = \$2.38$$

b. The cost of the protective put portfolio is the cost of one share plus the cost of one put: \$100 + \$2.38 = \$102.38

c. The goal is a portfolio with the same exposure to the stock as the hypothetical protective put portfolio. Since the put's hedge ratio is – .5, we want to hold (1 – .5) = .5 shares of stock, which costs \$50, and place the remaining funds (\$52.38) in bills, earning 5% interest.

Stock price	S = 90	S = 110
Half share	45	55
Bills	55	55
Total	100	110

This payoff is identical to that of the protective put portfolio. Thus, the stock plus bills strategy replicates both the cost and payoff of the protective put.

40. $u = \exp(\sigma\sqrt{\Delta t})$; $d = \exp(-\sigma\sqrt{\Delta t})$

a. 1 period of one year
$u = \exp(.40\sqrt{1}) = 1.4918$; $d = \exp(-.40\sqrt{1}) = .6703$

b. 4 subperiods, each 3 months
$u = \exp(.40\sqrt{1/4}) = 1.2214$; $d = \exp(-.40\sqrt{1/4}) = .8187$

c. 12 subperiods, each 1 month
$u = \exp(.40\sqrt{1/12}) = 1.1224$; $d = \exp(-.40\sqrt{1/12}) = .8909$

41. $u = 1.5 = \exp(\sigma\sqrt{\Delta t}) = \exp(\sigma\sqrt{1}) \Rightarrow \sigma = .4055$
$d = 2/3 = \exp(-\sigma\sqrt{\Delta t}) = \exp(-\sigma\sqrt{1}) \Rightarrow \sigma = .4055$
The volatility of return is assumed to be .4055.

42. Given $S_0 = X$ when the put and the call are at-the-money, the relationship of put-call parity, $P = C - S_0 + PV(X)$ can be written as: $P = C - S_0 + PV(S_0)$.

Because $PV(S_0) = \dfrac{S_0}{(1 + r_f)^T} \leq S_0$

$\Rightarrow C - P = S_0 - PV(S_0) \geq 0 \Rightarrow C \geq P$

43. We first calculate the risk neutral probability that the stock price will increase:

$$p = \frac{1 + r_f - d}{u - d} = \frac{1 + .1 - .8}{1.2 - .8} = .75$$

Then use the probability to find the expected cash flow at expiration, and discount it by the risk free rate:

$$E(CF) = .75 \times \$20 + .25 \times 0 = \$15$$

$$C = \frac{E(CF)}{1 + r_f} = \frac{\$15}{1.1} = \$13.64$$

It matches the value we found in problem 35.

44. We first calculate the risk neutral probability that the stock price will increase:

$$p = \frac{1 + r_f - d}{u - d} = \frac{1 + .05 - .95}{1.1 - .95} = .6667.$$

Then use the probability to find the expected cash flows at expiration, and discount it by the risk free rate to find P_u and P_d:

$$uE(CF) = .6667 \times 0 + .3333 \times \$5.5 = \$1.8333$$

$$P_u = \frac{E(CF)}{1 + r_f} = \frac{\$1.8333}{1.05} = \$1.7460$$

$$dE(CF) = .6667 \times \$5.5 + .3333 \times \$19.75 = \$10.25$$

$$P_d = \frac{E(CF)}{1 + r_f} = \frac{\$10.25}{1.05} = \$9.7619$$

Finally, compute the expected cash flow in 6 month, and discount the E(CF) by the 6 month risk free rate:

$$E(CF) = .6667 \times 1.7460 + .3333 \times \$9.7619 = \$4.4180$$

$$P = \frac{E(CF)}{1 + r_f} = \frac{\$4.4180}{1.05} = \$4.208$$

It matches the value we found in problem 37.

CFA 1

Answer:

a. i. The combined portfolio will suffer a loss. The written calls will expire in the money. The protective put purchased will expire worthless. Each short call will payout \$27, less the short option price of \$8.60, while each put will lose the option price of \$16.10. For each strategy the portfolio will gain \$927 − \$883 = \$44. Thus, the loss will be \$52.90 − \$44 = \$8.90 per index unit.

ii. Both options expire out of the money, and are thus not exercised. The proceeds are slightly higher on the short calls than the long put since the option price from 2 short calls was \$17.20 versus a cost of \$16.10 on the long put, and thus there is a gain on the strategy of \$1.1 × 301 = \$331.1.

iii. The calls will expire worthless and the portfolio will retain the short call option price. The put option will be exercised and the proceeds used to offset the purchase price of the put and the decline in value of the portfolio.

b. i. The delta of the call will approach 1.0 as the stock goes deep into the money, while expiration of the call approaches and exercise becomes essentially certain. The put delta will approach zero.

ii. Both options expire out of the money. Delta of each will approach zero as expiration approaches and it becomes certain that the options will not be exercised.

iii. The call is out of the money as expiration approaches. Delta approaches zero. Conversely, the delta of the put approaches –1.0 as exercise becomes certain.

c. The call sells at an implied volatility (20.00%) that is less than recent historical volatility (21.00%); the put sells at an implied volatility (22.00%) that is greater than historical volatility. The call seems relatively cheap; the put seems expensive.

CFA 2

Answer:

a. i. The option price will decline.

ii. The option price will increase.

b. i. Besides Weber's belief that the implied volatility may differ from the market, the Black Scholes model assumes the volatility, risk-free rate, and dividend payments are constant, while in reality, they change overtime.

ii. An American option may be exercised early, and the value of early exercise cannot be calculated using the Black Scholes model. The flexibility of early exercise may make the market price higher than the price calculated by the Black-Scholes model.

CFA 3

Answer:

a. Over two periods, the stock price must follow one of four patterns: up-up, up-down, down-down, or down-up.

The binomial parameters are:

u = 1 + percentage increase in a period if the stock price rises = 1.20
d = 1 + percentage decrease in a period if the stock price falls = 0.80
r = 1 + risk-free rate = 1.06

The two-period binomial tree is as follows:

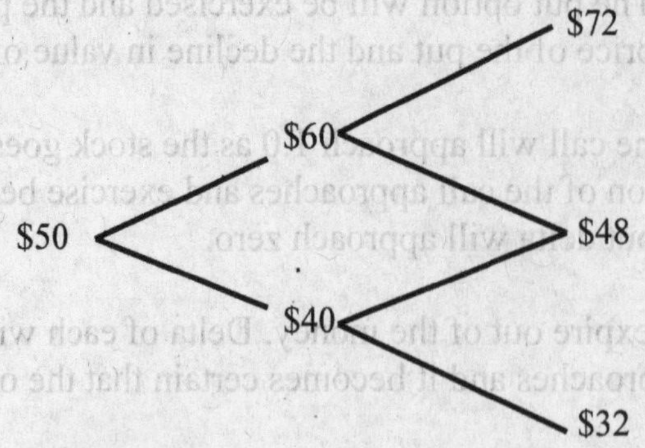

The calculations for the values shown above are as follows:

$uS_0 = \$50 \times 1.20 = \$60$

$dS_0 = \$50 \times 0.80 = \$40$

$uuS_0 = \$60.00 \times 1.20 = \$72$

$udS_0 = \$60.00 \times 0.80 = \$48$

$duS_0 = \$40 \times 1.20 = \$48$

$ddS_0 = \$40 \times 0.80 = \$32$

a. The value of a call option at expiration is: Max(0, S − X)

$C_{uu} = \text{Max}(0, \$72 - \$60) = \$12$

$C_{ud} = C_{du} = \text{Max}(0, \$48 - \$60) = 0$

$C_{dd} = \text{Max}(0, \$32 - \$60) = 0$

We use a portfolio combining the underlying stock and bond to replicate the payoffs: $S_T\Delta + (1+ r_f)\,B = \text{Payoff}$

$72\Delta + 1.06B = 12$
$48\Delta + 1.06B = 0$

Solve the equations for Δ and B ⇒ $\Delta = 0.5$, $B = -22.6415$

Therefore, the $C_u = 60\Delta + B = 7.3585$

$48\Delta + 1.06B = 0$
$32\Delta + 1.06B = 0$

Solve the equations for Δ and B ⇒ $\Delta = 0$, $B = 0$

Therefore, the $C_d = 40\Delta + B = 0$

The two-period binomial tree for the option values is as follows:

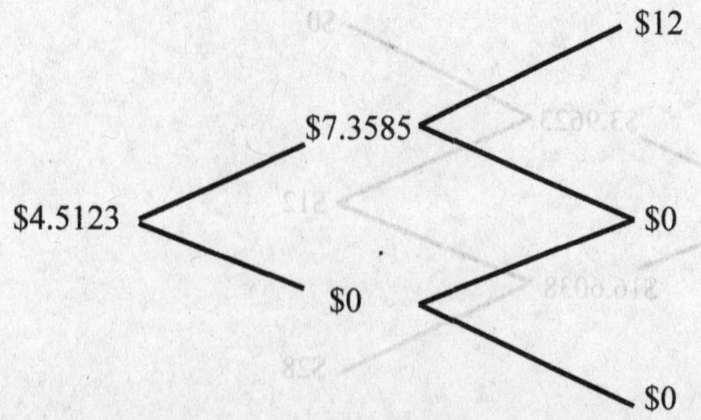

$60\Delta + 1.06B = 7.3585$
$40\Delta + 1.06B = 0$

Solve the equations for Δ and B $\Rightarrow \Delta = 0.3679$, $B = -13.8840$

Therefore, the $C = 50\Delta + B = 4.5123$

b. The value of a call option at expiration is: Max(0, X − S)

$P_{uu} = \text{Max}(0, \$60 - \$72) = \$0$

$P_{ud} = P_{du} = \text{Max}(0, \$60 - \$48) = \$12$

$P_{dd} = \text{Max}(0, \$60 - \$32) = \$28$

We use a portfolio combining the underlying stock and bond to replicate the payoffs: $S_T\Delta + (1+ r_f)B = \text{Payoff}$

$72\Delta + 1.06B = 0$
$48\Delta + 1.06B = 12$

Solve the equations for Δ and B $\Rightarrow \Delta = -0.5$, $B = 33.9623$

Therefore, the $P_u = 60\Delta + B = 3.9623$

$48\Delta + 1.06B = 12$
$32\Delta + 1.06B = 28$

Solve the equations for Δ and B $\Rightarrow \Delta = -1$, $B = 56.6038$

Therefore, the $P_d = 40\Delta + B = 16.6038$

The two-period binomial tree for the option values is as follows:

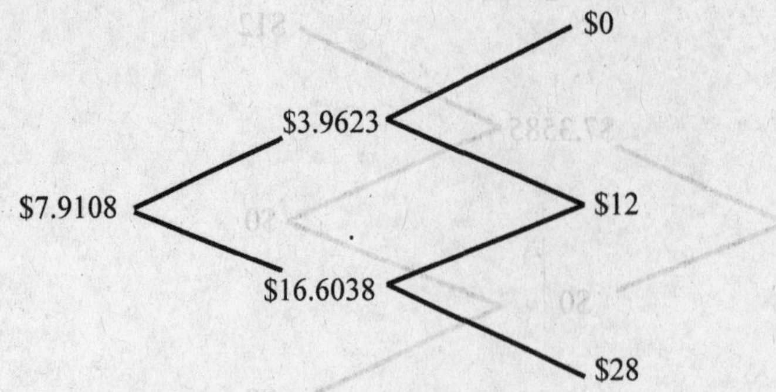

$60\Delta + 1.06B = 3.9623$
$40\Delta + 1.06B = 16.6038$

Solve the equations for Δ and B $\Rightarrow \Delta = -0.6321$, $B = 39.5158$

Therefore, the $C = 50\Delta + B = 7.9108$

c. The put-call parity relationship is:

$C - P = S_0 - PV(X)$

Substituting the values for this problem:

$\$4.5123 - \$7.9108 = -\$3.3985$
$\$50.00 - \$60/(1.06)^2 = -\$3.3998$

Despite a small rounding error, the put-call parity relationship stands.

CHAPTER 17
FUTURES MARKETS AND RISK MANAGEMENT

1. Selling a contract is a short position. If the price rises, you lose money.
   Loss = (1,250 − 1,200) × $250 = $12,500

2. Futures price = $S_0(1+r_f-d)^T$ = $1,200 × (1 + .01 − .02) = $1,188

3. The theoretical futures price = $S_0(1+r_f)^T$ = $1,700 × (1 + .02) = $1,734. At $1,641, the gold futures contract is underpriced. To benefit from the mispricing, we sell gold short $1,700 today, lend the money at risk-free rate, and long gold future of $1,641. One year from today we'll have cash inflows from the loan of $1,734 and the proceeds from future position of (S_T −$1,641), and outflow to close the short position of gold at spot price (−S_T). The arbitrage profit is thus $1,734 + ($S_T$ −$1,641) + (−$S_T$) = $93.

   This answer presumes that that the commodity is available for short sale without fees and with full access to the proceeds of the short sale. In real-world practice, failure to satisfy these conditions may limit the apparent arbitrage opportunity.

4. Margin = $115,098 × .15 = $17,264.70
   Total $ Loss = $115,098 −$108,000 = $7,098
   Total % Loss = $7,098/$17,264.70 = 41.11 % loss

5.
   a. The required margin is 1,164.50 × $250 × .10 = $29,112.50

   b. Total Return = (1,200 −1,164.50) × $250 = $8,875
      Percentage Return = $8,875/$29,112.5 = .3049 = 30.49%

   c. Total Loss = [1,164.5 × (1 −.01)] − 1,164.5) × $250 = −$2,911.25
      Percentage Loss = −$2,911.25/$29,112.5 = − .10 or 10% loss

6. The ability to buy on margin is one advantage of futures. Another is the ease with which one can alter holdings of the asset. This is especially important if one is dealing in commodities, for which the futures market is far more liquid than the spot market so that transaction costs are lower in the futures market.

7. Short selling results in an immediate cash inflow, whereas the short futures position does not:

Action	Initial Cash Flow	Cash Flow at Time T
Short sale	$+S_0$	$-S_T$
Short futures	0	$F_0 - S_T$

8. $F_0 = S_0 (1 + r_f - d) = \$1,200 \times (1 + .03 - .02) = \$1,212$

9. According to the parity relationship, the proper price for December futures is:

$$F_{Dec} = F_{June} \times (1 + r_f)^{1/2} = \$1,646.30 \times (1.04)^{1/2} = \$1,678.90$$

The listed futures price for December is too low relative to the June price. We could long the December contract and short the June contract to exploit the opportunity.

10.

a.

Action	Initial Cash Flow	Cash Flow at Time T
Buy stock	$-S_0$	$S_T + D$
Short futures	0	$F_0 - S_T$
Borrow	S_0	$-S_0(1 + r)$
Total	0	$F_0 + D - S_0(1 + r)$

b. The net initial investment is zero, whereas the final cash flow is not zero. Therefore, in order to avoid arbitrage opportunities, the equilibrium futures price will be the final cash flow equated to zero. Accordingly:

$$F_0 = S_0 (1 + r) - D$$

c. Noting that $D = (d \times S_0)$, we substitute and rearrange to find that:

$$F_0 = S_0 (1 + r - d)$$

11.

a. $F_0 = S_0 (1 + r_f)^T = \$150 \times 1.03 = \$154.50$

b. $F_0 = S_0 (1 + r_f)^T = \$150 \times (1.03)^3 = \$163.91$

c. $F_0 = S_0 (1 + r_f)^T = \$150 \times (1.05)^3 = \$173.64$

12.

a. Use the spreadsheet template from **www.mhhe.com/bkm**, input spot price, dividend yield, interest rate, and the dates, and get the expected future prices of each maturity dates.

Spot price	1200		
Income yield (%)	2	Futures prices versus maturity	
Interest rate (%)	1		
Today's date	2012/1/1	Spot price	1,200.00
Maturity date 1	2012/2/14	Futures 1	1,198.56
Maturity date 2	2012/5/21	Futures 2	1,195.32
Maturity date 3	2012/11/18	Futures 3	1,189.43
Time to maturity 1	0.12		
Time to maturity 2	0.39		
Time to maturity 3	0.88		

b. If the risk-free rate is higher than the dividend yield, the future price with longer maturity will be higher than those with shorter maturities.

Spot price	1200		
Income yield (%)	2	Futures prices versus maturity	
Interest rate (%)	3		
Today's date	2012/1/1	Spot price	1,200.00
Maturity date 1	2012/2/14	Futures 1	1,201.43
Maturity date 2	2012/5/21	Futures 2	1,204.65
Maturity date 3	2012/11/18	Futures 3	1,210.56
Time to maturity 1	0.12		
Time to maturity 2	0.39		
Time to maturity 3	0.88		

13.

a. $F_0 = S_0 (1 + r_f) = \$120 \times 1.06 = \$127.20$

b. The stock price falls to: $120 × (1 − .03) = $116.40
The futures price falls to: $116.40 × 1.06 = $123.384
The investor loses: ($127.20 − $123.384) × 1,000 = $3,816.00

c. The percentage return is: −$3,816/$12,000 = −31.8%

14.

a. The initial futures price is:

$F_0 = S_0 (1 + r_f - d) = 800 \times (1 + .005 - .002)^{12} = 829.28$

In one month, the futures price will be:

$F_0 = 810 \times (1 + .005 - .002)^{11} = 837.13$

The increase in the futures price is 7.85, so the cash flow will be:

7.85 × $250 = $1,962.50

b. The holding period return is: $1,962.50/$10,000 = .1963 = 19.63%

15. The parity value of F_0 is: $S_0 (1 + r_f - d) = 1{,}200 \times (1 + .03 - .02) = 1{,}212$
The actual futures price is 1,233, overpriced by 21.

Action	Initial Cash Flow	Cash Flow at Time T (one year)
Buy index	−1,200	S_T + (.02 × 1,200) [CF includes 2% dividend]
Short futures	0	1,233 −S_T
Borrow	1,200	−1,200 × 1.03
Total	0	21 [A riskless cash flow]

16.

a. The current yield on bonds (coupon interest divided by price) plays the role of the dividend yield.

b. When the yield curve is upward sloping, the current yield exceeds the short-term interest rate. Hence, net cost of carry is negative, and distant futures prices will be lower than near-term futures prices.

c. In Figure 17.1, the longer-term T-bond contracts do in fact sell at lower prices than near-term contracts.

17. The actual dollar cost of funds will be determined by LIBOR. The percentage cost, however, will always be 1% above LIBOR since the company sold its 7% fixed rate loan for 6% in the SWAP. Since firms typically only enter into SWAPs to create a net gain, their natural floating rate is likely above LIBOR + 1%.

18. The speculator who believes interest rates will fall wants to pay the floating rate and receive the fixed rate. This investor will benefit if the short-term reference rate does in fact fall, resulting in an increase in the net cash flow from the swap.

19. The dollar value of the index is: $\$250 \times 1{,}200 = \$300{,}000$
Therefore, the position requires margin of $30,000.

If the futures price decreases by 1% to 1,188, then the decline in the futures price is 12.
The decrease in the margin account would be: $12 \times \$250 = \$3{,}000$
This is a percent return of: $-\$3{,}000/\$30{,}000 = -10\%$
Cash in the margin account is now: $\$30{,}000 - \$3{,}000 = \$27{,}000$

20.

a. The initial futures price is: $F_0 = 1{,}000 \times (1 + .002 - .001)^{12} = 1{,}012.07$

In one month, the maturity of the contract will be only 11 months, so the futures price will be: $F_0 = 1{,}020 \times (1 + .002 - .001)^{11} = 1{,}031.28$

The increase in the futures price is 19.21, so the cash flow will be:

$19.21 \times \$250 = \$4{,}802.50$

b. The holding period return is: $\$4{,}802.50/\$10{,}000 = .48025 = 48.03\%$

21. The Treasurer would like to buy the bonds today, but cannot. As a proxy for this purchase, T-bond futures contracts can be purchased. If rates do in fact fall, the Treasurer will have to buy back the bonds for the sinking fund at prices higher than the prices at which they could be purchased today. However, the gains on the futures contracts will offset this higher cost.

22. She must sell: $\$1 \text{ million} \times \frac{8}{10} = \$.8$ million of T-bonds

23. If yield changes on the bond and the contracts are each 1 basis point, then the bond value will change by:

$\$10{,}000{,}000 \times .0001 \times 8 = \$8{,}000$

The contract will result in a cash flow of:

$100,000 × .0001 × 6 = $60

Therefore, the manager should sell: 8,000/60 = 133 contracts
The manager sells the contracts because she needs the profits on the contract to offset losses as a bond issuer if interest rates increase.

24.

a. Each contract is for $250 times the index, currently valued at 1,200. Therefore, each contract has the same exposure to the market as $300,000 worth of stock, and to hedge a $6 million portfolio, you need:
$6 million/$300,000 = 20 contracts

b. The parity value of the futures price = 1,200 × (1 + .02 − .01) = 1,212

Action	Initial Cash Flow	Cash Flow at Time T
Short 20 futures contracts	0	$20 \times \$250 \times (1{,}212 - S_T)$
Buy 5,000 "shares" of index (each share equals $1,200)	−$6 million	$(\$6 \text{ million} \times .01) + (5{,}000 \times S_T)$
Total	−$6 million	$6.12 million [which is riskless]

Thus the riskless return on the hedged strategy equals the T-bill rate of 2%.

c. Now, the stock swings only .6 as much as the market index. Hence, we need .6 as many contracts as in part (a): .60 × 20 = 12 contracts

In this case, however, the hedged position will not be riskless since the portfolio is exposed to the unsystematic risk. The beta of the hedged position is zero since all the systematic risk is hedged.

25. The firm should enter a swap in which it pays a 7% fixed rate and receives LIBOR on $10 million of notional principal. Its total payments will be as follows:

Interest payments on bond:	(LIBOR + .01) × $10 million par value
Net cash flow from swap:	(.07 − LIBOR) × $10 million notional principal
TOTAL	.08 × $10 million

The interest rate on the synthetic fixed-rate loan is 8%.

26.

a. From parity: $F_0 = S_0 (1 + r_f - d) = [1{,}200 \times (1 + .03)] - 15 = 1{,}221$
Actual F_0 is 1,218, so the futures price is $3 below its "proper" or parity value.

b. Buy the relatively cheap futures and sell the relatively expensive stock.

Action	Initial Cash Flow	Cash Flow at Time T
Short stock	+1,200	$-(S_T + 15)$
Buy futures	0	$S_T - 1{,}218$
Lend $1,200	−1,200	+1,236
Total	0	3

c. If you do not receive the proceeds of the short sales, then the $1,200 cannot be invested to gain interests at the risk-free rate. Thus, the proceeds from the strategy in part (b) becomes negative: the arbitrage opportunity no longer exists.

Action	Initial Cash Flow	Cash Flow at Time T
Short stock	+1,200	$-(S_T + 15)$
Buy futures	0	$S_T - 1{,}218$
Place $1,200 in margin account	−1,200	+1,200
Total	0	−33

d. If we call the original futures price F_0, then the proceeds from the long-futures, short-stock strategy are:

Action	Initial Cash Flow	Cash Flow at Time T
Short stock	+1,200	$-(S_T + 15)$
Buy futures	0	$S_T - F_0$
Place $1,200 in margin account	−1,200	+1,200
Total	0	$1{,}185 - F_0$

Therefore, F_0 can be as low as 1,185 without giving rise to an arbitrage opportunity. On the other hand, if F_0 is higher than the parity value (1,218) an arbitrage opportunity (buy stocks, sell futures) will open up. There is no short-selling cost in this case. Therefore, the no-arbitrage region is: $1{,}185 \le F_0 \le 1{,}218$

CFA 1

Answer:

a. Contrasts

CFA 2

Answer:

d. Maintenance margin

CFA 3

Answer:

Total losses may amount to $3,500 before a margin call is received. Each contract calls for delivery of 5,000 ounces. Before a margin call is received, the price per ounce can increase by: $3,500/5,000 = $ .70

The futures price at this point would be: $28 + $ .70 = $28.70

CFA 4

Answer:

a. Take a short position in T-bond futures, to offset interest rate risk. If rates increase, the loss on the bond will be offset by gains on the futures.

b. Again, a short position in T-bond futures will offset the bond price risk.

c. If bond prices increase, you will need extra cash to purchase the bond with the anticipated contribution. Thus, a long futures position on the bond will generate a profit if prices increase.

CFA 5

Answer:

The important distinction between a futures contract and an options contract is that the futures contract is an obligation. When an investor purchases or sells a futures contract, the investor has an obligation to accept or deliver, respectively, the underlying commodity on the delivery date. In contrast, the buyer of an option contract is not obligated to accept or deliver the underlying commodity but instead has the right, or choice, to accept or deliver the underlying commodity anytime during the life of the contract.

Futures and options modify a portfolio's risk in different ways. Buying or selling a futures contract affects a portfolio's upside risk and downside risk by a similar magnitude. This is commonly referred to as symmetrical impact. On the other hand, the addition of a call or put option to a portfolio does not affect a portfolio's upside risk and downside risk to a similar magnitude. Unlike futures contracts, the impact of options on the risk profile of a portfolio is asymmetrical.

CFA 6

Answer:

a. The strategy that would take advantage of the arbitrage opportunity is a Reverse Cash and Carry. A Reverse Cash and Carry arbitrage opportunity results when the following relationship does not hold true: $F_{0,t} \geq S_0 (1 + C)$

If the futures price is less than the spot price plus the cost of carrying the goods to the futures delivery date, an arbitrage in the form of a Reverse Cash and Carry exists. A trader would be able to sell the asset short, use the proceeds to lend at the prevailing interest rate, and buy the asset for future delivery. At the future delivery, the trader then collects the proceeds from the loan with interest, accepts delivery of the asset, and covers the short position of the commodity.

b.

Opening Transaction Now	
Sell the spot commodity short	+$120.00
Buy the commodity futures expiring in 1 year	0.00
Contract to lend $120 at 8% for 1 year	−$120.00
Total cash flow	$ 0.00

Closing Transaction One Year from Now	
Accept delivery on expiring futures	−$125.00
Cover short commodity position	0.00
Collect on loan of $120	+$129.60
Total arbitrage profit	$ 4.60

CFA 7

Answer:

a. In an interest rate swap, one firm exchanges (or "swaps") a fixed payment for another payment that is tied to the level of interest rates. One party in the swap agreement pays a fixed interest rate on the notional principal of the swap. The other party pays the floating interest rate (typically LIBOR) on the same notional principal. For example, in a swap with a fixed rate of 8% and notional principal of $100 million, the *net* cash payment for the firm that pays the fixed rate and receives the floating rate would be: (LIBOR − .08) × $100 million

Therefore, if LIBOR exceeds 8%, then this firm receives a payment; if LIBOR is less than 8%, then the firm makes a payment.

b. There are several applications of interest rate swaps. For example, suppose that a portfolio manager is holding a portfolio of long-term bonds, but is worried that interest rates might increase, causing a capital loss on the portfolio. This portfolio manager can enter a swap to pay a fixed rate and receive a floating rate, thereby converting the holdings into a synthetic floating rate portfolio. Or, a pension fund manager might identify some money market securities that are paying excellent yields compared to other comparable-risk short-term securities.

However, the fund manager might believe that such short-term assets are inappropriate for the portfolio. The fund can hold these securities and enter a swap in which the fund receives a fixed rate and pays a floating rate. The fund thus captures the benefit of the advantageous *relative* yields on these securities, but still establishes a portfolio with interest-rate risk characteristics more like those of long-term bonds.

CFA 8

Answer:

a. Delsing should sell stock index futures contracts and buy bond futures contracts. This strategy is justified because buying the bond futures and selling the stock index futures provides the same exposure as buying the bonds and selling the stocks. This strategy assumes high correlations between the movements of the bond futures and bond portfolio and also between the stock index futures and the stock portfolio.

b. Compute the number of contracts in each case as follows:

i. 5 × $200,000,000 × 0.0001 = $100,000

$100,000/97.85 = 1,022 contracts

ii. $200,000,000/($1,378 × 250) = 581 contracts

CFA 9

Answer:

a. Short the contract. As rates rise, prices will fall. Selling the futures contract will benefit from falling prices.

b. In 6 months the bond will accrue $25 of interest, which, when subtracted from the price of 978.40, leaves a bond value of 953.40. This implies a YTM of 5.30%. Assuming the underlying bond on the contract also has a 5% coupon and 10 years to maturity, the YTM on the contract is 4.68%. A drop in the price of the bond implies an increase in the YTM of .30%. If the YTM on the contract increases to 4.98% the contract price in 6 months will be 976.72.

c. The contract drops in price by 47.98, while the bond drops in price 46.60. Both exclude accrued interest. Thus, the combined portfolio will increase in value by 1.38, since the investor has a short position in the contract.

CHAPTER 18
PORTFOLIO PERFORMANCE EVALUATION

1.

a. Possibly. Alpha alone does not determine which portfolio has a larger Sharpe ratio. Sharpe measure is the primary factor, since it tells us the real return per unit of risk. We only invest if the Sharpe measure is higher. The standard deviation of an investment and its correlation with the benchmark are also important. Thus, positive alpha is not a sufficient condition for a managed portfolio to offer a higher Sharpe measure than the passive benchmark.

b. Yes. It is possible for a positive alpha to exist, but the Sharpe measure declines. Thus, we would experience inferior performance.

2. Maybe. Provided the addition of funds creates an efficient frontier with the existing investments, and assuming the Sharpe measure increases, the answer is yes. Otherwise, no.

3. No. The M-squared is an equivalent representation of the Sharpe measure, with the added difference of providing a risk-adjusted measure of performance that can be easily interpreted as a differential return relative to a benchmark. Thus, it provides in a different format the same information as the Sharpe measure.

4. Definitely the FF model. Research shows that passive investments (e.g., a market index portfolio) will appear to have a zero alpha when evaluated using the multi-index model but not when using the single-index one. The nonzero alpha appears even in the absence of superior performance. Thus, the single-index alpha can be misleading.

5.

a.

	E(r)	σ	β
Portfolio A	11%	10%	.8
Portfolio B	14%	31%	1.5
Market index	12%	20%	1.0
Risk-free asset	6%	0%	0.0

The alphas for the two portfolios are:

$$\alpha_A = E(r_A) - \text{required return predicted by CAPM}$$

$$= .11 - [.06 + .8 \times (.12 - .06)] = 0.2\%$$

$$\alpha_B = E(r_B) - \text{required return predicted by CAPM}$$

$$= .14 - [.06 + 1.5 \times (.12 - .06)] = -1.0\%$$

Ideally, you would want to take a long position in Portfolio A and a short position in Portfolio B.

b. If you hold only one of the two portfolios, then the Sharpe measure is the appropriate criterion:

$$S_A = \frac{E(r_A) - r_f}{\sigma_A} = \frac{.11 - .06}{.10} = .5$$

$$S_B = \frac{E(r_B) - r_f}{\sigma_B} = \frac{.14 - .06}{.31} = .26$$

Therefore, using the Sharpe criterion, Portfolio A is preferred.

6. We first distinguish between timing ability and selection ability. The intercept of the scatter diagram is a measure of stock selection ability. If the manager tends to have a positive excess return even when the market's performance is merely "neutral" (i.e., the market has zero excess return) then we conclude that the manager has, on average, made good stock picks. In other words, stock selection must be the source of the positive excess returns.

   Timing ability is indicated by the curvature of the plotted line. Lines which become steeper as you move to the right of the graph show good timing ability. The steeper slope shows that the manager maintained higher portfolio sensitivity to market swings (i.e., a higher beta) in periods when the market performed well. This ability to choose more market-sensitive securities in anticipation of market upturns is the essence of good timing. In contrast, a declining slope as you move to the right indicates that the portfolio was more sensitive to the market when the market performed poorly and less sensitive to the market when the market performed well. This indicates poor timing.

   We can therefore classify performance ability for the four managers as follows:

	Selection Ability	Timing Ability
A	Bad	Good
B	Good	Good
C	Good	Bad
D	Bad	Bad

7.

a. Actual: $(.70 \times .02) + (.20 \times .01) + (.10 \times .005) = .0165 = 1.65\%$

   Bogey: $(.60 \times .025) + (.30 \times .012) + (.10 \times .005) = .0191 = 1.91\%$

   *Under*performance $= .0191 - .0165 = .0026 = .26\%$

b. *Security Selection*:

Market	(1) Portfolio Performance	(2) Index Performance	(3) Excess Performance	(4) Manager's Portfolio Weight	(5) = (3) × (4) Contribution
Equity	2.0%	2.5%	−.5%	.70	−.35%
Bonds	1.0%	1.2%	−.2%	.20	−.04%
Cash	.5%	.5%	0%	.10	.00%
			Contribution of Security Selection:		−.39%

c. *Asset Allocation*:

Market	(1) Actual Weight	(2) Benchmark Weight	(3) Excess Weight	(4) Index Return	(5) = (3) × (4) Contribution
Equity	.70	.60	.10	2.5%	.25%
Bonds	.20	.30	−.10	1.2%	−.12%
Cash	.10	.10	0	.5%	0%
			Contribution of Asset Allocation:		.13%

Summary	
Security selection	−.39%
Asset allocation	.13%
Excess performance	−.26%

8. Support: A manager could be a better forecaster in one scenario than another. For example, a high-beta manager will do better in up markets and worse in down markets. Therefore, we should observe performance over an entire cycle. Also, to the extent that observing a manager over an entire cycle increases the number of observations, it would improve the reliability of the measurement.

   Contradict: If we adequately control for exposure to the market (i.e., adjust for beta), then market performance should not affect the relative performance of individual managers. It is therefore not necessary to wait for an entire market cycle to pass before you evaluate a manager.

9. It does, to some degree. If those manager groups are sufficiently homogeneous with respect to style, then relative performance is a decent benchmark. However, one would like to be able to adjust for the additional variation in style or risk choice that remains among managers in any comparison group. In addition, investors might prefer an "investable" alternative such as a passive index to which they can compare a manager's performance. After all, passive investors do not have the choice of investing in "the median manager," since the identity of that manager is not known until *after* the investment period.

10. The manager's alpha is: Actual return − Required return predicted by CAPM
$= .1 - [.06 + .5 \times (.14 - .06)] = 0$
The manager didn't show superior performance in the particular year.

11. a. The most likely reason for a difference in ranking is due to the absence of diversification in Fund A. The Sharpe ratio measures excess return per unit of total risk, while the Treynor ratio measures excess return per unit of systematic risk. Since Fund A performed well on the Treynor measure and so poorly on the Sharpe Measure, it seems that the fund carries a greater amount of unsystematic risk, meaning it is not well-diversified and systematic risk is not the relevant risk measure.

12. The within sector selection calculates the return according to security selection. This is done by summing the weight of the security in the portfolio multiplied by the return of the security in the portfolio minus the return of the security in the benchmark:
Selection effect = (Portfolio return − Bogey return) × Portfolio weight
Large-cap growth: $(.17 - .16) \times .6 = .006 = .6\%$
Mid-cap growth: $(.24 - .26) \times .15 = -.003 = -.3\%$
Small-cap growth: $(.20 - .18) \times .25 = .005 = .5\%$
$\Rightarrow$ Total effect: $.006 + (-.003) + .005 = .008 = .8\%$

13. Primo return $= 0.6 \times 17\% + 0.15 \times 24\% + 0.25 \times 20\% = 18.8\%$

Benchmark return $= 0.5 \times 16\% + 0.4 \times 26\% + 0.1 \times 18\% = 20.2\%$

Primo − Benchmark $= 18.8\% - 20.2\% = -1.4\%$ (Primo underperformed benchmark)

To isolate the impact of Primo's pure sector allocation decision relative to the benchmark, multiply the weight difference between Primo and the benchmark portfolio in each sector by the benchmark sector returns:

$$(0.6 - 0.5) \times (.16) + (0.15 - 0.4) \times (.26) + (0.25 - 0.1) \times (.18) = -2.2\%$$

To isolate the impact of Primo's pure security selection decisions relative to the benchmark, multiply the return differences between Primo and the benchmark for each sector by Primo's weightings:

$$(.17 - .16) \times (.6) + (.24 - .26) \times (.15) + (.2 - 0.18) \times (.25) = 0.8\%$$

14. Because the passively managed fund is mimicking the benchmark, the R^2 of the regression should be very high (and thus probably higher than the actively managed fund).

15. a. The euro appreciated while the pound depreciated. Primo had a greater stake in the euro-denominated assets relative to the benchmark, resulting in a positive currency allocation effect. British stocks outperformed Dutch stocks resulting in a negative market allocation effect for Primo. Finally, within the Dutch and British investments, Primo outperformed with the Dutch investments and under-performed with the

British investments. Since they had a greater proportion invested in Dutch stocks relative to the benchmark, we assume that they had a positive security allocation effect in total. However, this cannot be known for certain with this information. It is the best choice, however.

16.

a. $S_P = \dfrac{E(r_P) - r_f}{\sigma_P} = \dfrac{.102 - .02}{.37} = .2216$

$S_M = \dfrac{E(r_M) - r_f}{\sigma_M} = \dfrac{-.225 - .02}{.44} = -.5568$

b. To compute M^2 measure, blend the Miranda Fund with a position in T-Bills such that the "adjusted" portfolio has the same volatility as the market index. Using the data, the position in the Miranda Fund should be .44/.37 = 1.1892 and the position in T-Bills should be 1 − 1.1892 = −.1892. (assuming borrowing at the risk free rate)

The adjusted return is: $r_{P^*} = (1.1892)\times 10.2\% - (.1892)\times 2\% = .1175 = 11.75\%$

Calculate the difference in the adjusted Miranda Fund return and the benchmark:

$M^2 = r_{P^*} - r_M = 11.75\% - (-22.50\%) = 34.25\%$

[Note: The adjusted Miranda Fund is now 59.46% equity and 40.54% cash.]

c. $\dfrac{r_P - r_f}{\beta_P} \rightarrow T_{Miranda} = \dfrac{.102 - .02}{1.10} = .0745 \qquad T_{S\&P} = \dfrac{-.225 - .02}{1.00} = -.245$

d. $\alpha_P = E(r_P) - \{r_f + \beta_P\,[E(r_M) - r_f]\} = .102 - [.02 + 1.10 \times (-.225 - .02)] = .3515$

17. The spreadsheet below displays the monthly returns and excess returns for the Vanguard U.S. Growth Fund, the Vanguard U.S. Value Fund and the S&P 500.

	Total monthly returns				Excess Returns		
Month	Vanguard	Value Fund	S&P	T-bills	Vanguard	Value Fund	S&P
Jan-04	1.52	-0.07	1.35	0.07	1.45	-0.14	1.28
Feb-04	-0.53	-0.99	-1.32	0.06	-0.59	-1.05	-1.38
Mar-04	-2.69	-2.46	-1.89	0.09	-2.78	-2.55	-1.98
Apr-04	0.22	2.52	1.70	0.08	0.14	2.44	1.62
May-04	2.53	1.39	1.85	0.06	2.47	1.33	1.79
Jun-04	-1.93	-7.46	-3.22	0.08	-2.01	-7.54	-3.30
Jul-04	0.99	-0.78	0.25	0.1	0.89	-0.88	0.15
Aug-04	1.52	2.49	1.00	0.11	1.41	2.38	0.89
Sep-04	0.21	1.46	1.29	0.11	0.10	1.35	1.18
Oct-04	5.22	4.66	4.46	0.11	5.11	4.55	4.35
Nov-04	3.24	3.60	3.01	0.15	3.09	3.45	2.86
Dec-04	-2.36	-3.48	-2.24	0.16	-2.52	-3.64	-2.40
Jan-05	3.62	0.79	2.09	0.16	3.46	0.63	1.93
Feb-05	-2.33	-2.86	-1.83	0.16	-2.49	-3.02	-1.99
Mar-05	-2.68	-2.41	-1.87	0.21	-2.89	-2.62	-2.08
Apr-05	4.08	7.13	3.22	0.21	3.87	6.92	3.01
May-05	2.25	0.51	0.15	0.24	2.01	0.27	-0.09
Jun-05	3.55	5.28	3.82	0.23	3.32	5.05	3.59
Jul-05	-1.85	-0.85	-0.93	0.24	-2.09	-1.09	-1.17
Aug-05	0.38	1.34	0.80	0.3	0.08	1.04	0.50
Sep-05	-1.88	0.30	-2.36	0.29	-2.17	0.01	-2.65
Oct-05	2.87	5.04	4.39	0.27	2.60	4.77	4.12
Nov-05	0.93	0.46	-0.19	0.31	0.62	0.15	-0.50
Dec-05	3.41	3.30	2.41	0.32	3.09	2.98	2.09
Jan-06	0.00	-1.82	0.57	0.35	-0.35	-2.17	0.22
Feb-06	0.71	0.34	1.65	0.34	0.37	0.00	1.31
Mar-06	0.53	-0.45	1.26	0.37	0.16	-0.82	0.89
Apr-06	-3.00	-5.84	-3.01	0.36	-3.36	-6.20	-3.37
May-06	-0.27	-1.55	0.26	0.43	-0.70	-1.98	-0.17
Jun-06	1.09	-2.36	0.45	0.4	0.69	-2.76	0.05
Jul-06	2.70	3.60	2.18	0.4	2.30	3.20	1.78
Aug-06	2.63	2.87	2.70	0.42	2.21	2.45	2.28
Sep-06	2.56	1.92	3.16	0.41	2.15	1.51	2.75
Oct-06	0.75	1.94	1.99	0.41	0.34	1.53	1.58
Nov-06	2.32	0.22	0.77	0.42	1.90	-0.20	0.35
Dec-06	1.86	2.18	1.51	0.4	1.46	1.78	1.11
Jan-07	-2.30	-1.69	-1.96	0.44	-2.74	-2.13	-2.40
Feb-07	0.81	0.89	1.16	0.38	0.43	0.51	0.78
Mar-07	3.87	2.92	4.42	0.43	3.44	2.49	3.99
Apr-07	3.65	3.37	3.39	0.44	3.21	2.93	2.95

May-07	-2.02	-1.14	-1.46	0.41	-2.43	-1.55	-1.87
Jun-07	-4.74	-0.79	-3.13	0.4	-5.14	-1.19	-3.53
Jul-07	1.12	1.11	1.28	0.4	0.72	0.71	0.88
Aug-07	2.54	4.91	3.88	0.42	2.12	4.49	3.46
Sep-07	0.39	2.19	1.35	0.32	0.07	1.87	1.03
Oct-07	-5.86	-3.90	-3.87	0.32	-6.18	-4.22	-4.19
Nov-07	0.25	0.00	-1.13	0.34	-0.09	-0.34	-1.47
Dec-07	-5.39	-10.34	-6.04	0.27	-5.66	-10.61	-6.31
Jan-08	-2.67	-2.38	-2.58	0.21	-2.88	-2.59	-2.79
Feb-08	-0.89	-0.06	-0.90	0.13	-1.02	-0.19	-1.03
Mar-08	5.64	6.32	4.77	0.17	5.47	6.15	4.60
Apr-08	1.44	3.00	1.51	0.17	1.27	2.83	1.34
May-08	-7.18	-6.25	-8.35	0.17	-7.35	-6.42	-8.52
Jun-08	-1.80	-0.40	-0.90	0.17	-1.97	-0.57	-1.07
Jul-08	1.37	0.45	1.55	0.15	1.22	0.30	1.40
Aug-08	-7.50	-11.63	-9.42	0.12	-7.62	-11.75	-9.54
Sep-08	-18.16	-15.45	-16.52	0.15	-18.31	-15.60	-16.67
Oct-08	-7.16	-7.93	-6.96	0.08	-7.24	-8.01	-7.04
Nov-08	2.70	0.57	0.99	0.02	2.68	0.55	0.97
Dec-08	-10.76	-4.49	-8.22	0.09	-10.85	-4.58	-8.31
				Average	-0.59	-0.60	-0.55
			b	SD	4.05	4.21	3.81
			c	Beta	1.03	1.02	1.00
			d	Sharpe rat	-0.15	-0.14	-0.14
				Alpha	-0.03	-0.04	0.00
				Treynor	-0.57	-0.58	-0.55

a. The excess returns are noted in the spreadsheet.

b. The standard deviations for the U.S Growth Fund and the U.S. Value Fund are 4.21% and 4.05%, respectively, as shown in the Excel spreadsheet above.

c. The betas for the U.S. Growth Fund and the U.S. Value Fund are 1.02 and 1.03, respectively, as shown in the Excel spreadsheets below.

d. The formulas for the three measures are below and results listed above.

Sharpe: $$\frac{E(r_P) - r_f}{\sigma_P}$$

Treynor: $$\frac{E(r_P) - r_f}{\beta_P}$$

Jensen: $$\alpha_P = E(r_P) - \{r_f + \beta_P\,[E(r_M) - r_f]\}$$

SUMMARY OUTPUT Vanguard

Regression Statistics	
Multiple R	0.97
R Square	0.94
Adjusted R Square	0.94
Standard Error	1.02
Observations	60.00

ANOVA

	df	*SS*	*MS*	*F*
Regression	1.00	907.97	907.97	876.67
Residual	58.00	60.07	1.04	
Total	59.00	968.04		

	Coefficients	*Standard Error*	*t Stat*	*P-value*
Intercept	(0.03)	0.13	(0.22)	0.83
S&P	1.03	0.03	29.61	0.00

SUMMARY OUTPUT Value Fund

Regression Statistics	
Multiple R	0.93
R Square	0.86
Adjusted R Square	0.85
Standard Error	1.61
Observations	60.00

ANOVA

	df	*SS*	*MS*	*F*
Regression	1.00	896.12	896.12	343.89
Residual	58.00	151.14	2.61	
Total	59.00	1,047.26		

	Coefficients	*Standard Error*	*t Stat*	*P-value*
Intercept	(0.04)	0.21	(0.17)	0.86
S&P	1.02	0.06	18.54	0.00

18. See the Black-Scholes formula. Substitute:

Current stock price = S_0 = \$1.0

Exercise price = $X = (1 + r_f) = 1.01$

Standard deviation = $\sigma = .055$

Risk-free interest rate = $r_f = .01$

Time to maturity of option = $T = 1$

Recall that ln(1 + y) is approximately equal to y, for small y, and that $N(-x) = [1 - N(x)]$. Then the value of a call option on \$1 of the equity portfolio, with exercise price $X = (1 + r_f)$, is:

$C = 2N(\sigma/2) - 1$

$N(\sigma/2)$ is the cumulative standard normal density for the value of half the standard deviation of the equity portfolio.

$C = 2N(.0275) - 1$

Interpolating from the standard normal table:

$C = 2 \times [.5080 + .375 \times (.5160 - .5080)] - 1 = .0220 = 2.2\%$

Hence the added value of a perfect timing strategy is 2.2% per month.

19.

a. Using the relative frequencies to estimate the conditional probabilities P_1 and P_2 for timers A and B, we find:

	Timer A	Timer B
P_1	78/135 = 0.58	86/135 = 0.64
P_2	57/92 = 0.62	50/92 = 0.54
$P^* = P_1 + P_2 - 1$	0.20	0.18

The data suggest that timer A is the better forecaster.

b. Use the following equation and the previous answer to value the imperfect timing services of Timer A and Timer B:

$C(P^*) = C(P_1 + P_2 - 1)$

$C_A(P^*) = .022 \times .20 = .0044 = .44\%$ per month

$C_B(P^*) = .022 \times .18 = .0040 = .40\%$ per month

Timer B's added value is greater by 4 basis points per month.

CFA 1

Answer:

d. Russell 2000 Index

CFA 2

Answer:

a. $\alpha_A = .24 - [.12 + 1.0 \times (.21 - .12)] = 3.0\%$

$\alpha_B = .30 - [.12 + 1.5 \times (.21 - .12)] = 4.5\%$

b. (i) The managers may have been trying to time the market. In that case, the SCL of the portfolios may be non-linear.

(ii) One year of data is too small a sample.

(iii) The portfolios may have significantly different levels of diversification. If both have the same risk-adjusted return, the less diversified portfolio has a higher exposure to risk because of its higher diversifiable risk. Since the above measure adjusts for systematic risk only, it does not tell the entire story.

CFA 3

Answer:

a. Indeed, the one year results were terrible, but one year is a poor statistical base from which to draw inferences. Moreover, the fund manager was directed to adopt a long-term horizon. The Board specifically instructed the investment manager to give priority to long term results.

b. The sample of pension funds held a much larger share in equities compared to the Alpine pension fund. The stock and bond indexes indicate that equity returns significantly exceeded bond returns. The Alpine fund manager was explicitly directed to hold down risk, investing at most 25% of fund assets in common stocks. (Alpine's beta was also somewhat defensive.) Alpine should not be held responsible for an asset allocation policy dictated by the client.

c. Over the five-year period, Alpine's alpha, which measures risk-adjusted performance compared to the market, was positive:

$$\alpha = .133 - [.075 + 0.9 \times (.138 - .075)] = .13\%$$

d. Note that, over the last five years, and particularly the last one year, bond performance has been poor; this is significant because this is the asset class that Alpine had been encouraged to hold. Within this asset class, however, the Alpine fund fared much better than the index, as shown in the last two lines of the table. Moreover, despite the fact that the bond index underperformed both the actuarial return and T-bills, the Alpine fund outperformed both for the five-year period. On a risk-adjusted basis, Alpine's performance *within* each asset class has been superior. The overall disappointing returns were the result of the heavy asset allocation weighting towards bonds, which was the Board's, not the fund manager's, choice.

e. A trustee may not care about the time-weighted return, but that return is more indicative of the manager's performance. After all, the manager has no control over the cash inflow to the fund.

CFA 4

Answer:

a.

Alpha (α): $\alpha_i = E(r_i) - \{r_f + \beta_i [E(r_M) - r_f]\}$	Expected excess return: $E(r_i) - r_f$
$\alpha_A = .20 - [.08 + 1.3 \times (.16 - .08)] = 1.6\%$	$.20 - .08 = 12\%$
$\alpha_B = .18 - [.08 + 1.8 \times (.16 - .08)] = -4.4\%$	$.18 - .08 = 10\%$
$\alpha_C = .17 - [.08 + 0.7 \times (.16 - .08)] = 3.4\%$	$.17 - .08 = 9\%$
$\alpha_D = .12 - [.08 + 1.0 \times (.16 - .08)] = -4.0\%$	$.12 - .08 = 4\%$

Stocks A and C have positive alphas, whereas stocks B and D have negative alphas.

The residual variances are:

$\sigma^2(e_A) = .58^2 = .3364$

$\sigma^2(e_B) = .71^2 = .5041$

$\sigma^2(e_C) = .60^2 = .3600$

$\sigma^2(e_D) = .55^2 = .3025$

b. To construct the optimal risky portfolio, we first determine the optimal active portfolio. Using the Treynor-Black technique, we construct the active portfolio:

	$\frac{\alpha}{\sigma^2(e)}$	$\frac{\alpha/\sigma^2(e)}{\Sigma\alpha_i/\sigma^2(e_i)}$
A	.0476	−0.6136
B	−.0873	1.1261
C	.0944	−1.2185
D	−.1322	1.7060
Total	−.0775	1.0000

Do not be disturbed by the fact that the positive alpha stocks get negative weights and vice versa. The entire position in the active portfolio will turn out to be negative, returning everything to good order.

With these weights, the forecast for the active portfolio is:

$$\alpha = [-.6136 \times .016] + [1.1261 \times (-.044)] - [1.2185 \times .034]$$
$$+ [1.7060 \times (-.04)] = -16.90\%$$

$$\beta = [-.6136 \times 1.3] + [1.1261 \times 1.8] - [1.2185 \times 0.70] + [1.7060 \times 1.0] = 2.08$$

The high beta (higher than any individual beta) results from the short positions in the relatively low beta stocks and the long positions in the relatively high beta stocks.

$$\sigma^2(e) = [(-.6136)^2 \times .3364] + [1.1261^2 \times .5041]$$
$$+ [(-1.2185)^2 \times .36] + [1.7060^2 \times .3025]$$
$$= 2.18082$$

$$\sigma(e) = 147.68\%$$

Here, again, the levered position in stock B [with the high $\sigma^2(e)$] overcomes the diversification effect, and results in a high residual standard deviation. The optimal risky portfolio has a proportion w* in the active portfolio, computed as follows:

$$w_0 = \frac{\alpha/\sigma^2(e)}{[E(r_M) - r_f]/\sigma^2_M} = \frac{-.1690/2.18082}{.08/.23^2} = -.05124$$

The negative position is justified for the reason given earlier.
The adjustment for beta is:

$$w^* = \frac{w_0}{1+(1-\beta)w_0} = \frac{-.05124}{1+(1-2.08)\times(-.05124)} = -.0486$$

Because w* is negative, we end up with a positive position in stocks with positive alphas and vice versa. The position in the index portfolio is:

$1 - (-0.0486) = 1.0486$

c. To calculate Sharpe's measure for the optimal risky portfolio we compute the appraisal ratio for the active portfolio and Sharpe's measure for the market portfolio. The appraisal ratio of the *active portfolio* is:

$A = \alpha/\sigma(e) = -.1690/1.4768 = -.1144$

$A^2 = .0131$

Hence, the square of Sharpe's measure (S) of the *optimized risky portfolio* is:

$$S^2 = S_M^2 + A^2 = \left(\frac{8}{23}\right)^2 + 0.0131 = 0.1341$$

$S = .3662$

Compare this to the market's Sharpe measure: $S_M = 8/23 = .3478$

The difference is: .0184

Note that the only-moderate improvement in performance results from the fact that only a small position is taken in the active portfolio A because of its large residual variance.

We calculate the "Modigliani-squared" (M^2) measure, as follows:

$E(r_{P*}) = r_f + S_P\,\sigma_M = .08 + (.3662 \times .23) = 16.423\%$

$M^2 = E(r_{P*}) - E(r_M) = .16423 - .16 = .423\%$

CHAPTER 19
GLOBALIZATION AND INTERNATIONAL INVESTING

1. False. Investments made in a local currency have the added risk associated with exchange rates. If an investment were made in dollars, the business risk of the firm would be the only risk borne by the investor. If the investment is made in the local currency, the investor takes on both business risk and exchange rate risk.

2. False. In almost all cases the statement is true, however, such diversification benefit is not assured. In those cases where there is no correlation coefficient between the international investment and the U.S. portfolio, a diversification gain cannot be assured. In fact, should a high standard deviation security with zero or one correlation with the U.S. portfolio be added, the overall standard deviation of the portfolio would increase.

3. False. Evidence shows that the minimum-variance portfolio is not the efficient choice. A capitalization-weighted portfolio of world indexes is likely to produce a better risk-return trade-off than the minimum-variance portfolio.

4. True. By hedging, it is possible to virtually eliminate exchange rate risk. The result is a set of returns based on the foreign stocks and not the currency fluctuations.

5.
   a. \$10,000/\$2 = £5,000
      £5,000/£40 = 125 shares
      ⇒The investor can buy 125 shares.

   b. To fill in the table, we use the relation:

      $1 + r(US) = [(1 + r_f(UK)] E_1/E_0$

Price per	Pound-Denominated	Dollar-Denominated Return (%) for Year-End Exchange Rate		
Share (£)	Return (%)	\$1.80/£	\$2.00/£	\$2.20/£
£35	−12.5%	−21.25%	−12.5%	−3.75%
£40	0.0%	−10.00%	0.0%	10.00%
£45	12.5%	1.25%	12.5%	23.75%

   c. The dollar-denominated return equals the pound-denominated return when the exchange rate at year-end equals the exchange rate at initial investment.

6. The standard deviation of the pound-denominated return (using 3 degrees of freedom) is 10.21%. The dollar-denominated return has a standard deviation of 13.10% (using 9 degrees of freedom), greater than the pound-denominated standard deviation. This is due to the addition of exchange rate risk.

7.

a. First we calculate the dollar value of the 125 shares of stock in each scenario. Then we add the profits from the forward contract in each scenario.

Price per Share (£)	Exchange Rate:	Dollar Value of Stock at Given Exchange Rate $1.80/£	$2.00/£	$2.20/£
£35		7,875	8,750	9,625
£40		9,000	10,000	11,000
£45		10,125	11,250	12,375
Profits on Forward Exchange: [= 5000 × (2.10 − E_1)]		1,500	500	−500

Price per Share (£)	Exchange Rate:	Total Dollar Proceeds at Given Exchange Rate $1.80/£	$2.00/£	$2.20/£
£35		9,375	9,250	9,125
£40		10,500	10,500	10,500
£45		11,625	11,750	11,875

Finally, calculate the dollar-denominated rate of return, recalling that the initial investment was $10,000:

Price per Share (£)	Exchange Rate:	Rate of return (%) at Given Exchange Rate $1.80/£	$2.00/£	$2.20/£
£35		−6.25%	−7.50%	−8.75%
£40		5.00%	5.00%	5.00%
£45		16.25%	17.50%	18.75%

b. The standard deviation is now 10.24%. This is lower than the unhedged dollar-denominated standard deviation, and is only slightly higher than the standard deviation of the pound-denominated return.

8. <u>Currency Selection</u>

EAFE: [.30 × (− .10)] + (.10 × 0) + (.60 × .10) = .03 or 3.0%

Manager: [.35 × (− .10)] + (.15 × 0) + (.50 × .10) = .015 or 1.5%

⇒ Loss of 1.5% relative to EAFE.

<u>Country Selection</u>

EAFE: (.30 × .20) + (.10 × .15) + (.60 × .25) = .225 or 22.50%

Manager: (.35 × .20) + (.15 × .15) + (.50 × .25) = .2175 or 21.75%

⇒ Loss of 0.75% relative to EAFE.

<u>Stock Selection</u>

$[(.18 - .20) \times .35] + [(.20 - .15) \times .15] + [(.20 - .25) \times .50] = -.0247$ or -2.45%
$\Rightarrow$ Loss of 2.45% relative to EAFE.

9. $1 + r(US) = [1 + r_f(UK)] \times (F_0/E_0) = 1.08 \times (1.85/1.75) = 1.1417 \Rightarrow r(US) = 14.17\%$

10. You can now purchase: \$10,000/\$1.75 = £5,714.29

    This will grow with 8% interest to £6,171.43. Therefore, to lock in the return, you need to sell forward £6,171.43 at the forward exchange rate.

11. The relationship between the spot and forward exchange rates indicates that the U.S. dollar is expected to appreciate against the Euro. Therefore, the interest rate in the U.S. is higher in order to induce investors to invest in the U.S.

12.

a. Using the relationship:

$$F_0 = E_0 \times \frac{1 + r_f(US)}{1 + r_f(UK)} = 1.50 \times \frac{1.04}{1.03} = 1.515$$

b. If the forward rate is 1.53 dollars per pound, then the forward rate is overpriced. To create an arbitrage profit, use the following strategy:

Action	Initial Cash Flow	Cash Flow at Time T
Enter a contract to sell £1.03 at a (futures price) of F_0 = \$1.53	0	$1.03 \times (1.53 - E_1)$
Borrow \$1.50 in the U.S.	1.50	-1.50×1.04
Convert the borrowed dollars to pounds and lend in the U.K. at a 3% interest rate	−1.50	$1.03 \times E_1$
Total	0	.0159

13.

a. Lend in the U.K.

b. Borrow in the U.S.

c. According to the interest rate parity relationship, the forward rate should be:

$$F_0 = E_0 \times \frac{1 + r_f(US)}{1 + r_f(UK)} = 2.00 \times \frac{1.05}{1.07} = 1.9626$$

The strategy will involve:

Action	Initial Cash Flow	Cash Flow at Time T
Enter a contract to sell £1.07 at a (futures price) of F_0 = $1.97	0	$1.07 \times (1.97 - E_1)$
Borrow $2.00 in the U.S.	2,00	-2.00×1.05
Convert the borrowed dollars to pounds, and lend in the U.K. at a 7% interest rate	−2.00	$1.07 \times E_1$
Total	0	.0079

14. See the results below.

The table below includes all cells of the U.S. index and seven international portfolios from Table 19.9B.
In the following cells, actual performance is replaced by forecasts:
1. Average return on the U.S. portfolio was replaced by a forecast of the U.S. risk premium of 0.5% per month.
2. Alpha values of the seven portfolios were replaced by arbitrary forecast as shown in the column "Alpha."
3. Average return of the seven portfolios were recalculated with the new alpha values.
4. The Information and Sharpe ratios were recalculated with the forecasts.

	Monthly Excess Return		Regression on U.S. returns				Performance	
Market	Av. Return	SD	Correlation	Beta	Alpha	Resid SD	Info ratio	Sharpe
USA	0.50	4.81	1	1	0	0	0	0.10
Large-market portfolio	0.40	4.71	0.79	0.77	0.0100	2.90	0.0035	0.08
EU-dev portfolio	0.55	6.08	0.84	1.06	0.0220	3.33	0.0066	0.09
Aust+FE portfolio	0.54	6.21	0.80	1.04	0.0250	3.68	0.0068	0.09
Europe-dev portfolio	0.43	4.95	0.79	0.82	0.0260	3.01	0.0086	0.09
EM-FE-SA portfolio	0.54	7.10	0.69	1.01	0.0330	5.17	0.0064	0.08
EM- LA portfolio	0.71	7.83	0.78	1.27	0.0700	4.90	0.0143	0.09
EM-Europe portfolio	0.77	9.54	0.70	1.38	0.0750	6.84	0.0110	0.08

Optimization follows the index-model (Treynor-Black) procedure.

	alpha/residual variance	weights in active pf
Large-market portfolio	0.00119	0.08742
EU-dev portfolio	0.00198	0.14530
Aust+FE portfolio	0.00184	0.13511
Europe-dev portfolio	0.00286	0.21010
EM-FE-SA portfolio	0.00123	0.09059
EM- LA portfolio	0.00291	0.21376
EM-Europe portfolio	0.00160	0.11772
sum	0.01363	1.00000

Active pf alpha	0.03969
Active pf residual varianc	2.91188
Active pf info ratio	0.02326
Active pf beta	1.05958
w(0)	0.62981
w*	0.65436 Optimal position in active pf
Optimal position in U.S.	0.34564
Optimal position in pfs	
Large-market port	0.05721
EU-dev portfolio	0.09508
Aust+FE portfolio	0.08841
Europe-dev portfolio	0.13748
EM-FE-SA portfolio	0.05928
EM- LA portfolio	0.13988
EM-Europe portfolio	0.07703
sum	0.65436
Optimal pf Sharpe	0.10660

CFA 1

Answer:

a. We exchange $1 million for foreign currency at the current exchange rate and sell forward the amount of foreign currency we will accumulate 90 days from now. For the yen investment, we initially receive:

$1 million × 133.05 = ¥133.05 million

Invest for 90 days to accumulate:

¥133.05 × [1 + (.076/4)] = ¥135.57795 million

(We divide the quoted 90-day rate by 4, since quoted money market interest rates typically are annualized using simple interest and assuming a 360-day year.)

If we sell this number of yen forward at the forward exchange rate of ¥133.47/dollar, we will end up with:

$$\frac{\$135.57795 \text{ million}}{133.47} = \$1.015793 \text{ million}$$

The 90-day dollar interest rate is 1.5793%.

Similarly, the dollar proceeds from the 90-day Swiss franc investment will be:

$$[\$1 \text{ million} \times 1.526] \times \frac{1+(.086/4)}{1.5348} = \$1.015643 \text{ million}$$

The 90-day dollar interest rate is 1.5643%, almost the same as that in the yen investment.

b. The nearly identical results in either currency are expected and reflect the interest-rate parity relationship. This example thus asserts that the pricing relationships between interest rates and spot and forward exchange rates must make covered investments in any currency equally attractive.

c. The dollar-hedged rate of return on default-free government securities in Japan is 1.5793% and in Switzerland is 1.5643%. Therefore, the 90-day interest rate available on U.S. government securities must be between 1.5643% and 1.5793%. This corresponds to an annual rate between 6.2572% and 6.3172%, which is less than the APR in Japan or Switzerland. (For consistency with our earlier calculations, we annualize the 90-day rate using the convention of the money market, assuming a 360-day year and simple interest). The lower interest rate in the U.S. makes sense, as the relationship between forward and spot exchange rates indicates that the U.S. dollar is expected to appreciate against both the Japanese yen and the Swiss franc.

CFA 2

a. The primary rationale is the opportunity for diversification. Factors that contribute to low correlations of stock returns across national boundaries are:

   i. imperfect correlation of business cycles
   ii. imperfect correlation of interest rates
   iii. imperfect correlation of inflation rates
   iv. exchange rate volatility

b. Obstacles to international investing are:

   i. Availability of information, including insufficient data on which to base investment decisions. It is difficult to interpret and evaluate data that is different in form and/or content than the routinely available and widely understood U.S. data. Also, much foreign data is reported with a considerable lag.

   ii. Liquidity, in terms of the ability to buy or sell, in size and in a timely manner, without affecting the market price. Most foreign exchanges offer (relative to U.S. norms) limited trading, and experience greater price volatility. Moreover, only a (relatively) small number of individual foreign stocks enjoy liquidity comparable to that in the U.S., although this situation is improving steadily.

   iii. Transaction costs, particularly when viewed as a combination of commission plus spread plus market impact costs, are well above U.S. levels in most foreign markets. This, of course, adversely affects return realization.

   iv. Political risk.

   v. Foreign currency risk, although to a great extent, this can be hedged.

c. The asset-class performance data for this particular period reveal that non-U.S. dollar bonds provided a small incremental return advantage over U.S. dollar bonds, but at a considerably higher level of risk. Each category of fixed income assets outperformed the S&P 500 Index measure of U.S. equity results with regard to both risk and return, which is certainly an unexpected outcome. Within the equity area, non-U.S. stocks, represented by the EAFE Index, outperformed U.S. stocks by a considerable margin with only slightly more risk. In contrast to U.S. equities, this asset category performed as it should relative to fixed income assets, providing more return for the higher risk involved.

   Concerning the Account Performance Index, its position on the graph reveals an aggregate outcome that is superior to the sum of its component parts. To some extent, this is due to the beneficial effect on performance resulting from multi-market diversification and the differential covariances involved. In this case, the portfolio manager(s) (apparently) achieved an on-balance positive alpha, adding to total portfolio return by their actions. The addition of international (i.e., non-U.S.) securities to a portfolio that would otherwise have held only domestic (U.S.) securities clearly worked to the advantage of this fund over this time period.

CFA 3

Answer:

The return on the Canadian bond is equal to the sum of:

coupon income +

gain or loss from the premium or discount in the forward rate relative to the spot exchange rate +

capital gain or loss on the bond.

Over the six-month period, the return is:

Coupon + forward premium/discount + capital gain =

$$\frac{7.50\%}{2} + (-0.075\%) + \text{Price change in } \% = 3.00\% + \%\text{ capital gain}$$

The expected semiannual return on the U.S. bond is 3.25%. Since the U.S. bond is selling at par and its yield is expected to remain unchanged, there is no expected capital gain or loss on the U.S. bond. Therefore, in order to provide the same return, the Canadian bond must provide a capital gain of 0.25% (i.e., 1/4 point relative to par value of 100) over and above any expected capital gain on the U.S. bond.

CFA 4

Answer:

a. The following arguments could be made in favor of active management:
Economic diversity: the diversity of the Otunian economy across various sectors may offer the opportunity for the active investor to employ "top down" sector timing strategies.

High transaction costs: very high transaction costs may discourage trading activity by international investors and lead to inefficiencies that may be exploited successfully by active investors.

Good financial disclosure and detailed accounting standards: good financial disclosure and detailed accounting standards may provide the well-trained analyst an opportunity to perform fundamental research analysis in order to identify inefficiently priced securities.

Capital restrictions: restrictions on capital flows may discourage foreign investor participation and serve to segment the Otunian market, thus creating exploitable market inefficiencies for the active investor.

Developing economy and securities market: developing economies and markets are often characterized by inefficiently priced securities and by rapid economic change and growth. The active investor may exploit these characteristics.

Settlement problems: long delays in settling trades by non-residents may serve to discourage international investors, leading to inefficiently priced securities which may be exploited by active management.

The following arguments could be made in favor of indexing:
Economic diversity: economic diversity across a broad sector of industries implies that indexing may provide a diverse representative portfolio that is not subject to the risks associated with concentrated sectors.

High transaction costs: indexing would be favored by the implied lower levels of trading activity and costs.

Settlement problems: indexing would be favored by the implied lower levels of trading activity and settlement requirements.

Financial disclosure and accounting standards: wide public availability of reliable financial information presumably leads to greater market efficiency, reducing the value of both fundamental analysis and active management, and favoring indexing.

Restrictions of capital flows: indexing would be favored by the implied lower levels of trading activity and thus smaller opportunity for regulatory interference.

b. A recommendation for active management would focus on short-term inefficiencies in, and long term prospects for, the developing Otunian markets and economy, inefficiencies and prospects which would not generally be found in more developed markets.

A recommendation for indexing would focus on the factors of economic diversity, high transaction costs, settlement delays, capital flow restrictions, and lower management fees.

CHAPTER 20
HEDGE FUNDS

1. No, a market-neutral hedge fund would not be a good candidate for an investor's entire retirement portfolio because such a fund is not a diversified portfolio. The term 'market-neutral' refers to a portfolio position with respect to a specified market inefficiency. However, there could be a role for a market-neutral hedge fund in the investor's overall portfolio; the market-neutral hedge fund can be thought of as an approach for the investor to add alpha to a more passive investment position, such as an index mutual fund.

2. # of contracts = 1,200,000,000/(250 × 800) × .6 = 3,600 contracts

3. At the end of two years, the fund value must reach at least 104% of its base value. Since the value of the fund at the end of the first year is 92% of its base value, the fund must earn 13% during the second year. This is merely the IRR of a 92 investment over one year with a FV of 104.

4. a. Survivorship bias and backfill bias both result in upwardly biased hedge fund index returns. Survivorship bias happens when unsuccessful funds cease operation, stop reporting returns and leave the database; backfill bias happens because hedge funds report returns to the public only if they choose to—at times they are doing well.

5. b. The S&P 500. The shared goal of all types of hedge funds is seeking absolute returns— finding positive alpha which is above the required returns of the market exposure. In evaluating hedge fund performance, we frequently use S&P 500 as a proxy of the market to compare the return of the hedge fund with its expected CAPM return.

6. c. The extra layer of fees only.

7. a. A market-neutral hedge fund. Using the strategy, the fund tries to achieve a net zero exposure to the market (0 beta), and therefore the fair equilibrium expect return is the risk-free rate.

8. The incentive fee of a hedge fund is part of the hedge fund compensation structure; the incentive fee is typically equal to 20% of the hedge fund's profits beyond a particular benchmark rate of return. Therefore, the incentive fee resembles the payoff to a call option, which is more valuable when volatility is higher. Consequently, the hedge fund portfolio manager is motivated to take on high-risk assets in the portfolio, thereby increasing volatility and the value of the incentive fee.

9. There are a number of factors that make it harder to assess the performance of a hedge fund portfolio manager than a typical mutual fund manager. Some of these factors are:
   - Hedge funds tend to invest in more illiquid assets so that an apparent alpha may be in fact simply compensation for illiquidity.
   - Hedge funds' valuation of less liquid assets is questionable.
   - Survivorship bias and backfill bias result in hedge fund databases that report performance only for more successful hedge funds.
   - Hedge funds typically have unstable risk characteristics making performance evaluation that depends on a consistent risk profile problematic.
   - Tail events skew the distribution of hedge fund outcomes, making it difficult to obtain a representative sample of returns over relatively short periods of time.

10. No, statistical arbitrage is not true arbitrage because it does not involve establishing risk-free positions based on security mispricing. Statistical arbitrage is essentially a portfolio of risky bets. The hedge fund takes a large number of small positions based on apparent small, temporary market inefficiencies, relying on the probability that the expected return for the totality of these bets is positive.

11. Management fee = .02 × \$1 billion = \$20 million

	Portfolio Rate of Return (%)	Incentive Fee (%)	Incentive Fee (\$ million)	Total Fee (\$ million)	Total Fee (%)
a.	−5	0	0	20	2
b.	0	0	0	20	2
c.	5	0	0	20	2
d.	10	20	10	30	3

12. The incentive fee is typically equal to 20% of the hedge fund's profits beyond a particular benchmark rate of return. However, if a fund has experienced losses in the past, then the fund may not be able to charge the incentive fee unless the fund exceeds its previous high water mark. The incentive fee is less valuable if the high-water mark is \$67, rather than \$66. With a high-water mark of \$67, the net asset value of the fund must reach \$67 before the hedge fund can assess the incentive fee. The high-water mark for a hedge fund is equivalent to the exercise price for a call option on an asset with a current market value equal to the net asset value of the fund.

13.

a. First, compute the Black-Scholes value of a call option with the following parameters:

$S_0 = 62$
$X = 66$
$R = .04$
$\sigma = .50$
$T = 1$ year

Therefore: C = \$11.685

The value of the annual incentive fee is:

$.20 \times C = .20 \times \$11.685 = \$2.337$

b. Here we use the same parameters used in the Black-Scholes model in part (a) with the exception that: $X = 62$

Now: $C = \$13.253$

The value of the annual incentive fee is

$.20 \times C = .20 \times \$13.253 = \$2.651$

c. Here we use the same parameters used in the Black-Scholes model in part (a) with the exception that:

$X = S_0 \times e^{0.04} = 62 \times e^{0.04} = 64.5303$

Now: $C = \$12.240$

The value of the annual incentive fee is

$.20 \times C = .20 \times \$12.240 = \$2.448$

d. Here we use the same parameters used in the Black-Scholes model in part (a) with the exception that: $X = 62$ and $\sigma = .60$

Now: $C = \$15.581$

The value of the annual incentive fee is

$.20 \times C = .20 \times \$15.581 = \$3.116$

14.

a. The spreadsheet indicates that the end-of-month value for the S&P 500 in September 1977 was 96.53, so the exercise price of the put written at the beginning of October 1977 would have been:

$.95 \times 96.53 = 91.7035$

At the end of October, the value of the index was 92.34, so the put would have expired out of the money and the put writer's payout was zero. Since it is unusual for the S&P 500 to fall by more than 5 percent in one month, all but ten of the 120 months between October 1977 and September 1987 would have a payout of zero. The first month with a positive payout would have been January 1978. The exercise price of the put written at the beginning of January 1978 would have been:

$.95 \times 95.10 = 90.3450$

At the end of January, the value of the index was 89.25 (more than a 6% decline), so the option writer's payout would have been:

$90.3450 - 89.25 = 1.0950$

The average gross monthly payout for the period would have been 0.2437 and the standard deviation would have been 1.0951.

b. In October 1987, the S&P 500 decreased by more than 21%, from 321.83 to 251.79. The exercise price of the put written at the beginning of October 1987 would have been:

$.95 \times 321.83 = 305.7385$

At the end of October, the option writer's payout would have been:

$305.7385 - 251.79 = 53.9485$

The average gross monthly payout for the period October 1977 through October 1987 would have been 0.6875 and the standard deviation would have been 5.0026. Apparently, tail risk in naked put writing is substantial.

15.

a. In order to calculate the Sharpe ratio, we first calculate the rate of return for each month in the period October 1982-September 1987. The end of month value for the S&P 500 in September 1982 was 120.42, so the exercise price for the October put is:

$.95 \times 120.42 = 114.3990$

Since the October end of month value for the index was 133.72, the put expired out of the money so that there is no payout for the writer of the option. The rate of return the hedge fund earns on the index is therefore equal to:

$(133.72/120.42) - 1 = .11045 = 11.045\%$

Assuming that the hedge fund invests the $0.25 million premium along with the $100 million beginning of month value, then the end of month value of the fund is:

$100.25 million × 1.11045 = $111.322 million

The rate of return for the month is:

($111.322/$100.00) − 1 = .11322 = 11.322%

The first month that the put expires in the money is May 1984. The end of month value for the S&P 500 in April 1984 was 160.05, so the exercise price for the May put is:

$.95 \times 160.05 = 152.0475$

The May end of month value for the index was 150.55, and therefore the payout for the writer of a put option on one unit of the index is:

$152.0475 - 150.55 = 1.4975$

The rate of return the hedge fund earns on the index is equal to:

$(150.55/160.05) - 1 = -.05936 = -5.936\%$

The payout of 1.4975 per unit of the index reduces the hedge fund's rate of return by:

$1.4975/160.05 = .00936 = .936\%$

The rate of return the hedge fund earns is therefore equal to:

$-.05936 - .0936 = -6.872\%$

The end of month value of the fund is:

$100.25 million × .93128 = $93.361 million

The rate of return for the month is:

($93.361/$100.00) − 1 = − .06639 = −6.639%

For the period October 1982-September 1987:

Mean monthly return = 1.898%

Standard deviation = 4.353%

$$\text{Sharpe ratio} = \frac{E(r_P) - r_f}{\sigma_P} = (.01898 - .007)/.04353 = .275$$

b. For the period October 1982-October 1987:

Mean monthly return = 1.238%

Standard deviation = 6.724%

$$\text{Sharpe ratio} = \frac{E(r_P) - r_f}{\sigma_P} = (.01238 - .007)/\ .06724 = .080$$

16.

a. Since the hedge fund manager has a long position in the Waterworks stock, he should sell six contracts, computed as follows:

$$\text{Hedge ratio} = \frac{\$3{,}000{,}000 \times .75}{\$250 \times 1{,}000} = 9 \text{ contracts}$$

b. The standard deviation of the monthly return of the hedged portfolio is equal to the standard deviation of the residuals, which is 6%. The standard deviation of the residuals for the stock is the volatility that cannot be hedged away. For a market-neutral (zero-beta) position, this is also the total standard deviation.

c. The expected rate of return of the market-neutral position is equal to the risk-free rate plus the alpha: .005 + .02 = .025 = 2.5%

We assume that monthly returns are approximately normally distributed. The z-value for a rate of return of zero is:

$$Z = \frac{X - \mu}{\sigma} = \frac{0 - .025}{.06} = -\ .4167$$

Therefore, the probability of a negative return is: N(−.4167) = .3385

17.

a. The residual standard deviation of the portfolio is smaller than each stock's standard deviation by a factor of $\sqrt{100}$ = 10 or, equivalently, the residual variance of the portfolio is smaller by a factor of 100. So, instead of a residual standard deviation of 6%, residual standard deviation is now .6%.

b. The expected return of the market-neutral position is still equal to the risk-free rate plus the alpha: .005 + .02 = .025 = 2.5%

Now the z-value for a rate of return of zero is:

$$Z = \frac{X - \mu}{\sigma} = \frac{0 - .025}{.006} = -4.1667$$

Therefore, the probability of a negative return is: $N(-4.1667) = 1.55 \times 10^{-5}$
A negative return is very unlikely.

18.

a. For the (now improperly) hedged portfolio:

$$\text{Variance} = (.25^2 \times .05^2) + .06^2 = .00375625$$

$$\text{Standard deviation} = \sqrt{.00375625} = .06129 = 6.129\%$$

b. Since the manager has misestimated the beta of Waterworks, the manager will sell four S&P 500 contracts:

$$\text{Hedge ratio} = \frac{\$3{,}000{,}000 \times .50}{\$250 \times 1{,}000} = 6 \text{ contracts}$$

The portfolio is not completely hedged so the expected rate of return is no longer 2.5%. We can determine the expected rate of return by first computing the total dollar value of the stock plus futures position. The dollar value of the stock portfolio is:

$$\$3{,}000{,}000 \times (1 + r_{Portfolio})$$

$$= \$3{,}000{,}000 \times [1 + r_f + \beta(r_M - r_f) + \alpha + e]$$

$$= \$3{,}000{,}000 \times [1 + .005 + .75\,(r_M - .005) + .02 + e]$$

$$= \$3{,}063{,}750 + (\$2{,}250{,}000 \times r_M) + (\$3{,}000{,}000 \times e)$$

The dollar proceeds from the futures position equal:

$$6 \text{ contracts} \times \$250 \times (F_0 - F_1) = \$1{,}500 \times [(S_0 \times 1.005) - S_1]$$

$$= \$1{,}500 \times S_0\,[1.005 - (1 + r_M)] = \$1{,}500 \times [1{,}000 \times (.005 - r_M)]$$

$$= \$7{,}500 - (\$1{,}500{,}000 \times r_M)$$

The total value of the stock plus futures position at the end of the month is:

$$\$3{,}063{,}750 + (\$2{,}250{,}000 \times r_M) + (\$3{,}000{,}000 \times e) +$$

$$\$7{,}500 - (\$1{,}500{,}000 \times r_M)$$

$$= \$3{,}071{,}250 + (\$750{,}000 \times r_M) + (\$3{,}000{,}000 \times e)$$

$= \$3,071,250 + (\$750,000 \times 0.01) + (\$3,000,000 \times e)$
$= \$3,078,750 + (\$3,000,000 \times e)$

The expected rate of return for the (improperly) hedged portfolio is:

($\$3,078,750/\$3,000,000) - 1 = .02625 = 2.625\%$

Now the z-value for a rate of return of zero is:

$$Z = \frac{X - \mu}{\sigma} = \frac{0 - .02625}{.06129} = -.4283$$

The probability of a negative return is: N(− .4283) = .3342
Here, the probability of a negative return is very close to the probability computed earlier.

c. The variance for the diversified (but improperly hedged) portfolio is:

$(.25^2 \times .05^2) + .006^2 = 1.9225 \times 10^{-4}$

Standard deviation $= \sqrt{1.9225 \times 10^{-4}} = 1.3865\%$

The z-value for a rate of return of zero is:

$$Z = \frac{X - \mu}{\sigma} = \frac{0 - .02625}{.013865} = -1.8933$$

The probability of a negative return is: N(−1.8933) = .0292
The probability of a negative return is now far greater than the result with proper hedging.

d. The market exposure from improper hedging is far more important in contributing to total volatility (and risk of losses) in the case of the 100-stock portfolio because the idiosyncratic risk of the diversified portfolio is so small.

19. a., b., c.

	Hedge Fund 1	Hedge Fund 2	Hedge Fund 3	Fund of Funds	Stand-Alone Fund
Start of year value (millions)	$100.0	$100.0	$100.0	$300.0	$300.0
Gross portfolio rate of return	20%	10%	30%		
End of year value (before fee)	$120.0	$110.0	$130.0		$360.0
Incentive fee (Individual funds)	$ 4.0	$ 2.0	$ 6.0		$ 12.0
End of year value (after fee)	$116.0	$108.0	$124.0	$348.0	$348.0
Incentive fee (Fund of Funds)				$ 9.6	
End of year value (Fund of Funds)				$338.4	
Rate of return (after fee)	16.0%	8.0%	24.0%	12.8%	16.0%

Note that the end of year value (after-fee) for the Stand-Alone (SA) Fund is the same as the end of year value for the Fund of Funds (FF) before FF charges its extra layer of incentive fees. Therefore, the investor's rate of return in SA (16.0%) is higher than in FF (12.8%) by an amount equal to the extra layer of fees (16% × 0.2 = 3.2%, or $9.6 million) charged by the Fund of Funds.

d.

	Hedge Fund 1	Hedge Fund 2	Hedge Fund 3	Fund of Funds	Stand-Alone Fund
Start of year value (millions)	$100.0	$100.0	$100.0	$300.0	$300.0
Gross portfolio rate of return	20%	10%	–30%		
End of year value (before fee)	$120.0	$110.0	$ 70.0		$300.0
Incentive fee (Individual funds)	$ 4.0	$ 2.0	$ 0.0		$ 0.0
End of year value (after fee)	$116.0	$108.0	$ 70.0	$294.0	$300.0
Incentive fee (Fund of Funds)				$ 0.0	
End of year value (Fund of Funds)				$294.0	
Rate of return (after fee)	16.0%	8.0%	–30.0%	–2.0%	0.0%

Now, the end of year value (after fee) for SA is $300, while the end of year value for FF is only $294, despite the fact that neither SA nor FF charges an incentive fee. The reason for the difference is the fact that the Fund of Funds pays an incentive fee to each of the component portfolios. If even one of these portfolios does well, there will be an incentive fee charged. In contrast, SA charges an incentive fee only if the aggregate portfolio does well (at least better than a 0% return). The fund of funds structure therefore results in total fees at least as great as (and usually greater than) the stand-alone structure.

CHAPTER 21
TAXES, INFLATION, AND INVESTMENT STRATEGY

1. Moral hazard. The owner now has an incentive to cause a loss and file a claim.

2. The owner will suffer from adverse selection. The owner will attract cargo that would normally cost more than the flat fee being charged.

3. Passive investors who are not sophisticated and looking for reduced fees. These investors are unable to frequently review their portfolio and reallocate the investment assets. The target date fund does this automatically for the investor.

4. The social security annuity is paid out for the balance of your life, regardless of how long you live. The amount is determined based on the calculation of a Primary Insurance Amount (PIA). This determines the monthly annuity paid. Like insurance, once the worker works the minimum number of years, the policy is fully paid and the recipient is guaranteed an income when reaching the designated age. There are other components of SS that are pure insurance such as survivorship benefits that are paid upon the death of a SS recipient to beneficiaries designated by law.

5. The progressive tax code sharpens the importance of taxes during the retirement years. High tax rates during retirement reduce the effectiveness of a tax shelter. In the case of social security, the progressive tax code allocates a relatively larger share of retirement benefits to low-income individuals. Additionally, the lower tax brackets of a progressive system during the retirement years allow you to pay lower taxes over time, significantly increasing retirement consumption. The use of an IRA-style tax shelter increases the retirement annuity, thus an improvement over what you obtain from a tax shelter with the flat tax.

6. With a savings rate of 16%, the retirement annuity would be $205,060 (compared to $192,244 with the 15% savings rate).

Spreadsheet 21.1: Adjusted for Change in Savings Rate

Retirement Years	Income Growth	Savings Rate	ROR	
25	**0.07**	**0.16**	**0.06**	
Age	Income	Saving	Cumulative Savings	Consumption
30	50,000	8,000	8,000	42,000
31	53,500	8,560	17,040	44,940
32	57,245	9,159	27,222	48,086
35	70,128	11,220	65,769	58,907
45	137,952	22,072	329,450	115,879
55	271,372	43,419	1,006,376	227,952
65	533,829	85,413	2,621,352	448,416
Total	**7,445,673**	**1,191,308**	**Retirement Annuity**	**205,060**

7. With a savings rate of 16%, the retirement annuity will be $52,979 (vs. $49,668). The growth in the real retirement annuity (6.67%) is the same as with the case of no inflation.

Spreadsheet 21.2: Adjusted for Change in Savings Rate

Retirement Years	Income Growth	Rate of Inflation	Savings Rate	ROR	rROR
25	**0.07**	**0.03**	**0.16**	**0.06**	**0.0291**
Age	Income	Deflator	Saving	Cumulative Savings	rConsumption
30	50,000	1.00	8,000	8,000	42,000
31	53,500	1.03	8,560	17,040	43,631
35	70,128	1.16	11,220	65,769	50,814
45	137,952	1.56	22,072	329,450	74,379
55	271,372	2.09	43,419	1,006,376	108,871
65	533,829	2.81	85,413	2,621,352	159,360
Total	**7,445,673**		**1,191,308**	**Real Annuity**	**52,979**

8. The objective is to obtain a real retirement annuity of $49,668, as in Spreadsheet 21.2. In Spreadsheet 21.3: Backloading the Real Savings Plan, select Data/Solver from the menu bar. Set the objective value of Real Annuity to 49,668; Assign the value of Saving Rate as the variable. Then we can solve for the saving rate from real income:

Spreadsheet 21.3: With Objective Value of Desired Real Annuity

Retirement Years	Income Growth	Rate of Inflation	Savings Rate	ROR	rROR
25	**0.07**	**0.03**	**0.083**	**0.06**	**0.0291**
Age	Income	Deflator	Saving	Cumulative Savings	rConsumption
30	50,000	1.00	4,145	4,145	45,855
31	53,500	1.03	4,568	8,961	47,507
35	70,128	1.16	6,739	36,764	54,680
45	137,952	1.56	17,816	216,291	77,111
55	271,372	2.09	47,099	785,093	107,114
65	533,829	2.81	124,516	2,457,508	145,463
Total	**7,445,673**		**1,303,467**	**Real Annuity**	**49,668**

We find that a savings rate of 8.3% from real income yields the desired real retirement annuity.

9. Because of the exemption from taxable income, only part of income is subject to tax, while a change in ROR affects all savings.

   As a result, we find from Spreadsheet 21.4 that the increase in tax rate reduces the real annuity by a relatively small amount, while the increase in ROR increases the annuity substantially. A 1% increase in the tax rate, from 25% to 26% (all else equal), reduces the real annuity from $37,882 to $37,426. A 1% increase in ROR, from 6% to 7%, increases the real annuity from $37,882 to $49,107. Making both changes simultaneously yields a real annuity of $48,505.

10. In the original Spreadsheet 21.5, real consumption during retirement is $60,789. A 1% increase in the rate of inflation will reduce real consumption during retirement to $15,780.

    A 1% increase in the flat-tax rate reduces real consumption during retirement to $58,983.

The root of the difference is similar to that of the case of ROR compared to tax rates. While the tax rate affects only part of the income, an increase in the rate of inflation affects all savings, and the reduction in real savings compound over time.

Note that in this example, real consumption during the saving period is fixed, set to equal consumption in Spreadsheet 21.4. To sustain this level of real consumption with a 4% inflation rate, investors must withdraw funds from the saving account as of age 60. In reality, however, households reduce consumption in the face of deteriorating circumstances in order to protect the retirement annuity.

Spreadsheet 21.5: Adjusted for Higher Rate of Inflation

Retirement Years	Income Growth	Rate of Inflation	Exemption Now	Tax Rate	Saving Rate	ROR	rROR
25	**0.07**	**0.04**	**15000**	**0.25**	**0.15**	**0.06**	**0.0192**
Age	Income	Deflator	Exemption	Taxes	Savings	Cumulative Savings	rConsumption
30	50,000	1.00	15,000	5,016	9,922	9,922	35,063
31	53,500	1.04	15,600	5,518	10,309	20,826	36,224
35	70,128	1.22	18,250	8,005	11,852	75,503	41,319
45	137,952	1.80	27,014	19,299	14,442	312,148	57,864
55	271,372	2.67	39,988	44,501	8,877	728,674	81,773
65	533,829	3.95	59,191	99,999	-25,356	1,246,974	116,365
Total				**1,203,168**	**265,856**	**Real Annuity**	**16,040**
RETIREMENT							
Age	Nom Withdraw	Deflator	Exemption	Taxes		Fund left	rConsumption
66	65,827	4.10	61,559	1,067		1,255,966	15,780
70	77,008	4.80	72,015	1,248		1,268,594	15,780
75	93,692	5.84	87,618	1,519		1,210,836	15,780
80	113,991	7.11	106,600	1,848		1,028,069	15,780
85	138,688	8.65	129,696	2,248		655,161	15,780
90	168,735	10.52	157,794	2,735		0	15,780
Total	**2,741,427**			**44,437**			

11. In Spreadsheet 21.6, the real retirement annuity is $37,059.

A 1% increase in the lowest tax bracket reduces the real retirement annuity to $36,815.
A 1% increase in the highest tax bracket reduces the real retirement annuity to $37,033.

The increase in the highest tax bracket has a smaller impact because it applies to a small part of income.

[Note that the adjustments to the tax rates in Spreadsheet 21.6 must be made directly in the cell formulas for Column E: Taxes.]

Retirement Years	Income Growth	Rate of Inflation	Exemption Now	Tax Rates in	Saving Rate	ROR	rROR
25	**0.07**	**0.03**	**10000**	**Table 21.1**	**0.15**	**0.06**	**0.0291**
Age	Income	Deflator	Exemption	Taxes	Savings	Cumulative Savings	rConsumption
30	50,000	1.00	10,000	8,400	6,240	6,240	35,360
31	53,500	1.03	10,300	9,151	6,652	13,267	36,599
35	70,128	1.16	11,593	13,061	8,560	50,802	41,842
45	137,952	1.56	15,580	33,609	15,651	245,813	56,927
55	271,372	2.09	20,938	77,541	29,075	725,893	78,688
65	533,829	2.81	28,139	187,472	51,954	1,821,534	104,626
Total		Total	**632,759**	**2,145,101**	**795,086**	**Real Annuity**	**36,815**

RETIREMENT

Age	Nom Withdraw	Deflator	Exemption	Taxes		Fund left	rConsumption
66	106,699	2.90	28,983	16,865		1,824,127	30,996
70	120,090	3.26	32,620	15,987		1,801,160	31,914
75	139,218	3.78	37,816	13,594		1,672,523	33,220
80	161,391	4.38	43,839	9,150		1,382,861	34,727
85	187,097	5.08	50,821	1,762		858,991	36,468
90	216,896	5.89	58,916	0		0	36,815
Total	**3,890,156**			**236,400**			

Example of adjustment

Cell E4 =MAX(0,(B4-D4)*0.21)+MAX(0,(B4-D4-50000*C4)*0.09)+MAX(0,(B4-D4-150000*C4)*0.1)

Retirement Years	Income Growth	Rate of Inflation	Exemption Now	Tax Rates in	Saving Rate	ROR	rROR
25	**0.07**	**0.03**	**10000**	**Table 21.1**	**0.15**	**0.06**	**0.0291**
Age	Income	Deflator	Exemption	Taxes	Savings	Cumulative Savings	rConsumption
30	50,000	1.00	10,000	8,000	6,300	6,300	35,700
31	53,500	1.03	10,300	8,716	6,718	13,396	36,958
35	70,128	1.16	11,593	12,489	8,646	51,310	42,262
45	137,952	1.56	15,580	32,866	15,763	248,018	57,333
55	271,372	2.09	20,938	76,587	29,218	731,514	79,076
65	533,829	2.81	28,139	188,156	51,851	1,832,347	104,420
Total		Total	**632,759**	**2,124,073**	**798,240**	**Real Annuity**	**37,033**

RETIREMENT

Age	Nom Withdraw	Deflator	Exemption	Taxes		Fund left	rConsumption
66	107,332	2.90	28,983	16,192		1,834,955	31,446
70	120,803	3.26	32,620	15,355		1,811,852	32,326
75	140,044	3.78	37,816	13,069		1,682,452	33,577
80	162,349	4.38	43,839	8,818		1,391,069	35,022
85	188,207	5.08	50,821	1,748		864,090	36,689
90	218,184	5.89	58,916	0		0	37,033
Total	**3,913,248**			**229,781**			

Example of adjustment

Cell E4 =MAX(0,(B4-D4)*0.2)+MAX(0,(B4-D4-50000*C4)*0.1)+MAX(0,(B4-D4-150000*C4)*(

12. The real retirement annuity in Spreadsheet 21.7 is $83,380.

A decrease of 2% in the ROR reduces the real retirement annuity to $50,900.
An increase of 2% in the ROR increases the real retirement annuity to $137,819.

The percent reduction in the real annuity resulting from the decrease in ROR (39%) is much smaller than the percent increase resulting from the increase in ROR (65%). The reason the IRA shelter works as a hedge is that, if savings decline, then the marginal tax rate declines. The reverse is true when savings increase.

Retirement Years	Income Growth	Rate of Inflation	Exemption Now	Tax Rates in	Saving Rate	ROR	rROR
25	**0.07**	**0.03**	**10000**	**Table 21.1**	**0.15**	**0.04**	**0.0097**
Age	Income	Deflator	Exemption	Taxes	Savings	Cumulative Savings	rConsumption
30	50,000	1.00	10,000	5,140	9,160	9,160	35,700
31	53,500	1.03	10,300	5,553	9,880	19,406	36,958
35	70,128	1.16	11,593	7,480	13,654	73,648	42,262
45	137,952	1.56	15,580	14,749	33,880	383,219	57,333
55	271,372	2.09	20,938	32,920	72,885	1,190,868	79,076
65	533,829	2.81	28,139	66,100	172,359	3,165,652	104,970
Total			**632,759**	**879,430**	**2,036,474**	**Real Annuity**	**50,900**
RETIREMENT							
Age	Nom Withdraw	Deflator	Exemption	Taxes		Fund left	rConsumption
66	147,522	2.90	28,983	23,708		3,144,756	42,720
70	166,037	3.26	32,620	26,683		3,005,037	42,720
75	192,483	3.78	37,816	30,933		2,674,804	42,720
80	223,140	4.38	43,839	35,860		2,116,733	42,720
85	258,680	5.08	50,821	41,572		1,256,567	42,720
90	299,881	5.89	58,916	48,193		0	42,720
Total	**5,378,537**			**864,369**			

Retirement Years	Income Growth	Rate of Inflation	Exemption Now	Tax Rates in	Saving Rate	ROR	rROR
25	**0.07**	**0.03**	**10000**	**Table 21.1**	**0.15**	**0.08**	**0.0485**
Age	Income	Deflator	Exemption	Taxes	Savings	Cumulative Savings	rConsumption
30	50,000	1.00	10,000	5,140	9,160	9,160	35,700
31	53,500	1.03	10,300	5,553	9,880	19,773	36,958
35	70,128	1.16	11,593	7,480	13,654	80,752	42,262
45	137,952	1.56	15,580	14,749	33,880	496,093	57,333
55	271,372	2.09	20,938	32,920	72,885	1,806,095	79,076
65	533,829	2.81	28,139	66,100	172,359	5,546,345	104,970
Total			**632,759**	**879,430**	**2,036,474**	**Real Annuity**	**137,819**
RETIREMENT							
Age	Nom Withdraw	Deflator	Exemption	Taxes		Fund left	rConsumption
66	399,437	2.90	28,983	96,645		5,590,616	104,473
70	449,569	3.26	32,620	108,775		5,672,462	104,473
75	521,174	3.78	37,816	126,099		5,463,256	104,473
80	604,184	4.38	43,839	146,184		4,698,518	104,473
85	700,415	5.08	50,821	169,467		3,044,675	104,473
90	811,972	5.89	58,916	196,459		0	104,473
Total	**14,563,165**			**3,523,597**			

13. The real retirement annuity in Spreadsheet 21.8 is $ 49,153.
    A 1% increase in ROR increases the real retirement annuity to $63,529.
    A 1% decrease in the rate of inflation increases the real retirement annuity to $119,258.

    The reason inflation is more potent than ROR is that inflation affects the entire savings. Here, too, consumption during the labor years is fixed and hence the entire effect is transferred to the retirement annuity.

Retirement Years	Income Growth	Rate of Inflation	Exemption Now	Tax Rates in	Saving Rate	ROR	rROR
25	**0.07**	**0.03**	**10000**	**Table 21.1**	**0.15**	**0.07**	**0.0388**
Age	Income	Deflator	Exemption	Taxes	Savings	Cumulative Savings	rConsumption
30	50,000	1.00	10,000	8,000	6,300	6,300	35,700
31	53,500	1.03	10,300	8,640	6,793	13,534	36,958
35	70,128	1.16	11,593	11,764	9,370	54,231	42,262
45	137,952	1.56	15,580	28,922	19,707	298,059	57,333
55	271,372	2.09	20,938	64,661	41,143	987,189	79,076
65	533,829	2.81	28,139	145,999	92,460	2,827,329	104,970
Total	**7,445,673**		**632,759**	**1,752,425**	**1,163,478**	**Real Annuity**	**63,529**

RETIREMENT

Age	Nom Withdraw	Deflator	Exemption	Taxes		Fund left	rConsumption
66	184,124	2.90	28,983	0		2,841,119	63,529
70	207,233	3.26	32,620	0		2,845,645	63,529
75	240,240	3.78	37,816	0		2,692,973	63,529
80	278,504	4.38	43,839	0		2,272,075	63,529
85	322,862	5.08	50,821	0		1,442,043	63,529
90	374,286	5.89	58,916	0		0	63,529
Total	**6,713,023**			**0**			

Retirement Years	Income Growth	Rate of Inflation	Exemption Now	Tax Rates in	Saving Rate	ROR	rROR
25	**0.07**	**0.02**	**10000**	**Table 21.1**	**0.15**	**0.06**	**0.0392**
Age	Income	Deflator	Exemption	Taxes	Savings	Cumulative Savings	rConsumption
30	50,000	1.00	10,000	8,000	6,300	6,300	35,700
31	53,500	1.02	10,200	8,660	7,143	13,821	36,958
35	70,128	1.10	11,041	12,206	11,261	59,264	42,262
45	137,952	1.35	13,459	30,619	30,170	362,197	57,333
55	271,372	1.64	16,406	69,174	72,466	1,293,122	79,076
65	533,829	2.00	19,999	165,534	158,367	3,756,978	104,970
Total	**7,445,673**		**519,944**	**1,929,174**	**1,901,289**	**Real Annuity**	**119,258**

RETIREMENT

Age	Nom Withdraw	Deflator	Exemption	Taxes		Fund left	rConsumption
66	243,272	2.04	20,399	0		3,739,125	119,258
70	263,325	2.21	22,080	0		3,603,662	119,258
75	290,733	2.44	24,379	0		3,250,278	119,258
80	320,992	2.69	26,916	0		2,613,730	119,258
85	354,401	2.97	29,717	0		1,581,215	119,258
90	391,288	3.28	32,810	0		0	119,258
Total	**7,792,077**			**0**			

14. When deferring taxes to the last year of retirement, you must set money aside every year in order to accumulate a fund sufficient to pay the capital gains tax in a lump sum. To leave consumption fixed in real terms, a fixed real amount is set aside each year.

    We calculate the cumulative capital gains in cells D45 through D69. The nominal capital gains tax due in the final year appears in cell F69, and its real value is computed in cell F71. The real annuity required in order to pay the tax in cell F71 is shown in cells I45 through I69. The real amounts set aside in cells I45 through I69 are deducted from real consumption.

    With annual payments of capital gains taxes (Spreadsheet 21.9), real consumption starts at $46,808 and ends at $43,955. When taxes are deferred to the last year of retirement, real consumption is fixed at $46,190. Thus, the progressivity of the tax code makes this option preferable.

Retirement Years	Income Growth	Rate of Inflation	Exemption Now	Tax Rates in	Saving Rate	ROR	rROR
25	**0.07**	**0.03**	**10000**	**Table 21.1**	**0.15**	**0.06**	**0.0291**
Age	Income	Deflator	Exemption	Taxes	Savings	Cumulative Savings	rConsumption
30	50,000	1.00	10,000	8,000	6,300	6,300	35,700
35	70,128	1.16	11,593	11,764	9,370	52,995	42,262
45	137,952	1.56	15,580	28,922	19,707	278,528	57,333
55	271,372	2.09	20,938	64,661	41,143	883,393	79,076
65	533,829	2.81	28,139	145,999	92,460	2,432,049	104,970
Total				**1,752,425**	**1,163,478**	**Real Annuity**	**49,153**

RETIREMENT Tax rate on capital gains **0.15**

Age	Nom Withdraw	Deflator	Cum Cap Gains	Exemption	Taxes	Fund Left	rConsumption	rSaving	Adj rConsumption
66	142,460	2.90	1,414,494	28,983	0	2,435,512	49,153	2,964	46,190
70	160,340	3.26	1,997,710	32,620	0	2,404,847	49,153	2,964	46,190
75	185,879	3.78	2,702,767	37,816	0	2,233,096	49,153	2,964	46,190
80	215,484	4.38	3,332,479	43,839	0	1,846,348	49,153	2,964	46,190
85	249,805	5.08	3,811,381	50,821	0	1,146,895	49,153	2,964	46,190
86	257,299	5.23	3,880,195	52,346	0	958,409	49,153	2,964	46,190
87	265,018	5.39	3,937,700	53,917	0	750,895	49,153	2,964	46,190
88	272,969	5.55	3,982,753	55,534	0	522,980	49,153	2,964	46,190
89	281,158	5.72	4,014,132	57,200	0	273,201	49,153	2,964	46,190
90	289,593	5.89	4,030,524	58,916	629,410	0	49,153	2,964	46,190
Total				**1,056,691**	**629,410**				

15. Answers will vary.

16. The present value of labor income is $ 2,010,917 (at the rate of the applicable ROR). The present value of college tuition is $167,741. This is equal to:

($167,741/$2,010,917) = 8.34% of the present value of labor income. When college tuition increases by 1%, to $40,400, the present value of college tuition increases to $169,419, which is equal to 8.42% of labor income. Note that the present value of college tuition for two children makes up almost 10% of the present value of the entire household lifetime income.

Retirement Years	Income Growth	Rate of Inflation	Savings Rate	ROR	rROR	Extra-Cons
25	**0.07**	**0.03**	**0.15**	**0.06**	**0.0291**	**40,000**
Age	Income	Deflator	Saving	Cumulative Savings	rConsumption	Expenditures
30	50,000	1.00	7,500	7,500	42,500	0
31	53,500	1.03	8,025	15,975	44,150	0
35	70,128	1.16	10,519	61,658	51,419	0
45	137,952	1.56	20,693	308,859	75,264	0
48	168,997	1.70	25,349	375,099	84,378	68,097
49	180,826	1.75	27,124	354,588	87,654	70,140
50	193,484	1.81	29,023	260,397	91,058	144,489
51	207,028	1.86	31,054	158,252	94,595	148,824
52	221,520	1.92	33,228	124,331	98,268	76,644
53	237,026	1.97	35,554	88,401	102,084	78,943
54	253,618	2.03	38,043	131,748	106,049	0
55	271,372	2.09	40,706	180,359	110,167	0
65	533,829	2.81	80,074	1,090,888	161,257	0
Total			**1,116,851**	**Real Annuity**	**22,048**	

PV (labor income)	2,010,917.42
PV (College Tuition)	167,741.16
PV(college tuition)/PV(labor incom	8.34%

Retirement Years	Income Growth	Rate of Inflation	Savings Rate	ROR	rROR	Extra-Cons
25	**0.07**	**0.03**	**0.15**	**0.06**	**0.0291**	**40,400**
Age	Income	Deflator	Saving	Cumulative Savings	rConsumption	Expenditures
30	50,000	1.00	7,500	7,500	42,500	0
31	53,500	1.03	8,025	15,975	44,150	0
35	70,128	1.16	10,519	61,658	51,419	0
45	137,952	1.56	20,693	308,859	75,264	0
48	168,997	1.70	25,349	374,418	84,378	68,778
49	180,826	1.75	27,124	353,165	87,654	70,842
50	193,484	1.81	29,023	257,444	91,058	145,934
51	207,028	1.86	31,054	153,633	94,595	150,312
52	221,520	1.92	33,228	118,668	98,268	77,411
53	237,026	1.97	35,554	81,609	102,084	79,733
54	253,618	2.03	38,043	124,549	106,049	0
55	271,372	2.09	40,706	172,727	110,167	0
65	533,829	2.81	80,074	1,077,222	161,257	0
Total			**1,116,851**	**Real Annuity**	**21,771**	

PV (labor income)	2,010,917.42
PV (College Tuition)	169,418.58
PV(college tuition)/PV(labor income	8.42%

17. Adverse selection is a concept that is generally associated with insurance; however, in a broader sense, adverse selection is a potential issue in any contract where one party has more complete information about the transaction than the other. In insurance, the insured has more information about one's own health (e.g., in life insurance and health insurance) or, in general, the risk of loss (e.g., one's driving ability in the context of automobile insurance). The insurance company attempts to price an insurance contract based on the average characteristics of a population, but, in the case of life insurance, for example, those whose health is worse than average are more likely to buy the policy that is priced in terms of the company's average risk of loss because this price is a bargain for the person with above-average risk. On the other hand, the person in good health will regard the price of such a contract as too high and will not buy the insurance. The consequence for the insurance company is that those who buy the contract are higher risks than average, resulting in higher losses for the insurance company. Insurance companies try to resolve such problems by measuring the risk (e.g., requiring medical examinations before issuing an insurance policy) in order to price the insurance contracts correctly. In the broader economic sense, adverse selection affects product prices because the seller of a product knows more about the quality of the product than does the buyer. The buyer may tend to assume that the quality is worse than it actually is, and may not be willing to pay the high price that would be appropriate for a high-quality product. The seller is then forced to reduce both the price and the quality of the product.

18. The major traits are the degree of risk aversion and the bequest motive.

19. In general, moral hazard is a term associated with insurance contracts and with government programs that essentially function as insurance. When an individual or a business entity insures against loss of property due to fire, theft or other hazard, the insured may have a tendency to take greater risks than one would in the absence of insurance. In the extreme, the insured may be motivated to damage or destroy one's own property in order to collect payment from the insurer. Even health insurance might lead the insured to be less cautious about one's health. In addition, the existence of government programs that provide assistance to those in poverty or those who have suffered a loss due to natural disaster may encourage those at risk to be less attentive to these risks. Examples include unemployment compensation, food stamps and public housing which serve as a form of insurance against financial difficulties. Also, government disaster relief programs may serve to encourage people to live in disaster-prone locations. Similarly, government bailouts of financial institutions and other corporations may also encourage risky behavior.

CHAPTER 22
INVESTORS AND THE INVESTMENT PROCESS

1. The investment objectives of the Masons should be expressed in terms of return and risk. These return and risk preferences should be portrayed in terms of the Mason's preferences, their current financial status, and the stage in their life cycle.

   Investment Objectives
   Return Requirement: Dr. Mason is nearing retirement. Therefore, the overriding objective is to provide the Masons with sufficient retirement income. This objective should be easily satisfied by investing the original $1,000,000 payment from ACS to provide a moderate current income level. This income, combined with the Masons' Social Security and pension benefits, will provide sufficient retirement income. Because of the large cash payment from ACS (even after payment of capital gains taxes), the Masons will have a large enough financial base to pursue their other objectives, specifically, for the grandchildren and for scholarships to the Essex Institute. These latter two objectives suggest a portfolio seeking long-term capital appreciation. Therefore, the substantial size of the assets permits a growth-oriented posture with a secondary emphasis on current income. Common stocks and equity real estate provide growth opportunities, and the latter may also provide tax benefits.

   Risk Tolerance: Given the substantial size of the Masons' assets, this portfolio can tolerate a larger amount of risk than is normal for a family in the later stage of their life cycle. Coupled with the Masons' retirement benefits, a moderate income from the portfolio will provide sufficient retirement income. Therefore, the portfolio can accept greater risk in the pursuit of higher long-term capital appreciation. A significant portion of the Masons' assets can be invested in growth assets, such as common stocks and real estate, with secondary emphasis on investments with a high current income yield. The greater the amount of royalties received, the greater the risk-tolerance for the portfolio.

   Investment Constraints
   Liquidity: The substantial size of the Masons' assets and the prospects for continued high royalty income lessen the importance of the liquidity constraint. A major portion of the portfolio should be invested in relatively non-liquid assets in order to achieve long-term capital growth.

   Time Horizon: Because the Masons are in the later part of their life cycle, one would ordinarily expect them to have a relatively short time horizon. The size of the Masons' assets, however, and the objectives of providing for the education of their grandchildren and for scholarships, dictate that a substantial portion of the portfolio be invested for the longer term. Common stocks and real estate would be appropriate.

   Regulatory and Legal: Since this is a personal portfolio, regulatory and legal constraints are not important.

Tax Considerations: The income from royalties and investments will require that the portfolio be structured for favorable tax treatment. Long-term growth assets, which enjoy deferral of gains until the sale of the assets, are suitable. Real estate, in the form of rental property, provides tax deductions that might also be desirable, and rental income would supplement common stock dividends to provide the moderate current income required.

Investment Policy
Given the Masons' substantial assets, the investment policy should emphasize capital appreciation and provide moderate current income. The large size of the portfolio allows the purchase of growth-oriented common stocks while providing sufficient retirement income. This policy will provide the opportunity to achieve the objectives of educating the grandchildren and funding the scholarships to the Essex Institute, while providing enough retirement income. Growth assets should also be a better inflation hedge. Real estate, tax-exempt bonds, and low-risk money market investments would provide the necessary diversification.

2.

a. Mature pension fund:

Investment Objectives
Return requirement: Return must exceed the fund's actuarially assumed rate of return based in part on the anticipated 5% rate for wage cost increases.

Risk tolerance: Proximity of payouts limits tolerance for risk taking. As a result, the portfolio's asset mix should lean toward intermediate-maturity fixed-income assets of relatively high quality.

Investment Constraints
Liquidity: Proximity of payouts requires liquidity above that required for less mature plans. This additional liquidity may limit returns.

Time horizon: Again, maturity of plan results in an emphasis on a short- to intermediate-term time horizon, which may limit returns.

Tax considerations: Non-taxable.

Regulatory and legal: Federal (U.S.-ERISA) and state laws will affect asset mix and quality.

b. Conservative endowment fund:

Investment Objectives
Return requirement: Return must meet or exceed 5% spending rate with 3% inflation rate. Return can be from income or capital gains but budget requirements would place the emphasis on income. Inflation considerations require some consideration of long-term growth.

Risk tolerance: With a 8.15% ($1.05 \times 1.03 - 1 = .0815$) return objective, moderate level of risk tolerance may be required but the certainty of return will temper this risk tolerance.

Investment Constraints
Liquidity: Budget needs will require some liquidity to meet expenses; this may limit returns.

Time horizon: Budget considerations will require funding immediate needs but inflation considerations require some attention to a longer-term growth horizon.

Tax considerations: Non-taxable.

Regulatory and legal: State regulation.
It would also be important to recognize the dichotomy of objectives of the endowment fund: maximizing assured returns to fund current needs over a short-term time horizon, and maximizing more risky returns to maintain long-term real value of the endowment's principal value over a long-term time horizon.

c. Life insurance company specializing in annuities:
Investment Objectives
Return requirement: Return should exceed new money rate by sufficient margin to meet expenses and profit objectives. Lower minimum accumulation rate tempers return objective.

Risk tolerance: With a 7% new money return objective, moderate level of risk tolerance may be required, but certainty of return and avoidance of reinvestment rate risk virtually mandates the use of an immunized fixed income portfolio.

Investment Constraints
Liquidity: Some liquidity may be required for surrenders and rollover of funds to protect against locking in noncompetitive rates.

Time horizon: Shorter than normal time horizon because annuities are subject to disintermediation.

Tax considerations: A minor factor because competition will require a high rate of return, most of which will accumulate for the policyholder and thus not be subject to tax.

Regulatory and legal: Significant state regulation will affect asset mix and quality.

CFA 1

Answer:

b. Purchasing power risk.

CFA 2

Answer:

b. Organizing the management process itself.

CFA 3

Answer:

d. All investors.

CFA 4

Answer:

b. The level of the market.

CFA 5

Answer:

a. Paying benefits to retired employees.

CFA 6

Answer:

a. Determines most of the portfolio's returns and volatility over time.

CFA 7

Answer:

Investment Objectives

Return Requirement: Often, the return is stated in terms of minimum levels required to fund a specific liability or budget requirements, as indicated by the Wood Museum Treasurer. The minimum returns to meet the budget requirements are: 2013 – 12%; 2014 – 12.8%; and 2015 – 14%. The trustees have to clarify how capital gains should be treated relative to the budget.

Risk Tolerance: This section specifies the client's willingness or ability to bear risk in the pursuit of specified return requirements. For Wood Museum, the tight budget position and the trustees' fears of a financial crisis indicate a low tolerance for risk.

Investment Constraints

Liquidity Requirements: The client's need for cash or cash availability from securities that can be sold quickly and without substantial price risk (concessions). Wood Museum's liquidity needs are a significant factor given the budget considerations.

Time Horizon: The client's expected holding period, which is generally determined by such factors as the nature of the client's liabilities, cash flow requirements or expectations. Investment managers also have an expectational time horizon, which is the length of time into the future that the manager feels he can predict important financial variables, such as earnings and dividends, with reasonable accuracy. For Wood Museum, the immediacy of the budget requirements (1 to 3 years) suggests a very short time horizon for at least a major portion of the portfolio.

Tax Considerations: Wood Museum is tax exempt.

Regulatory and Legal Considerations: In the case of an endowment fund, prudent-man factors must be considered as well as the legal structure of the fund and any state or federal regulation that might influence the management of the investment portfolio.

Unique Needs and Circumstances: Particular conditions or requirements that reflect the discretion of the fund trustees. For example, social factors might be a concern of the Museum that the trustees want reflected in the types of investment deemed appropriate for the fund.

CFA 8

Answer:

The most important area of change concerns taxes. Mrs. Atkins pays income tax, but the endowment fund will be free of taxes.

<u>Investment Objectives</u>

Return Requirement: The fund should strive to provide a predictable stream of income growing in line with the rising costs. An initial income target of 6% of portfolio assets should enable the fund to support the hospital's operating budget, while still favoring future growth.

Risk Tolerance: In view of the relatively long time horizon, limited liquidity needs, and adequacy of already existing endowment assets to offset the operating deficit, the Atkins Fund has an above average ability to assume risk.

<u>Investment Constraints</u>

Liquidity: Liquidity needs are low. Except for investment reasons and periodic payment of accumulated income, there is no reason to maintain any sizable liquid reserves in the fund.

Time Horizon: Endowment funds typically have very long time horizons and there is no reason to believe that the current case is any exception. Certainly the time horizon extends well beyond normal market cycles.

Tax Considerations: Since endowment funds are normally free from taxes, with the exception of minimal estate taxes, taxes would not be a meaningful constraint for this fund.

Legal: Most endowment funds are governed by state regulations, and since most states have moved to a "prudent man" standard, regulatory and legal constraints should not be significant investment factors (certainly no more so than during the time that Mrs. Atkins is alive).

Unique Needs: Although the details provided concerning Good Samaritan are somewhat sketchy, and additional information might be appropriately requested, it would appear that this hospital is experiencing financial difficulties which have been characteristic of this industry for several years. The existence of an operating deficit, and the possibility that this deficit may grow, suggest that a slightly more conservative posture relative to other endowment funds might be appropriate.

CFA 9

Answer:

a. An appropriate investment policy statement for the endowment fund will be organized around the following major and specific aspects of the situation:

   i. The primacy of the current income requirement;

   ii. The inability to accept significant risk as to 85% of the original capital;

   iii. The payout of $8,500,000 on June 30, 2014, restricting the time horizon within the fund's infinite life span;

   iv. The unique and dominating circumstance represented by the June 30, 2014, capital payout requirement; and

   v. The requirements of the "spending rule."

   A proposed IPS might be:

   "The endowment fund's investment assets shall be managed in a Prudent Man context to provide a total return of at least 8% per year, including an original $500,000 (5%) current income component growing at 3% annually. Meeting this current income goal is the primary return objective. Inasmuch as $8,500,000 of capital must be distributed in cash on June 30, 2014, no significant risk can be taken on the sum that is required to guarantee this payout; a normal risk capacity shall be assumed with respect to remaining investment assets. The fund's horizon is very long term as to assets not required for the 2014 distribution. The endowment fund 'spending rule' shall be taken into account in determining investment strategy and annual income distributions."

b. The account circumstances will affect the initial asset allocation in the following major ways:

   i. The aggregate portfolio will have much larger than normal holdings of U.S. Treasury and Treasury-related securities. Maximum use will be made of discount Treasuries and related zero-coupon securities in order to minimize the risk and the amount of total assets that must be "frozen" in order to assure the availability of $8,500,000 on June 30, 2014.

   ii. The aggregate portfolio will have much smaller than normal holdings of equity securities, given the need to "lock up" the 2014 distribution requirement in virtually riskless form. The initial mix here might well be

15% zeros, 55% discount Treasuries, and only 30% equities; normally, 60 to 70% in equities would not be uncommon.

iii. The equity portfolio will emphasize a growth orientation. Income in excess of the current income requirement will be added to equity. Not only must building of future value and income be derived from the rather small equity component of the portfolio, but it must also serve an inflation protection need as well. Since it does not appear that meeting the annual current income target will be difficult initially, there is plenty of room for lower yielding issues to be included in the equity mix.

iv. The aggregate portfolio risk level will be well below average. The 2014 payout requirement dictates a zero risk posture on a large part of the total while the prudent man environment will act to prevent overzealous risk taking in the "remainder" portion.

v. The fund's tax-exempt status maximizes allocation flexibility, both as to income aspects and as to planning for future capital growth.

vi. A short horizon to 2014 must be accommodated as to a major portion of total capital funds, while a very long-term horizon applies to the rest.

CFA 10

Answer:

a. Investment *objectives* are goals; investment *constraints* are the limits within which the responsible party must operate in order to achieve the objectives; investment *policies* define the ways in which the effort to achieve the objectives will be undertaken.

The primary function of an *investment objective* is to identify the risk/return relationship sought for an account. Emphasis may be on maximizing return while accepting an appropriate level of risk. Objectives may be specified in either absolute or relative form. For example:
"8% total return while experiencing a risk level equivalent to the S&P 500" or, "a target total return of 3% per annum greater than the rate of inflation with a standard deviation no greater than that of the S&P 500 in the post-World War II period."

An *investment constraint* is a limitation on the investment decision-making which can be identified as a requirement in terms of liquidity, time horizon, tax considerations, legal or regulatory considerations and unique needs. The realism of both the investment objectives and the practical policies adopted for managing the account must be tested against any investment constraints. For example: an investment advisor to an ERISA plan is legally constrained by virtue of inclusion as a fiduciary under the law, and cannot purchase for the plan portfolio more than 10% of the common stock of the plan sponsor.

An *investment policy* is an operational statement or guideline that specifies the actions to be taken in order to achieve the investment objective within the constraints imposed.

b. Investment Objectives

Return: Total return equal to or greater than the foundation's annual spending plus the rate of inflation.

Risk Tolerance: Moderate; no less volatility than long-term bonds and no more volatility than a diversified portfolio of common stocks.

Investment Constraints

Time Horizon: Long-term (perpetuity).

Liquidity: Modest percentage (5% to 10%) of assets must be available for annual distribution.

Legal and Regulatory: State regulation and/or the endowment documents.

Taxes: None.

c. Investment Policies

A portfolio balance, to be averaged over time, of a maximum position of 67% in equity-type investments and a minimum position of 33% in fixed income type investments.

Qualified equity and fixed income investments to consist of the following:

Equity Related	Fixed Income
Common stocks and warrants	Government and agency obligations
Convertible securities	Corporate obligations
Option writing	Real estate mortgages

In the case of convertible securities, corporate obligations and preferred stocks carrying a credit rating, qualifying for purchase are securities rated no less than BBB ("regarded as having an adequate capacity to pay interest / dividends and repay principal") as defined by S&P, or its equivalent as defined by other recognized rating agencies. Stocks are to be of high quality with betas not to exceed 1.2 for portfolio as a whole.

The Office of the Treasurer shall have direct responsibility for no more than 50% of total marketable endowment funds. Remaining funds to be the responsibility of outside managers as selected from time to time. All managers shall have full investment discretion within defined statements of objectives and policies.

As a charitable foundation, minimum of 5% of assets must distribute annually in order to avoid loss of tax-exempt status. Sufficient funds shall be available for annual disbursement. Money market instruments rated A-1 may be utilized for a liquidity reserve.